THE FOOTBALL SOLUTION

ALSO BY GEORGE MEGALOGENIS

The Australian Moment
Australia's Second Chance
Faultlines
The Longest Decade
Quarterly Essay 40: Trivial Pursuit
Quarterly Essay 61: Balancing Act

THE FOOTBALL SOLUTION

HOW RICHMOND'S PREMIERSHIP CAN SAVE AUSTRALIA

GEORGE MEGALOGENIS

VIKING
an imprint of
PENGUIN BOOKS

VIKING

UK | USA | Canada | Ireland | Australia
India | New Zealand | South Africa | China

Penguin Books is part of the Penguin Random House group of companies
whose addresses can be found at global.penguinrandomhouse.com.

First published by Penguin Random House Australia Pty Ltd, 2018

Cover design by Adam Laszczuk © Penguin Random House Australia Pty Ltd
Graph in picture section by Guy Holt
Typeset in Adobe Caslon Pro by Midland Typesetters, Australia
Printed and bound in Australia by Griffin Press, an accredited ISO AS/NZS 14001
Environmental Management Systems printer.

A catalogue record for this
book is available from the
National Library of Australia

ISBN: 978 0 14379 172 0

penguin.com.au

For Mum and Dad

CONTENTS

Introduction

I have always wanted to write a book about Australia that takes as its central characters my football club and the inner-city suburb it sprang from. A club that rose from the slums to become the most popular in the country, but fell to earth when football went national. A club of very Australian contradictions.

I had a beginning and a middle, but it never occurred to me that there could be a happy ending. Richmond was the tragic character in a soap opera, destined for perpetual heartbreak. Each season would tease the possibility of fulfilment before taking a humiliating twist. The finale was never in doubt. The suspense was only in the timing and the detail of the dignity-shredding loss.

The 2017 premiership changed that plotline in a delightful, unexpected way. It went beyond sport, speaking to the very meaning of national life.

Across the world, sporting competitions were producing fairytales that gave their communities permission to enjoy themselves. Between 2016 and 2018, the cities of Leicester, Cleveland, Chicago and Philadelphia, and the suburbs of Footscray and Cronulla, celebrated their drought-breaking championships with street parties that recalled those that greeted the end of World War II.

Although Richmond's premiership was part of this global trend, I believe it sits in a category of its own. Partly because it was my club, and partly because it carried a lesson for leadership in Australia. Richmond didn't just win, it rewrote the rules for sporting success.

For the Tigers, there was no logical reason to think that 2017 would be different from the previous thirty-six years of disappointment.

The season began with the team winning while playing poorly. Hope. Then they placed themselves on the guillotine of public ridicule by losing a couple of close games in which their play merited a win. Let down.

Then they started winning again. Hang on?

I was reminded of the conversations I'd have with my mother as a ten-year-old, back when a Richmond premiership was a reasonable expectation. In 2017, we were talking that way again. One moment we were going to the footy out of habit, because it was the best time of the week for the family to catch up, the next we were thinking ahead to a top four finish and the path to a grand final.

As my confidence grew, I figured I should share my hunch with the handful of people who followed me on Twitter.

And so, with four games still left in the home and away season, I publicly predicted a Richmond premiership. To increase the degree of difficulty at my own expense, I declared my faith on a weekend when we didn't play all that well. I waited for the blowback. There was none.

I pinned the tweet to the top of my account, replacing a column I had written for the *New York Times* on Australia's stellar migration record. Still, no blowback.

The people who replied to my missives throughout August and September behaved in a manner completely abnormal for Twitter. That is, their engagement was thoroughly human.

There was none of the static that enters my feed when I tweet about politics. No misspelled insults. No accusations of bias. No random arguments between strangers based on obscure readings of past events. Just a series of funny conversations about a game.

The good humour in cyberspace was replicated in the physical world. Not a week went by without someone shouting across the street, or out of the window of a passing car, 'Hey George, go Tigers!'

After Richmond had won the premiership, I mentioned my prediction – its smart-arse timing, and the unexpected response – to Neil Balme. Few people in football can credibly claim to have seen it all, but Balme really has. He played in two premierships for Richmond in the 1970s, in the era of black and white television replays, coached two premierships at Norwood in the South Australian competition in the 1980s, and won another three premierships in the twenty-first century as an administrator at Geelong.

He tells me he didn't see Richmond's success coming. Which is to say he thought my premiership forecast was evidence-free and exceedingly heroic.

'That is why footy is so popular,' he laughs. 'Everyone is entitled to that opinion, however wrong it may be.'

Football had achieved what politics no longer aspires to, an ideal democratic space.

Public life in Australia has become strangely inverted in the twenty-first century. Politics is increasingly conducted like sport once was. Leaders yell at voters like the footy coaches of previous eras bellowed at their players. Prime ministers make a 'captain's call' without consulting their cabinet colleagues. The major parties drop their leaders as frequently as Richmond used to sack its coaches. The media egg them on, turning political journalism into something akin to an extended footy tipping competition, with Newspoll as the scoreboard. Meanwhile sport has been filling the vacuum left by the loss of respect for parliament, media and the churches.

Football is one of the few institutions that Australians still want to join. Collectively, the eighteen clubs of the national competition now have almost one million members, which is more than the trade unions have in the private sector. The four smallest Victorian clubs have more members between them than the four biggest federal political parties (the Liberals, Labor, the Nationals and the Greens). In 2018, Richmond has over 95 000 members, almost exceeding the combined total for Labor and the Liberals.

I hadn't realised this until my Twitter experiment, but football today is more civil than parliament because it keeps its tribalism in perspective. Consider the modern relationship between supporters of Richmond and Collingwood. Although our clubs have been vicious rivals for a century now, our mutual passion for football binds us. We can each picture our younger selves going to our first game with a parent or older sibling. We can imagine the generations of family and friends reunited in the joy of a drought-breaking premiership – theirs in 1990, after thirty-two years; ours in 2017, after thirty-seven years.

The partisanship in politics does the reverse: it closes the mind to the possibility of the other side's humanity. The main parties assume the electorate is too diverse to unite, so they divide it to prop up their respective base votes. This contest has created the most absurd impasse in which the Liberals and Labor define themselves primarily by what they hate about the other. I have lost count of the incoming governments, at both federal and state level, that devoted their first term in office to erasing every single program of their predecessor.

Politics played as a team sport offends the Australian character. We are wary of zealots, and when one like Tony Abbott does get to be prime minister they normally don't win a second election. But the other end of this bargain is that we don't want to be inspired by politics either. Gough Whitlam and Paul Keating, our two most imaginative leaders, suffered two of the biggest election defeats in Australian history.

We reserve our zealotry for – and seek inspiration in – pastimes like football. I didn't really understand why until Richmond's 2017 premiership prompted me to investigate the game's history, and my club's place in it. What I found, digging through the records, and re-evaluating my childhood passion for the game, is that football bridges the divides of class, ethnicity and religion better than any other sport in the country. It is by no means perfect. The bureaucracy that runs the game ranks alongside politics for dysfunction. Just like the main parties, the AFL intervenes when the game is best left alone and sits on its hands when leadership is required.

Nevertheless, football as it is played and followed is the closest thing we have to a common story between Indigenous, migrant and local-born Australians. I was genuinely, and pleasantly, surprised by this. The game did not make sense to me until I widened the frame to include the full sweep of its history: from the traditional version of football, marngrook, to the gold rush migrants who took up the Melbourne version of the game in the mid-nineteenth century, and finally to the Australian-born who turned football into a national obsession in the twentieth century.

This book is meant to be read with the one eye of a sports fan and the open mind of a citizen. It asks what our attachment to the game tells us about ourselves as people, and what the Richmond premiership can teach politics about leadership. This leadership question was the unexpected bonus of looking more deeply at the 2017 season. I learned that Richmond had broken with a century of macho habit and discovered a new way to win. What began as a book about the game I love became a book about how to run the country I love.

I also found that I couldn't contain the narrative to the Tigers alone. I wanted to know more about other clubs and codes, notably Collingwood and rugby league. So while Richmond remains the main character, there are a number of co-stars, from Victoria Park to North Queensland.

I follow the stories of Richmond, and the nation, in three acts. The first act is a fresh take on football's foundation in the nineteenth century and Sydney's rejection of the sport at the turn of the twentieth century. It traces the rise of Richmond the club and the decline of Richmond the suburb, explaining why the Tigers of old tended to win during periods of economic and political crisis and struggled during the good times. The second act contains my personal story – a declaration of baggage – and explores the politics of football from the establishment of a national competition to the booing of Adam Goodes. The final act reveals how Richmond transformed itself from laughing-stock to premiership role model, based on exclusive interviews with the club's off-field leaders. It is here that I draw out the lessons for politics.

PART ONE

THE PEOPLE AND THEIR GAME

1850s–1960s

I

FOOTBALL'S CONFLICTED ORIGINS

Australian Rules football begins with a paradox. The game is our most original thought and can credibly claim to be the world's first mass spectator sport because it was developed before soccer and rugby. Yet it could not even conquer the whole of the Australian continent.

In the early years of federation, when making football the national faith was still a reasonable prospect, the people of New South Wales and Queensland chose rugby league – a rebel code from northern England – over the indigenous game played by their fellow Australians in the southern states.

The nations we like to compare ourselves to are not this conflicted about their favourite football codes. There are no significant pockets of resistance to soccer in England, Gaelic football in Ireland, rugby union in New Zealand or American football in the United States.

The schism in Australian sport is one of the most curious aspects of our national character: an otherwise peaceful people bitterly divided over the game they play. The split reflects the historical accident of football, which was established in Victoria in the middle of the nineteenth century, before the mother country had any code of her own to export to the gold rush colony. It is also a legacy of the rivalry between Melbourne and Sydney at the turn of the twentieth century, when the two cities were competing for the right to lead Australia into federation.

Melbourne Rules Football, as it was first called, was conceived as an amateur game. It spread to neighbouring South Australia and Tasmania, and later to Western Australia. But that's as far it went. The former convict colonies of New South Wales and Queensland never showed much interest, and when they switched from rugby union to rugby league at the turn of twentieth century they did so, in part, because of money. Rugby league was a professionalised code – the clubs paid their players. For the working men of the northern states that made more material and emotional sense than the middle-class game from the south, which had not yet crossed the threshold to direct payment for players.

But there is another conflict, within football itself. The game can't agree on its own foundation. Perhaps this is the most Australian thing about football. It reflects our inability to understand our own past. Historians are divided between those who believe that the white man invented the game without help and those who believe he was inspired by Indigenous Australians.

After considering the evidence, I found myself in a third camp. Football is an Indigenous game taken up by free migrants. It sprang from a unique period of independence and experimentation in our colonial history, when we didn't look up to London, and when the rest of the world viewed us as a role model for democracy.

Football is a distinctively open game, with both a modern and traditional lineage. It resembles no other game on earth – except the one played by the local Indigenous people.

No other sport permits the same freedom of movement. Every other winter game developed in the nineteenth century has an offside rule. Even American football, which was consciously anti-British in its formation, accepted this British inhibition: the team with the ball was prohibited from having players between the opposition and the goal, waiting for the play to reach them. Australian football didn't care if the teams wandered into each other's territory. On the contrary, it was welcomed.

The men who first played it at the end of the 1850s, and the men and women who watched it, were predominantly middle-class migrants. These people did not carry the inferiority complex of those who came to the colonies before them, or the chip on the shoulder that would burden their Australian-born children and grandchildren. But here's the final paradox: the suburban rivalries that have sustained football for more than a century and a half were first formed in the economic depression of the 1890s, and reaffirmed between the two world wars. That is, we started playing the game in the long boom of the nineteenth century, when Melbourne and Victoria were marvellous, but it was the bust that taught us how to barrack.

Football's four most popular clubs – Collingwood, Richmond, Essendon and Carlton – grew up within a few of miles of the city centre. In any other aspect of their lives, the players and supporters might greet one another as fellow Melburnians. They might attend the same church, belong to the same trade union, or if they were higher up the social ladder, the same men's club. Yet on the football field and in the grandstands they were sworn enemies. The matches these sides play against one another during the regular season still generate passions normally only associated with sporting contests between nations. Rugby league can only work itself up to an equivalent level of enthusiasm in the state of origin games between New South Wales and Queensland.

The most unusual thing about football is its association with Victoria's political development. The ethos of open play suited the progressive character of the times.

In 1856 Victoria became the first settlement in the world to legislate for a secret ballot in elections, and in 1857 the men of the colony were granted the vote. Victoria was also the first to adopt an eight-hour day for workers in the building trade, in 1856. The rallying cry for the labour movement was 'eight hours work, eight hours recreation and eight hours rest'. And it was the question of what to do with their newly won free time that led Victorians to the epiphany of football two years later.

One thing was clear, they didn't want to play the British game of rugby because it carried risks that they had not considered when they were growing up. In their youth, the bruises and broken bones were worn as medals of courage. But as adults in this new land, they could not afford time off work for sporting injuries.

Tom Wills, the son of a wealthy squatter politician, and the grandson of a convict, had the visionary's gift for stating the obvious. Rugby, he said, was 'unsuitable for grown men engaged in making a livelihood'.

Wills had left Melbourne at fourteen to study and play sport at Rugby School in Warwickshire, England. Victoria was still known as Port Phillip, and part of New South Wales. The young émigré and the young colony grew up in tandem. In the seven years he was abroad, he developed a solid reputation as a cricketer and rugby player. In the same period, Victoria separated from New South Wales and, with the discovery of gold, became the world's richest settlement.

Wills returned home at the end of 1856, at age twenty-one, with the champion's strut. His local fame was assured when he led Victoria to its first win against New South Wales at an intercolonial cricket game in January 1858. But the coming of winter filled him with dread. The sport he loved was in recess and there was no other activity to take its place. Would his teammates lose their edge?

He shared his concerns in a letter to a local sporting journal, and offered the suggestion that Victorians follow the lead of his English schoolmates and devote themselves to sport all year round. Wills was writing for an audience that either played one of the versions of football in the mother country, or was reading about it in the most popular book of the time, *Tom Brown's School Days*, which was set in Rugby School.

'Rather than allow this state of torpor to creep over them, and stifle their now supple limbs, why can they not, I say, form a football club and form a committee of three or more to draw up a code of laws?' he asked.

If a football club could not be started, perhaps they could take up shooting, he went on.

> [W]hy, I say, do they not form themselves into a rifle club, so as at any rate they may some day be called upon to aid their adopted land against a tyrant's band, that may some day 'pop' upon us when we least expect a foe at our very doors.

Of the two things that troubled him – an idle winter or a sneak attack from the Russian navy – it was the call to play football that resonated with his fellow Victorians.

The handful of matches improvised in that winter of 1858 inspired a movement. The following April, *The Argus* reported that football clubs were being formed across Melbourne in anticipation of the end of the cricket season. The newspaper could not explain the fascination with this new game, but it welcomed the dedication to winter fitness.

> Whether that manly and healthy book, *Tom Brown's School Days*, or the natural anti-American tendencies of Victoria [. . .] or a little of both, have produced such a love for robust exercise, it matters not to inquire. Football, like cricket, has become an institution in and about the metropolis, and it would not be surprising if the epidemic spread wider. There are many well-grassed valleys and plains

> in the immediate neighborhood of the various diggings, where the miners, cramped in their limbs with working in constrained positions, and whose lungs would be none the worse for a little extra oxygen, might enjoy themselves on Saturday afternoons in straining for goals of easier attainment than that which is the aim of their ordinary occupations. Mechanics, too, and artizans, would find their health much improved by a good game of foot-ball once a week.

The first rules for a game to be played in the colony were drawn up at a meeting of the Melbourne Football Club in May 1859. Wills was one of the four officials in the room. He argued that the rugby he had played was not suited to local conditions. The paddocks were harder and the risk of injury far greater than the sodden playing fields of the mother country. Soccer might have been the natural choice for these men if they had pondered the question of recreation only a few years later; they were, after all, children of Queen Victoria's empire. But the rules of British association football, the game that would be favoured by the mother country's working class, were not codified until 1863, and the various forms of rugby played at elite public schools not until 1871.

With no established game to take up, they had the privilege of inventing a game of their own. They took the template of rugby and adapted it, with two critical differences. First, there was no offside rule to limit the movement of an attacking player, meaning the play was open. Second, the practice of hacking – kicking an opponent in the shins, which was common to rugby – was prohibited. Tripping was allowed at first, but after parents complained that young sons had been badly hurt, the rule was quickly amended to ban that as well.

Not everyone appreciated this less brutal sport. *The Argus* mocked the softness of the colonial men who played it. 'Under the humane legislation of the Melbourne Football Club tripping has been tabooed, and "hacking" renders a member liable to excommunication. These rare old "bullies," so famous, at one time at least, at Winchester, Eton, and Harrow, have no place in Victoria, and in vain do we in these degenerate days anticipate the spectacle of a dozen players rolling on the ground together,' the newspaper said, reviewing the opening match between Melbourne and Richmond, held on 12 May 1860.

> But if sore shins and aching shoulders are less common, and the excitement be less intense, we make up in some measure by increased good humour and the absence of severe accidents. So that perhaps, after all, football under the rules of the 'Humane Society' is preferable to the horse-play we so much gloried in as schoolboys, when our bruises were deemed trophies of pluck, and a good limp or a black eye a thing to talk about and be proud of. Besides, the football players here are grown men, and don't take a kick so kindly as they would a dozen years ago. Black eyes don't look well in Collins-street.

The match itself was a tie, with one goal for each team. Melbourne and Richmond met again a fortnight later, and although no goals were scored, the public were intrigued. 'There were a large number of spectators present, who appeared to take as much interest in the game as the players themselves.' Each good kick and every artful run with the ball was met with 'ready applause'. And every fumbled ball or tumbling player 'provoked a burst of merriment.'

The player they came to watch was the captain of the Richmond side, Tom Wills. As the catalyst for the game's origin and its first drawcard, his personal story is, in effect, the game's foundation story.

Wills had a family tree with roots in the earliest years of the convict settlement. His grandfather Edward Wills had been transported to New South Wales in 1799, accompanied by his free grandmother Sarah. Following Edward's emancipation, the couple prospered as Sydney merchants. Edward died in 1811, five months before his son Horatio was born. Sarah married George Howe, the publisher of the *Sydney Gazette*, on Horatio's first birthday. As an adult, Horatio Wills ran the *Gazette* and for a brief period a magazine called the *Currency Lad*, which pushed the cause of colonial offspring like himself under the banner of 'Rise Australia'. He married in 1833 and Tom was born in 1835.

Horatio was an ambitious man and when Victoria, then still known as the Port Phillip district of New South Wales, was opened up to settlers he joined the squatter rush. He moved his young family from their property in the Molonglo Plains of New South Wales to Victoria's Western District in 1840, where he laid claim to 200 000 acres of farmland. The measure of his wealth was his entourage – 500 sheep, 500 cattle, drovers, stockmen, shepherds and their families.

This is ground zero in football's history war. Tom was the district's only white child, and grew up playing with the local Indigenous children. He spoke their language and participated in their ceremonies; this much historians agree on. The argument is over whether he saw the locals play marngrook, the Indigenous version of football.

The official position of the AFL remains that there was no direct link between settler and Indigenous games, but the case for marngrook's influence has been strengthened by the recent work of historians Jenny Hocking and Nell Reidy. They have uncovered a description of the Indigenous game that places it in Victoria's Western District in the 1840s, when Wills was living there as a child. The recollection is from a local man named John Connolly. He played a game in which a ball was 'kicked about' between teams that represented their respective communities. There is also the oral history of the Wills family. Tom's grand-nephew, Lawton Wills Cooke, told author Martin Flanagan that the family has known for more than 100 years that Tom Wills played Aboriginal football as a kid.

The game itself gives further evidence. Wills and his colleagues got the idea that the ball could be kicked in the air and caught from rugby. But the footballing version of the 'mark' evolved into an exclamation point of the game, not the footnote it was in rugby. A mark wasn't just taken on the chest, the ball cradled like a newborn baby, it was an invitation to fly, arms reaching skywards to grab the ball above the head. The only other game that featured the 'high mark' was marngrook.

Consider this description from the pivotal year of 1858, written by William Thomas, the assistant protector of Aborigines:

> The Marngrook (or ball) is a favorite game with boys and men. [The] ball is kicked up and not thrown by the hand as white boys do. The ball is kicked into the air not along the ground. There is a general scramble to catch it in the air. The tall blackfellows stand the best chance. When caught it is again kicked up in the air with great force and ascends as straight up and as high as when thrown by the hand [. . .] The girls play at Marngrook but throw it up as white children.

He was referring to the game the locals played in the 1840s, before the gold rush. The ball was made of possum skin and would have been closer in shape and size to a soccer ball than the oval rugby ball.

Another possibility is that the influence was the other way around: the locals copied the settlers and were able to realise the game's potential by perfecting the high mark while the white men were still fumbling for the football on the ground. This is the theory historian Roy Hay offered in response to Hocking and Reidy's research:

> Indigenous people who played their traditional games, particularly in regional areas, saw or interacted with the white men at football. They would probably have been involved in it very quickly if they had been allowed to do so. But since they were effectively kept out,

they formed their own teams and played with each other, or tried to break into local activities or competitions when they could.

But why football and not cricket? After all, Wills taught the locals to play cricket and, in the summer of 1866–67, he led them onto the MCG for a game before 10 000 spectators, and then on a tour of New South Wales. They went to England without him in 1868. Yet the summer game did not flourish in the same way as football did later in the Aboriginal missions.

Although the game Wills and his colleagues pioneered has much more in common with marngrook than rugby, the former is never mentioned in their many letters, while the latter is a clear influence, if only to avoid its worst features. That could well reflect what people at the time wished to hear. While Wills was being schooled in England, the Indigenous population of Victoria had been virtually wiped out. The exact toll can never be known, let alone the breakdown between massacre, disease and starvation. But all the available statistics confirm that the migrant waves to Victoria triggered the fastest collapse of any Indigenous community on the continent. By 1861, there were 2384 locals remaining, a reduction of 84 per cent on the 15 000-strong population estimated in 1788. The colony that Wills returned to at the end of 1856 had no interest in hearing about his childhood or its Indigenous connections. They only wanted to know about his sporting conquests in the mother country.

Still, the colonial version of football did not have the creative spirit and athleticism of marngrook. The early games were a gridlock of good intentions and poor implementation. Hours could pass without a goal being scored. There are no celebrated accounts of a colonial Roy Cazaly taking gravity-defying marks, a Gordon Coventry kicking a bagful of goals, let alone a John Coleman doing both. To imagine the efforts of those early players, recall how awkward Australian politicians and international celebrities – even sports stars from other codes – look when they attempt to kick or handball a football for the television cameras. A generation of Victorians would need to be raised with a football in their hands before the adults could realise the game's magic and play it with childlike abandon.

In these years before football became an art form, the athlete who stood out was the defender. For Tom Wills, that meant a reversal of roles. In summer, he was the attacking all-rounder who belted the runs and bowled out the opposition. In winter, he stopped goals. At that first game against Melbourne in 1860 Wills was reportedly best on ground, defending 'his post against all comers with almost unvarying success'.

Wills was a contrarian. For instance, he wanted to remove the ban on hacking, and argued his case as the game grew in popularity in the early 1860s. Thankfully his colleagues brushed him off. By 1866, they had cracked the code for the game we know today, adding a rule that allowed a player to pick up the football in general play and run with it, provided they bounced or tapped it on the ground 'every five or six yards'. This change was introduced to prevent the quickest players, such as Henry Harrison, from simply grabbing the ball and sprinting towards the goals.

The question I kept coming back to as I read the early accounts of football is: why Victoria and nowhere else? What was so special about the people of this settlement that they made a sporting discovery that was missed by their cousins in the United Kingdom, Europe and the United States?

And this raises an awkward follow-up question: why was it that the only invention to come out of a colony with the world's highest standard of living was a code of football?

The people who took up football had their lives transformed by the gold rush. In 1859, Victoria was the richest colony in the world's richest settlement. Australia's gross domestic product per person was 6 per cent larger than Great Britain's and 36 per cent larger than in the United States. The Victorians built bigger houses, and lived in less densely populated cities and towns. They were better fed, breathed cleaner air and had a longer life expectancy. They bought more books per capita than any other people. A tradesman or a farmer in Victoria could earn double or treble the wage of their counterpart in the US.

It seems hard to credit that these comfortable, material people would be original thinkers in sport, but lack imagination in the sciences, arts or political philosophy. The industrial and political reforms of this era – the eight-hour day and the secret ballot – were ideals that the migrants brought with them to Victoria. These innovations arose peacefully, through collaboration and adaptation. Surely Tom Wills and his colleagues came to football by a similar means.

Here's what I think is the most plausible explanation. The initial inspiration for football was the game that Wills had played with the local Indigenous children in the 1840s. Into that sporting stew he added the games he played in England in the 1850s. By the time he returned to Victoria in 1856, the settlers were ready for a sport that reflected their free spirt. Once they tried this new type of game – without an offside rule, without the gratuitous violence, and with the invitation to fly – they were let into a secret that the locals had known for millennia. Football suited the egalitarian personality of the migrants from Britain, Ireland and Europe better than any class-conscious code they could have imported from the old world.

Rugby league and union, soccer and American football abhor chaos. The dominant sports in Britain and the US are regimented like board games. The two rugby codes do not allow the ball to be passed forward by hand, or, in practical terms, much scope for most players to kick it. In soccer you can only kick, or use your head – only the goalkeeper can pick the ball up.

By contrast, football's anxiety is not chaos but congestion. The rules are constantly tweaked in an effort to open up the play.

Running, jumping, marking and kicking. Both hands, both feet – only the head is excluded. The game is the greatest expression of the Australian faith in human nature. In William Thomas's account of marngrook, he observed how 'the men and boys joyfully assemble when this game is to be played'. They play for hours and 'never seem to tire of the exercise' of kicking and catching the ball.

Football arrived at a time when Victorians were developing the habit of watching sport in large numbers.

Prosperity brought passenger train lines that connected Melbourne's suburbs to each other, and the capital to the colony's three main towns of Ballarat, Bendigo and Geelong. The crowds at the cricket, football and especially the race track swelled from a few thousand in the early 1860s to 10 000 or more by the decade's end. The second phase of rail construction from the late 1870s to the end of the 1880s, and the introduction of cable trams in Melbourne from the mid-1880s, facilitated the movement of tens of thousands more.

The first Melbourne Cup horserace was held in 1861, three years after football was born, and seen by 4000 people. By 1877, there were at least 75 000 at the track, and well over 100 000 by the early 1880s.

The Melbourne Cup was a single annual event, worth the time and the travel. When the Victorian Football Association played its first season in 1877, it proved there was appetite for a sporting spectacle every week. In June that year, a football match drew its first 10 000 crowd, to watch Melbourne and Carlton at the MCG.

The South Australian Football Association, formed in the same year as the VFA, attracted an audience that was smaller and rougher. In July 1877, 'upwards of 500 spectators . . . including about 100 larrikins' watched an infamous night game at the Adelaide Football Club. Whenever the ball was kicked out of bounds, the larrikins would seize it and kick it among themselves. The players soon tired of the interruptions and the two twenty-man teams united to take on the mob. Tackles were laid, punches thrown and players and spectators crashed to the ground together. Eventually the ball was recovered and 'handed for safe-keeping to a gentleman on horseback, who galloped with it under his arm towards the city'. The crowd chased him 'shouting and jeering till the fleet steed left the excited multitude far behind, and the horseman was able to house the ball safely in the Gresham Hotel'.

What separated Victoria from the football colonies to its west and the football sceptics to the north was the discovery of gold. It created a mass middle-class society within the blink of a decade, providing a cashed-up supporter base with leisure time and the civility prosperity brings.

Before the gold rush of 1851, Victoria's population of 77 000 was not that much greater than South Australia's or Van Diemen's Land. By the time the rush ended ten years later, the total population had increased six-fold to 540 000 – 70 per cent larger than New South Wales (358 000); four times larger than South Australia (131 000) and six times larger than what was now Tasmania (90 000). In 1851, Melbourne had been a small, sewerless town of 23 000. Within a year it was the most visited port in the world, and by 1861 it had replaced Sydney as Australia's largest city, with 140 000 people.

Eighty-four per cent of Victoria's population boom came from overseas. This wave of fortune-seeking humanity was too diverse to worship in the same church, read the same books, or admire the same art. No single group was large enough to impose its tastes and prejudices on the others. Democracy was in its infancy: Victoria had six premiers in its first six years of self-government, between 1855 and 1861. In this tumultuous setting, football was social glue that bound the disparate tribes.

The landmark reform of the eight-hour day meant the game could be stitched into Victoria's social fabric. The clubs and their grounds became community centres – just as the racetrack had been in the earliest decades of Sydney's convict settlement, bringing the classes together in celebration of sport.

Attending a game of football became one of the things to do in Melbourne, and as the game grew in popularity in the 1870s and especially 1880s, it became the dominant social activity in winter. Workers on the city's building sites and in the small factories of the inner suburbs finished their shifts at midday on a Saturday and joined clerks, police officers, judges and politicians in the commute to the football. Many walked to the grounds, but many more boarded the trains and cable trams, which could take them to any part of the city in time for the 3 p.m. start of a game.

When the VFA expanded to ten teams in 1885, five games were often scheduled on the same Saturday afternoon. On 25 July, for instance, almost 25 000 people attended the four games across Melbourne and another 2000 watched Geelong play Williamstown at Corio Oval. While they were competitors on the field, the clubs had a shared sense of purpose as crowds and coffers swelled.

The following season delivered football's first blockbuster. South Melbourne and Geelong were both undefeated when they met late in the season, with the match deciding who would win the premiership, which was then awarded to the team that finished first on the ladder. Many of the rituals of the grand final were established on this day, from the columns of fans marching to the ground to the street party thrown for the premiership team after the game. An unprecedented crowd of 28 000 came to South Melbourne to watch, the equivalent of around 10 per cent of the city's population. Some mischievous South Melbourne fans tried but failed to interfere with the rail track between Werribee and Melbourne, hoping to delay the two special trains from Geelong that carried the players and 2000 supporters.

'In the city, from the intersection of Bourke and Swanston streets all the way to the South Melbourne cricket ground, the road between the hours of 2 and 3 o'clock resembled what is seen on a Melbourne Cup day,' *The Age* wrote.

> Everybody seemed to be going in the same direction, and the stream of overladen cabs [cable trams] crossing the Falls-bridge was something to see. No provision had been made for regulating the traffic, and consequently there were numerous narrow escapes from accident, though no serious casualties occurred.

Every available space at the ground was occupied. Younger fans climbed trees for a better view, while a small contingent watched the game from the roof of the South Melbourne pavilion. A fence collapsed from the weight of bodies pressed against it, but the spectators remained respectfully behind the boundary line. Nobody wanted to be the cause of an early end to the game.

Geelong, the fittest and the fastest team of the VFA, was victorious by four goals to one (at the time, behinds were not counted in the final score). Their post-match celebration confirmed the growing importance of football to the people. Thousands of wellwishers cheered the players as they were driven through South Melbourne's main road, Clarendon Street.

In its review of the game, *The Argus* declared that football had replaced cricket as Victoria's most popular sport. 'Cricket is the more scientific pastime, and the more graceful, but, like Parliament, it has been half ruined by the stonewallers.' Australia's Charles Bannerman and England's Dick Barlow were killing cricket with their defensive play. They would occupy the crease for an hour 'without scoring a run'.

In football, 'all was vivacity from start to finish'. The contest between South Melbourne and Geelong demonstrated that, with two well-matched teams, 'every moment brings its own excitement, and the stir and the strife certainly take mightily with young Victoria'.

A critical part of football's success, the paper argued, was its civility.

> No game so easily degenerates into rowdyism as football, but the association has kept a strict and stern watch, and has pretty well put down violence on the field and vehemence of expression among the spectators.

This was the first inflection of football's popularity, from the low-scoring games of the 1860s to the dashing contests of the 1880s. It coincided with Victoria's transition from a colony of migrants to one where the majority of the population were local-born. Nevertheless, football wasn't yet an obsession. It was still just one of the many forms of entertainment on offer to a people raised in affluence.

Melbourne held two opulent international exhibitions in 1880 and 1888, the second featuring the most extravagant concert tour the world had seen. One of England's top conductors, Frederick Cowen, was hired for the event on a generous six-month contract worth more than $750 000 in today's dollars. He brought with him fifteen instrumentalists, combined them with the best of the local talent, and a choir of 708 singers. They played ten times a week for six months. 'About 11 000 people attended every Saturday; the Beethoven symphonies and Wagner became immensely popular,' Australian historian Geoffrey Searle wrote. Australians were said to own the most pianos per head of population in the world. Although as footballer, journalist and newspaper editor Richard Twopeny wrote in his 1883 book *Town Life in Australia*, 'in no country is a good pianoforte player more rare, or do you hear greater trash strummed in a drawing-room'.

Up to this point, the colonial experience had been a series of long booms, interrupted by short busts. In the period from the white man's arrival in Melbourne in 1835 to the peak of the last of those booms in 1891, Australia's gross domestic product per person quadrupled. No other people came close to this level of wealth in the nineteenth century. The next best result over the same period was the United States, where GDP per person doubled. When the crash came in the 1890s, though, it turned Victoria into a riven settlement and brought Australians back to the same standard of living as the Americans and British.

Australia's reaction was to close itself off from the world – it introduced protection against foreign goods and restricted immigration to white people only. In this period of harder economic times and isolation, the meaning of football changed. The game became more violent and the crowds more vociferous. Supporters who had applauded visiting teams in the 1870s and 1880s would yell abuse at them in the 1890s and 1900s. In too many instances, they would jump the fence and attack the players of opposing clubs. The game became defined by the rivalries between suburban clubs, and a new mythology would be written around the annual tribal contest for the premiership. Football's cosmopolitan origins were forgotten along with marngrook.

2

A FOOTBALL CLUB RISES AS A SUBURB DIES

The opportunity for football to become the nation's winter pastime disappeared in the long depression of the 1890s. In that hungry decade the game still retained its aesthetic appeal, and its ability to convert non-believers: the Victorians who abandoned the colony for the Western Australian goldfields took football with them, completing the game's takeover of the southern half of the continent. But in its home base, the game split between the old guard of the Victorian Football Association and the rebel Victorian Football League, founded in 1896.

Divided, football did not have the resources to push into New South Wales, even though the working class there was losing interest in the traditional sport of rugby. The depression shaped both the suburban character of football in Victoria and the advance of the new game of rugby league in New South Wales and Queensland.

The depression was a global event, triggered by a financial panic in Britain in 1890. A second, more widespread financial crisis came in 1893, overwhelming banking systems from London to New York to Melbourne as people rushed to withdraw their deposits. Half the trading banks in Victoria closed their doors during the run. The extent of the fallout in individual countries was determined by the excesses of the 1880s. Those who had borrowed the most bore the brunt of the reckoning. In the US, that was the small-scale farmers who had expanded into the country's heartland. In states like Kansas and South Dakota they had borrowed up to half the value of their land and, when crop prices collapsed, many lost their livelihood.

In the colonies of Victoria and New South Wales, the hardest landing was felt in the cities by the middle-class property speculator. The data is not precise, but in Melbourne and Sydney land values appear to have doubled in a matter of years. The bust, as best as it can be measured, saw prices crash by 50 per cent in Melbourne and 25 per cent in Sydney by the mid-1890s.

Australia was one of the first to succumb to the global depression and the very last to recover. It would take twenty years for Australia's GDP per person to return to the level it had been in 1889. One of the reasons is that the White Australia Policy, introduced in 1901, ended mass migration, although restrictions based on race had been in place for many years before that. Between 1891 and 1906, more people left Australia than arrived from overseas.

These multiple shocks to the economy and society had a compounding effect, turning a once-confident people inward. In the depression the fault lines of class and sectarianism – which the colonies thought they had overcome in the golden decades – opened up, testing the unity of the people. Labour and capital clashed in the great strikes of the 1890s while the working class in the industrial suburbs of the inner city separated economically and culturally from the middle class in the so-called garden suburbs.

This is where the tribalism of football begins, and it is best understood through the story of Richmond, the suburb and the club.

Richmond had what turns out to be the ideal mix of advantages and curses to produce a successful football club. A struggling suburb, it was caught on the wrong side of the Yarra River, but on the right side of what is still Melbourne's best sporting address, Yarra Park.

The river flats in the suburb's south and east were a dumping ground for the waste produced by the colony's nascent industries. Tanneries, bootmakers, furniture makers, a brewery and a wool-washing plant cast a stench over the suburb.

On the other side, the river's bank was steeper. In Toorak to the south and Hawthorn to the east mansions were built, not factories. Today if you stand on the MacRobertson Bridge over the river, by the Burnley exit of the CityLink toll road, the divide between the two worlds is still apparent. On one side of the river you see the old workers' cottages and factories, on the other you see the mansions of Melbourne's most exclusive postcode.

Richmond did have its own pocket of colonial wealth. On its western boundary, a majestic hill gave the rich folk unrivalled views of the Dandenong Ranges on one side and the city on the other. Between the suburb and the city lay Melbourne's most inclusive piece of real estate – the vast reserve that was home to the Richmond Cricket Ground, the Melbourne Cricket Ground and the East Melbourne Cricket Ground, which was Essendon's inner-city base until it was demolished at the end of the 1921 season to allow for the extension of the Jolimont Yard railway sidings. The *Australian Handbook's* 1875 edition described this parkland as 'a very favourite place of resort for the people'.

For a brief, deceptive period in the 1880s it seemed as if Richmond would jump the trap of geography and join the rest of Melbourne in middle-class comfort. The suburb was the first to be connected to the Melbourne cable tram network in 1885, and the commuters who rode the service underwrote a boom in the local economy. The retail strip along Bridge Road received a facelift as the old stores built during the gold rush were knocked down and replaced with rows of modern two-storey buildings. Clothes makers, cobblers, hairdressers and the suburb's many pubs satisfied the people's mania for consumption.

The middle class moved into Richmond and new mansions rose on the Church Street hill. Among them was Lalor House, built by Joseph Lalor, son of Peter, the speaker of the Victorian parliament and leader of the Eureka Rebellion. Across the road, and a little further up the hill, the landmark St Ignatius' Catholic Church towered over the old St Stephen's Anglican Church.

The suburb's collective heart swelled with pride when local girl Nellie Melba made her debut as an opera singer at the Théâtre Royal de la Monnaie in Brussels in 1887. Richmond felt like the centre of the universe. People flocked to the suburb – the population exploded by 66 per cent, from 23 500 in 1881 to almost 39 000 in 1891 – and it was in this ebullient period that the Richmond Football Club was finally born, in 1885, after five previous ventures had failed. The original club had been captained by Tom Wills and then Henry Harrison. But once these pioneers of the game moved to Geelong, Richmond lost its impetus and that first incarnation of the club disbanded at the end of the 1861 season.

Other suburbs and towns had more luck establishing their clubs. Melbourne and Geelong had been playing continuously since 1858 and 1859 respectively, while Carlton, the suburb immediately to the north of the city centre, formed its club in 1864. In fact, of the ten Victorian clubs in the AFL today, only Collingwood, born in 1892, is younger than Richmond. What had separated the older clubs from the late starters was money. The nascent industrial suburbs did not become large enough to support football until the 1880s.

As with the invention of the game, the catalyst for Richmond FC was the cricket club, which was based at the oval on Punt Road. The heroes of summer wanted football played on their ground during the winter break to generate revenue for the cricket club. So, at a meeting at the Royal Hotel on 20 February 1885, as the cricket season drew to a close a football club was born. Six days later, the committee reconvened at Byrne's Hotel to pick the club's colours, 'all blue with yellow and black sash and cap to correspond'. The beer tap was turned off for the club's first general meeting at Temperance Hall on Church Street, where 'all supporters of the yellow and black stripes were urged to attend'.

Richmond entered the Victorian Football Association that season, with *The Argus* reporting 3000 people in attendance for the home game against Carlton on 20 June, more than had ever attended a cricket match at the ground. The following month, the Richmond Cricket Ground hosted an intercolonial soccer match between Victoria and New South Wales, which drew only 300 spectators. At the return encounter between Richmond and Carlton, at Prince's Oval on 1 August, the crowd was 7000-strong. Football had entered Richmond's bloodstream.

Although Richmond won just four of the eighteen matches it played in its first season, *The Australasian* judged this a 'fairly creditable' result for a new club.

> The general play of the team has been very good, and fully justified its determination to figure in the senior ranks; but its deficiency in goal-kicking quality has placed it in a much worse position than its general play would have warranted.

The contemporary equivalent of 'deficiency in goal-kicking' is 'butchering the football'. That would become a common criticism of Richmond teams during their many decades of underachievement.

The club's second season revealed one possible explanation for the poor kicking: the players liked a drink. On their trip to Ballarat in June 1886, they partied so hard that most members of the team had no sleep before the game. They suffered a heavy defeat. Upon their return home, Richmond's match committee decided to make an example of the captain Tom Graham and two of the best players, dropping them for the next match. Three other players protested that they would not play until their mates were reinstated. They were also dropped. Ultimately all six were kicked out of the club.

The VFA praised the committee for its moral stand and banned the six from playing for any other club for the rest of the year. The officials of the VFA and the Richmond Football Club were on a joint ticket of decency. Embarrassed by the team's 'rowdy' image, they urged players and spectators to curb their language at home games at the oval on Punt Road.

This dichotomy between the upwardly mobile suburb and its rugged football team reflected the class divide that emerged in Richmond during the land boom of the 1880s. With the hill and nearby streets redeveloped to accommodate the mansions and terraces for the newly rich, the workers were pushed into the filthy back lanes to the south. Slums of overcrowded cottages had formed even before the depression struck. The club also identified as Catholic and although sectarianism was not yet an open wound in Victoria, even in the 1880s, the club and the suburb still felt like outsiders in prosperous, Protestant Melbourne.

When the depression of the 1890s hit, the middle class moved out to the leafier suburbs, or left Melbourne altogether. Almost 50 000 people – around 10 per cent of Melbourne's total population – fled the capital between 1891 and 1893. Most headed to the Western Australian gold rush, taking football with them. Richmond was one of the suburbs most affected by the exodus. In these first three years of the depression, it lost 7000 people – almost 20 per cent of the suburb. Even by 1901, there were 1000 fewer residents than there had been ten years before. Left behind were rows of empty houses and stores, and a destitute people. The formerly rich gave up their mansions, and these monuments to the boom were repurposed in the bust as seedy boarding homes.

Victorians had thought slums only blighted the big cities in the mother country or the United States. But in the 1890s, they became the reality in the inner city of Melbourne. Unemployment soared as high as 20 per cent, while the men who did find work were paid a subsistence wage and could barely feed their families.

The Age ran a series of articles in 1893 titled 'Poorer than the Poor' that catalogued the plight of the inner city. Three case studies were reported, and it is the account of life in Collingwood that is closest to Richmond's experience.

> The working part of Collingwood was described as being in a state of industrial paralysis owing to the almost complete cessation of building operations throughout the city. It is found as a rule that the suffering families are mostly those whose bread winners were formerly employed in heavy labor of different descriptions, or were either dependent on the building and attendant trades.
>
> [Once] the 'boom' collapsed this class of people began to feel the pressure of the contracting markets, and ever since employment for them has become smaller by degrees and beautifully less. At first many of these men went up the country, earning a few shillings at one place, remitting as much as possible to their wives in town, and tramping on to other towns. But the country, it seems, soon became as overrun with men on the look out for work as the town, or at any rate many found that their journeys in search of work were not only fruit less but left them weaker in health than before.

Their families back in Collingwood were 'bearing the brunt of the suffering during these winter months'.

> In the hopeless periods when work failed utterly, their homes were sold piece by piece, and now when their situation seems to have come to the most desperate pass, they find that actual charitable relief, though very bitter indeed to swallow, is, in many cases, their only stand by to keep them from want.

The ladies who ran the charities described finding 'at least 10 families' living in a lane off Hoddle Street 'under circumstances of the most wretched discomfort and penury'.

'At the back of the Town Hall, whole clusters of people were found at their last crust, so to speak.'

The most striking anecdote is of an old man and his son living 'in an outhouse of an empty cottage'. 'The man's wife had died, his home had been sold up, and with no prospect of working at his trade of shipwright, he had been forced to seek this last forlorn shelter.'

Every one of Richmond's football neighbours suffered dramatic population losses in the 1890s – Carlton, Collingwood, Fitzroy, Melbourne, North Melbourne, Port Melbourne and South Melbourne. They became ghost suburbs, an urban version of the towns in South Australia and Tasmania that had been emptied of their young men during the Victorian gold rush.

Some football clubs thrived in this environment, able to retain a critical mass of men eager to prove themselves on the field. Collingwood was one of those. Other clubs were barely viable. Richmond was in that category.

In the 1890s the VFA competition became lopsided and violent. Spectators routinely disrupted games, and even attacked players. The sense of shared purpose that the clubs felt in the 1880s had vanished with the depression. The big clubs such as Essendon and South Melbourne resented subsidising poor clubs like Richmond and Footscray through their gate receipts. They even came to hate playing them, because although they would be easy to defeat, attendances fell precipitously. Especially in the economic circumstances, few people wanted to pay to watch a forgone conclusion. The big clubs urged the VFA to reform the competition, but the officials dithered until they lost patience and decided to break away and form a league of their own.

The tipping point for open rebellion appears to have been the haggling over the fixture to conclude the 1896 season. For the first time, the final round would feature the top two teams on the ladder, with the winner assured of the premiership. Collingwood and South Melbourne wanted to play on 26 September, the same day as four other scheduled matches. They made an arrangement to stage the premiership decider at the largest available venue, the East Melbourne Cricket Ground, where a bumper crowd was expected.

The VFA feared that the eight other clubs playing on that day would see their 'gate [receipts] spoiled by an all-absorbing contest' between the top two teams. And so it ordered Collingwood and South Melbourne to delay their game by a week, to 3 October. The two clubs protested and a special meeting of the VFA was held at the Young and Jackson's Hotel to hear their appeal.

Collingwood's president William Beazley argued that a delay would be unfair to the players of both teams. They wanted the game played on its merits, with both teams fit. 'In waiting for a week some of the men would be overtrained, others would not be sufficiently trained.'

The South Melbourne vice-president, a Mr J. Sloss, passed on the reaction of the players when they were first advised of the delay. He quoted Collingwood captain Bill Strickland, who'd said: 'Don't put it off, or half our players will be in the lunatic asylum.'

But they could not persuade a majority of the clubs needed to carry the appeal, and by a vote of ten to nine the VFA reaffirmed its decision to delay the 'premiership tie', as it was now being called.

On 2 October, the night before the postponed game, Collingwood and South Melbourne had their revenge. They met secretly with the officials of four other clubs, Essendon, Melbourne, Fitzroy and Geelong, to consider reform options for the VFA. The first was to split the competition into two divisions with promotion and relegation between them, the second was to reduce the number of clubs by weeding out the poorest, and the third was to leave the VFA.

They took the third option, inviting Carlton and St Kilda to join them in the new Victorian Football League. The criteria for entry was a mix of ladder position, age of club and reputation for good behaviour.

Five of the eight rebels, Collingwood, South Melbourne, Essendon, Melbourne and Fitzroy, were conveniently the top five teams on the ladder in 1896. Geelong had a poor season, but the other clubs agreed it should be included, 'having done more for Victorian football than any other', according to *The Argus*.

Carlton was given the benefit of 'its glorious past, not its present feebleness' while St Kilda was unanimously chosen as the eighth club due to its 'manly and decent conduct, both on the field and off it'.

Collingwood won the premiership the following day before a crowd of 12 000, fewer than half the number that had attended the blockbuster decider between South Melbourne and Geelong a decade earlier. The smaller audience reflected the effects of the depression as many supporters could not afford the admission price of one shilling.

Richmond was snubbed by the VFL rebels because, in 1986, it had the worst on-field record in the thirteen-club VFA competition, and its players and supporters were among the worst behaved.

As well as Richmond, the VFA was left with four other clubs – Footscray, North Melbourne, Port Melbourne and Williamstown. A sixth suburban club, Brunswick, was added to ensure the competition could continue. For its part, Richmond remained out of its depth, finishing last again in 1897.

It took several more years for the club to find its feet and begin its rise up the ladder. A third-place finish in 1900 in an expanded nine-team VFA provided cause for optimism, and a taste of the galvanising power of suburban rivalry. When Richmond recorded its first ever win against archenemy Port Melbourne in June that year, the 'penalty for their victory' was to be attacked by the supporters of the losing team. Special attention was paid to Archie McNair, who *The Age* said was Richmond's best player. '[He] had to be surrounded by his comrades and the visiting followers of the Richmond team, whose secretary had his shin cut by a kick.'

The Richmond contingent required a police escort to the train 'as a safeguard against' further attack from the 'mob of ruffians'. The enmity grew with each subsequent encounter.

In 1901, the players took a vow of sobriety: they agreed to stop drinking whiskey at half time. Drinking would be confined to after the game. With that level of commitment, and their early performances, they expected to win the premiership. But they dropped a match late in the season, handing top spot and the pennant to their bayside rival, Port Melbourne. When Richmond hosted Port Melbourne for the opening game of the 1902 season, it was the turn of the Richmond supporters to disgrace themselves. They pelted the opposition with stones, injuring two of Port Melbourne's star players. Port's captain called for a suspension of the game until police restored order and the ground was cleared.

'At the conclusion of the match there were further disturbances of a highly discreditable nature,' *The Argus* reported.

The rivals entered the final round with fourteen wins each, tied at the top of the ladder. If, as expected, they defeated their respective opponents, the two teams would play each other for the deciding 'premiership tie' the following week. But the VFA did not gets its wish. Port Melbourne lost its game at Williamstown, and when word got back to Toorak Park, where Richmond had just defeated Prahran, 'the delight of Richmondites was unbounded'. At last, a premiership.

A second premiership in 1905 confirmed Richmond's competitiveness, and its popularity. The club was now responsible for about one third of the VFA's total attendances. The VFL was ready to talk, and in 1908 they finally welcomed Richmond to the big league, along with the University club.

The VFL introduced two revolutionary changes to the game. First, players would be paid to play. Initially only their expenses were meant to be covered, but since extra cash was often being provided under the table, in 1911 the league took a pragmatic decision and permitted direct player payments. The second reform was the introduction of a finals series, involving the top four teams on the ladder in a knockout competition to decide the premiership.

What the league wasn't able to do was export the game to New South Wales. The time was ripe – there, the working class was losing interest in the amateur game of rugby union, which thrived in the private schools and at Sydney University but not in the suburbs. But there was no substantial Victorian diaspora in NSW to carry the game with them, as there had been in Western Australia. Some Victorians did move across the Murray River to the Riverina farming district, where football became the most popular winter sport, but not enough people made it as far as Sydney.

Without new arrivals to proselytise for it in the capital, the only way for football to convert the masses was by staging games for premiership points in Sydney. But that required money, and ambition, both of which football had lost in the 1890s. The VFL did make a belated pitch in 1903, when Collingwood and Fitzroy played an official game at the Sydney Cricket Ground in front of 20 000 spectators. A second game was played in Sydney that season, between Carlton and Geelong. But the VFL didn't come back. That left the door ajar for the recent invention of rugby league to supplant union.

Part of the problem was that no one respected, or envied, Melbourne anymore. As the city's population went into retreat, by 1902 Sydney was Australia's largest city again, only a year after the six colonies formed a federation. In this new country, the last place Sydneysiders would want to look for direction was their fallen neighbour. But that doesn't entirely explain why rugby league triumphed there. The other big reason was the hip pocket.

The foundation story rugby league tells itself is based around its most famous recruit. The Balmain-born Dally Messenger arrived on rugby's main stage in 1906, playing first grade for Eastern Suburbs and representing New South Wales against Queensland and New Zealand's All Blacks. Thousands, then tens of thousands, came to watch him play. According to his fawning entry in the *Australian Dictionary of Biography*, they were 'drawn by his great ball-skills, cheeky tricks (such as diving over defenders or carrying the ball behind his back) and his accurate, long-range kicking with either foot'. In 1907, only his second season, a then record 52 000 people attended the New South Wales game against New Zealand, exceeding by 7000 the crowd for the VFL grand final that same year between Carlton and South Melbourne.

Messenger was a profit maker for sport but he didn't see a penny of it himself. Rugby in Australia still operated on the assumption that men of honour would play for the love of the game alone.

In England the sport had already fractured on the question of money. In 1895, the clubs based around the industrial north broke away to form their own professional competition, known as rugby league, which paid its players. The middle-class south maintained its loyalty to the amateur code, rugby union.

The authorities in New South Wales clung to rugby union, which fundamentally misread the mood of the Australian people, who wanted to be entertained; and the players, who wanted to be paid. At a time of general economic hardship, Australians no longer had the luxury of being amateur sportsmen.

Even as Messenger was pulling big crowds to rugby union, a breakaway rugby league competition was being organised. Messenger's name was on the top of the rebel's wish list and they signed him up before the 1907 season ended. As part of the deal, he would play with the professional New Zealand team touring England in that northern winter, a mercenary twist to the game's origin that, to Victorian eyes, befits a settlement that began as an open-air prison.

Messenger returned to Sydney in April 1908, snappily dressed and with 200 pounds in his pocket, which was almost 100 times the basic weekly wage of 2 pounds and 2 shillings introduced under the Harvester judgement the previous year. He captained Eastern Suburbs in the inaugural New South Wales Rugby League competition and returned to England that year with the first touring Australian rugby league team. Over the next five seasons, rugby league established itself as the dominant winter sport in Sydney.

This polarisation between rugby league and football occurred when Australia was supposedly more independent of mind. At federation, 80 per cent of the population of New South Wales was born locally, yet they looked to the north of England, not to their immediate neighbour to the south, for a game to play. Conversely, when Victoria eschewed rugby union in the 1860s, 70 per cent of the population were migrants. The schism is even more remarkable given that at federation, Victoria retained sufficient political sway to write the economic model for Australia – industry protection and wages set by an independent umpire.

The author of the compromise between business and the trade unions was the Victorian Alfred Deakin, the most influential Australian politician of the early twentieth century. Indeed, Deakin commemorated football's fiftieth anniversary in 1908 with the assumption that it had already been confirmed as the national game, 'played wherever the sea washes the shore in Australia and all the interior between'.

Deakin underestimated the appeal of rugby league in New South Wales and Queensland, but there was a reminder in his otherwise triumphal speech that football had strayed from its foundational ideals of fair play. The tribal passions that were being aroused by the game troubled him. He did not like the barracking from spectators, who only applauded their own team.

> It has been found that the true sportsman, pitted at his best against his opponent under the rules of fair play is the manliest man who walks this planet today. We can say that, and a great deal more about the football player. I wish we could say as much for the football spectator, for I notice that whenever an adverse criticism is fairly and reasonably passed upon any game, ninety-nine times out of a hundred the fault lies not with those who are playing and putting their spirit and muscle and energy into the game but those who are putting their energy into their voices instead of the muscle.

It amuses me as a Victorian to concede this, but at that time rugby league was the more enlightened code. It was the first to use sport as an explicit tool of economic mobility. In Sydney, working-class men could aspire to a second wage playing the game they loved. In Melbourne, footballers had been paid under the table and supporters used the game as a means to settle scores, like street gangs defending their corner.

Rugby league made New South Wales feel important in the world. The state matches against Queensland and the international tests against New Zealand and England created the illusion of openness at a time when the nation was in retreat with the White Australia Policy. By contrast, football's gaze had narrowed to the suburb, reflecting Victoria's loss of self-esteem at the end of its golden age.

The competing narratives of football and rugby league in the early years of federation had a political subtext. New South Wales was the free-trade state while Victoria was the driving force for protection. Rugby league, not football, was the game best suited to a state that still wanted to engage with the rest of the world.

Yet football proved to be the more adaptable game because Victorians maintained their habit of attendance through hard times. The NSW rugby league competition could never match the crowds of the VFL because Sydney did not have a cluster of large inner-city grounds like Melbourne. When the next depression struck, at the end of the 1920s, football moved from mass entertainment to social safety net. The working-class clubs became literal representatives of their people, raising their spirits in a way that politics could not.

3

THE WORLD'S FIRST GREAT FOOTBALL RIVALRY

Richmond and Collingwood were neighbours in poverty, both of them on the wrong side of the Yarra River. Connected to the rest of the city by their industries but isolated from it by their Catholic religion and working class, they felt the rest of Melbourne looking down on them. Immediately to Collingwood's east was Kew, the suburb with the highest rate of home ownership during Melbourne's marvellous 1880s.

Football united these two inner-city suburbs in a mutual search for respect. The two clubs began as the best of friends. If one was not able to win the premiership, it was their ardent wish that the other be the champion. But it turns out that both clubs, and the game itself, were better off once they became fierce rivals.

Their falling out coincided with football's greatest period of spectator engagement. In the 1920s and 1930s, a typical round of VFL in Melbourne would attract between 10 and 12 per cent of the city's entire population, figures that have never been repeated. Home games at Richmond's Punt Road Oval and Collingwood's Victoria Park would be seen by the equivalent of half the suburb. The pattern held true in Geelong, where up to half the town would cheer their Cats at Corio Oval. The more alienated the suburb or the town felt from the cultural and economic life of Melbourne, the greater the connection to their football club.

This would be the last time that who you barracked for was determined by where you lived or worked. After World War II, the decisive factor was not where you were raised but who you were born to. Allegiances formed in the inner city between the wars were transferred when families moved to the suburbs in the 1950s and 1960s.

When Richmond joined the VFL in 1908, it was led by two former Collingwood champions. Charlie Pannam, the Daylesford-born son of a Greek migrant, was Richmond's captain. Dick Condon, reputedly the greatest and most argumentative player of the decade, was player-coach. Collingwood supporters didn't mind losing their talents because both were at the end of their careers. They viewed Richmond as something like a younger brother, while Richmond people admired the success of their neighbour.

In their first eleven seasons together in the VFL, between 1908 and 1918, the clubs faced each other twenty-five times. Collingwood won twenty of those matches. Richmond was not considered a threat to anyone, and the players accepted their losses with good humour. They were known by the nickname 'Tigers' from 1910 onwards, but in those formative years they were toothless.

'Week after week we went out and were trimmed,' recalled Richmond's best player in those years, Vic Thorp. 'One day something went wrong and we won. Ruckman Barney Herbert went home full of joy at our luck, but his wife [told him], "I won't believe it until I see it in the *Herald*."'

The relationship between the clubs shifted when Richmond finally became competitive after World War I. Collingwood was the most consistent team in 1919 and secured top spot on the ladder in the final round of the season, ahead of South Melbourne. Carlton was third and Richmond fourth.

Richmond shocked South Melbourne, the reigning premier, in their semi-final, and Collingwood defeated Carlton in the second semi-final. So certain was Collingwood of victory against Richmond in the following week's final that the Magpies booked a celebratory end of season trip to the Gippsland Lakes.

But before a crowd of almost 52 000 at the MCG, the upstarts from Punt Road won the game. The Collingwood president, Jim Sharp, reaffirmed the kinship with a generous speech in the Richmond dressing rooms. 'It was, he said, the wish of Collingwood that if the premiership should go to any team outside his own, that team should be Richmond,' *The Age* reported.

He could afford to be magnanimous because Richmond had to beat Collingwood twice to win the premiership. Under the rules, the team finishing first in the home and away season received a second chance if it lost any final. Despite their kindly concession, Collingwood knew they were entitled to a rematch, which they won by 25 points. They toasted their fifth VFL premiership of the young century.

The Age said the Richmond players cracked under the pressure. 'Flushed with success and weighed down by the responsibility of a final [they] broke down. To them it was a psychological defeat as well as a premiership loss.'

The friendship could not survive another season as the two proud working-class clubs succumbed to the forces that generate and sustain a sporting rivalry: ambition and envy.

The catalyst for the split was Dan Minogue, the former Collingwood captain. On his return home from war service in 1919, Richmond convinced him to switch clubs. He applied for a transfer three days after the 30 June deadline, but it was rejected by the league's officials. 'I felt that returned soldiers might have been given a few days grace,' Minogue said later. He sat out that season as a spectator and joined Richmond in the new year. The players elected him captain and coach.

Minogue led Richmond against his old club in round five of the 1920 season. More than 30 000 filled the Punt Road ground and this epic contest still resonates almost a century later.

Anyone who has witnessed a close game will appreciate the drama, tension, and ecstatic release. Time appears to accelerate as the ball moves frantically from one end of the ground to the other. Then it warps into two different speeds. It's like you're in a Dalí painting – the minute hand on the clock is melting while the hour hand is a whirling dervish. If your team is in front, but the other side is attacking, the final few minutes of a match can seem like an eternity. But if your team is the one staging a fightback, those same few minutes flash by in a panic of missed opportunities.

In 1920, Richmond were clinging to a 4-point lead late in the game, but Collingwood were resurgent. A snap shot hit the post, another point was kicked, and then another. With only three minutes left in the final quarter, Richmond were a solitary point in front. The Richmond players worked the ball forward, Collingwood repelled the attack, but the ball came back again. Richmond's Hughie James, the least reliable kick in the team, took a mark right in front of the goals.

'The stands rocked, the roof of the verandah of the cricket pavilion, crowded with spectators, gave way, and crashed to the ground,' *The Argus* reported.

The people tumbling off the roof must surely have feared for their lives, but no one was seriously injured. The attention of 30 000 people snapped back to the game.

'During the confusion James kicked the goal which made the game safe. They had lost a verandah but won a match.'

Years later Minogue would recall that the roof collapsed just as he knocked over a smaller Collingwood player, who had the front to 'flashily' poke the ball in the Tiger captain's face as he ran past him.

'I had a fixed rule in such a case. I always went straight into the man who baulked me, regardless of his size. So in I sailed this time. At that moment there were two crashes. My opponent hit the ground. Simultaneously the verandah of the old pavilion collapsed – but I had nothing to do with that!'

The story got taller as spectators repeated it for those who weren't there. In Janet McCalman's celebrated book on life in Richmond, *Struggletown*, one old-timer said that James had taken a 'sky-scraping mark' in the goal square. 'I didn't see any more – all the people on the roof jumped up in the air and down they came on top of me.' He was able to save himself by hanging onto the beams of what remained of the pavilion.

Just four weeks later, a stirring final-quarter comeback against Essendon transformed a 25-point Richmond deficit into a 20-point victory. The city was enthralled. It was 'the talk of Melbourne all this week', the *Herald* reported. After two decades of depression, four grinding years of war, and a year of the Spanish flu, the people were finally enjoying themselves again.

Richmond dominated the 1920 regular season and finished on top of the ladder. But the finals series opened with two upsets. Fourth-placed Collingwood defeated second-placed Fitzroy, while Richmond lost to third-placed Carlton before a crowd of 62 000, a new MCG record. Now Richmond was the beneficiary of the challenge system and as minor premier exercised its right to face the winner of the preliminary final in the grand final.

Collingwood then defeated Carlton in the preliminary final, setting up another showdown between the two working-class neighbours. But in the week leading up to the big game people noticed that Dan Minogue had disappeared from sight. Richmond's leader had missed the final against Carlton due to a bout of tonsillitis. He had gone back to Bendigo to recuperate but somehow a rumour started that he had passed away. On the day of the preliminary final distressed Richmond supporters rushed to his Albert Park home to pay their respects. No doubt loving the attention,

Minogue made a heroic return to the city to correct the reports of his demise.

On the day of the grand final, Minogue was still queasy, but he would play. In the dressing room before the game, Richmond's treasurer Jack Archer was in a vengeful mood. He told the players that the 'eyes of Richmond and the whole of the football world are upon you today so go out and win'.

He asked them to remember how rude the Collingwood people had been to Dan Minogue after he moved clubs. Collingwood, he said, had been a model for sportsmanship. 'Yes, they were good sports at social gatherings after the matches they won, but that scene changed at Collingwood this year when we beat them, and we're going to beat them again to-day.'

Archer regretted the loss of camaraderie between the clubs. 'I've come to the conclusion that it is all self, self, self with the league clubs, and from now on the Richmond club is going to be the same.'

He concluded with a rousing appeal to tribal identity.

> Set your mind on the goal in front, remember the injustices you have been burdened with, grind your teeth and stretch your nostrils wide. All Richmond are expecting great things from you, and let this flag I hold here 'Defiance' inspire you, and this flag 'Richmond on top' will be quite in order when you come back into the dressing room after the match.

The Richmond treasurer surely exaggerated his case against the Magpies. A month out from the grand final, Collingwood people were once again saying that 'if defeated' they hoped 'Richmond would be the team to win'.

On the day, there was no evidence of bad blood. Richmond were simply too good. They 'outpace and outplay' their opponents. Minogue was too weak to influence the game with his play. He served as an on-field general, directing his team. The Tigers dominated every aspect of the game except goal kicking. They won by 17 points but, with a little more composure in front of goal, could easily have doubled that margin.

'When the bell rang,' *The Age* wrote, 'there were the congratulations between friend and foe that make Australians such fine sportsmen and their game so enjoyable to watch'.

Richmond had secured its first VFL premiership, but Vic Thorp felt a letdown at that moment. 'Something turned in my stomach,' he wrote in his memoirs. 'I felt as if I was going to be ill.' He pushed his way through the crowd in the dressing room and wondered 'what was the premiership anyway'.

'Strange the way things affect you. Here was something I had been fighting for since 1910: a premiership. I didn't know what it was, or whether I wanted it.'

Sir Arthur Conan Doyle, creator of Sherlock Holmes, was a special guest at the grand final. After the game, he declared that football was the very best winter sport in the world.

'I know something about football,' he wrote, 'for I played rugby for the Edinburgh University and soccer with the Hampshire team. I have also seen the best American football. I consider the Australian game is magnificent, and from the spectacular point of view it is probably the best of them all.'

Doyle was particularly taken with the kicking game. 'I have never seen anything to touch the accuracy of both the punting and drop kicking.' The stab pass enthralled him, as did the snap shot for goal, which was then known as the screw kick.

He was also impressed to meet a founding father of the game, Henry Harrison, now aged eighty-five. They discussed one of football's unique rules, which Harrison had accepted at his own expense more than half a century earlier. 'I thought it was very sporting of him, as the fastest runner of his day, to introduce the bouncing rule, which robbed him of his advantage.'

Perhaps he was flattering his host. But his observations suggest the game had discovered the ingredients for spectacle well before comparable winter sports in Britain and the US.

The template for Richmond's first ten premierships was established on this day, from using an exaggerated sense of victimhood to motivate the players all the way to the jubilant street party that celebrated the win.

For dinner the players were driven in motor cars to St Kilda. After they finished eating, and made their final toasts, they poured back into the cars and were taken to the city, where the premiership convoy 'made several trips up and down Bourke Street through cheering crowds'. The next stop was Richmond Town Hall, where 2000 locals were waiting to greet their heroes.

Ruckman Barney Herbert climbed the statue of George Bennett, a former club president and mayor of Richmond, and orchestrated an eccentric rendition of the club's battle cry. Herbert had a crayfish in each hand, and yelled to the adoring mob: 'What did we do to them?'

'Eat 'em alive!' they roared.

For his part, Dan Minogue had already slipped quietly back home to Albert Park to resume his recovery from illness. In bed, he replayed the grand final 'in fitful, feverish dreams'.

The local paper the *Richmond Guardian* covered the triumph with a bolder front-page headline than it had used for the signing of the Armistice two years beforehand. 'Premiers at Last,' it declared. The end of the war was reported under the more earnest headline 'Kitchener's Task is Finished by Foch.'

But while the Richmond celebrations were charming, they were not the decade's most jubilant, nor the most revealing of the times.

The 1925 grand final between Geelong and Collingwood, between the football-mad town and the football-mad suburb, provides a vivid example of how the game reached into every part of Victorian society.

Geelong had not won a premiership since the VFA game of the century against South Melbourne in 1886. Depression had ravaged the town, and the Great War left it without enough young men to field a viable team. Geelong had been one of four clubs to temporarily drop out of the VFL competition in 1916.

The club's form improved noticeably from 1921 on, and it finally reached the top of the ladder in 1925. Although Geelong lost its semi-final, it exercised its right to challenge and faced Collingwood in the grand final. It was momentous enough for labour and capital to declare a truce in their class war. Employers granted their workers flexible hours for grand final week. They could work an extra hour a day in exchange for having Saturday free to go to the game.

Almost 6000 locals took trains to Melbourne for the game, while a further 2000 travelled by road. The town's population was 34 000, which meant almost one in four made the trip to the MCG. They would have been swamped on arrival by Collingwood fans, who accounted for the largest section of the new record MCG crowd of 64 000. All neutral fans, however, were said to be cheering for Geelong.

This game was the first to be broadcast through the wireless radio, and the new technology gave full expression to the prominence of football, as the remaining Geelong residents followed the action at communal listening posts around the town.

'At such places hundreds congregated,' *The Argus* reported.

> Wireless was installed into the bars of a number of hotels, and a temporary set was installed in two wards of the Geelong Hospital, by Mr W. Mullett, for the benefit of the patients. A set was also installed at Kardinia Park, where the Junior Association final match was in progress. The crowd took comparatively little interest in the game, but listened intently to the news from Melbourne,

> applauding any good play announced by Geelong players, growing despondent about injuries received, and cheering loudly the announcement of every goal by Geelong.

Geelong had established a commanding lead, but Collingwood staged a gallant recovery in the final quarter. The 3LO announcer was describing another Collingwood charge towards the forward line when he stopped mid-sentence to declare 'Geelong has won the premiership'.

The next few words were lost in the merriment until the crowd calmed down and turned a collective ear back to the wireless. The next sentence they heard from the announcer was: 'It will be a great night in Geelong tonight!'

> Literally the city went mad at night. Soon after 8 o'clock a crowd of 5000 people assembled in front of the railway station, and each special [train] from Melbourne added to the number and caused a block on the platform.

The train carrying the players announced its arrival with a loud whistle before it reached North Geelong station and 'whistled all the way' to Geelong station.

'[As] the train pulled into the station, upwards of 200 detonators were let off and the crowd cheered loudly.'

A reception of 7500 people greeted the team at the town hall. 'Such enthusiasm was not manifested on armistice night, and in the last decade the crowd in front of the hall has only been equalled by the one which gathered on the occasion of the visit of the Prince of Wales.'

The pecking order for the speeches showed that football was woven into the political life of the town. At the MCG after the game the first person to address the players had been the Country Party senator James Guthrie. In Geelong, it was the city mayor, then the club president, then a local councillor, and then a state politician. The captain, Cliff Rankin, was fifth in line.

The mayor, Francis Ritchie, said the premiership was 'a happy finale to his term of office'. The president, Dr J.E. Piper, said the match committee should be congratulated for appointing Rankin as captain. Rankin interrupted the flow of self-applause by thanking the players and supporters. 'I am captain of a great side, in which every player has been captain in his own part.' Even more speeches followed, from both players and politicians.

There is obedience and rapture in these celebrations. It did not occur to any of the politicians or club officials that they were gatecrashers. They lined up to speak, one pompous attention seeker after the other. But the crowd did not think it was out of order either. Supporters would not think to boo the prime minister at a football or rugby league grand final until the Whitlam–Fraser era half a century later.

Why were so many politicians there in the first place? The simple answer is that it was an opportunity to impress a large crowd. But a more nuanced explanation is that they were observing what was by then a six-decade-old tradition. It was common practice for a politician to wear the second hat of football club president. George Bennett and William Beazley, respectively the founding presidents of Richmond and Collingwood, were also lord mayors and local members of the colonial and Victorian state parliaments.

The game was established just three years after Victoria won the right to self-government from London and, as football welcomed all classes, the politicians who represented the people in this infant democracy could not afford to remain outside the gate of inclusion.

In the 1920s football moved to the heart of Victorian culture by serving as a pressure-release valve for the entire community following the cataclysm of the Great War.

Dan Minogue said sport was an 'outlet for pent-up emotions'. Soldier-footballers couldn't wait to throw off their khaki uniforms and wear the togs of their club, 'to career around the turf once more without having to do this or that "by numbers" as in the army'.

But here's the problem. This was all Victorians really had to enjoy.

While the Australian population grew from 3.5 million to 6.5 million, Geoffrey Searle observes, 'It is difficult to discern any coherent cultural development or much achievement in the first third of the century.'

In art, film and music, the people had simply lost their inspiration. Many of the best painters had relocated overseas during the depression of the 1890s. The nation's young film industry, which showed much promise in the early days of silent movies, was moribund by the 1920s. Not even a royal commission could restore it, leaving Australian movie goers to be entertained by Hollywood and British productions.

But it was Nellie Melba, still the most famous of Richmond's offspring, who provided unintended proof that the culture had frozen. For many Victorians her voice was the first they heard on the new technology of the wireless; a living echo from a long lost golden age. In October 1924, radio station 3LO launched onto the airwaves with her performance of *La bohème* at Her Majesty's Theatre in what was meant to be her farewell tour.

Football's mesmeric hold on Victoria tightened with each advance in technology and, counterintuitively, with each setback in the economy. The trains and cable trams brought bigger crowds in the 1870s and 1880s, the depression of the 1890s and 1900s galvanised the suburban identity of the big clubs, and the advances in media communication in the 1920s and 1930s embedded the sport in the home, the pub and the workplace.

Local newspapers such as the *Geelong Advertiser* and the *Richmond Guardian* began publishing action photographs from the games and portrait shots of the players. *The Sun News-Pictorial* was launched in 1922 and was soon devoting its entire front page to a single image from the football.

The most popular clubs of the era were Carlton and Richmond. On average they attracted more than 20 000 people to their home games. Carlton's strength at the gate did not translate to premierships during football's boom decades, only winning their first flag in twenty-three years in 1938. But the Blues had the VFL's largest ground other than the MCG, and a generation of supporters had been made loyal by success, with five premierships between 1906 and 1915.

While Carlton and Richmond drew the biggest crowds, the most successful club of this period was Collingwood. The Magpies won four premierships in a row between 1927 and 1930, and added two more by 1936. But Collingwood did not yet have the supporter base to match its trophy cabinet. It was ranked fifth on the home attendance ladder, behind South Melbourne and Melbourne. But those clubs had much larger populations to draw from. Adjust the figures for each suburb's population and Collingwood supporters were alongside Richmond, Fitzroy and Carlton as the most adoring. A home game would draw in almost half the total population of each inner-city suburb.

But not all suburbs followed their football clubs with the same degree of fanaticism as those of the inner city. The clubs with the poorest attendances at the time were the three most recent additions to the VFL, Hawthorn, North Melbourne and Footscray, who all joined in 1925. The weakest club in the competition was foundation member St Kilda. University had left the VFL at the end of the 1914 season, after just six years in the competition.

Hawthorn and St Kilda were middle-class suburbs, while North Melbourne and Footscray were working-class suburbs. Two different sets of people, but each of their clubs underperformed. Where Collingwood took just five years to win its first VFL premiership and Richmond twelve, Footscray would have to wait twenty-nine years, Hawthorn thirty-six, North Melbourne fifty and St Kilda an incredible sixty-nine.

One of the factors that separated these unsuccessful and less popular clubs from their competitors was migration. The suburbs that received people from overseas, or from other parts of Melbourne, tended to attract fewer spectators to the football. The new arrivals to the suburb had a weaker attachment to the local club, at least initially.

This pattern held true for uncompetitive clubs like St Kilda, the suburb that had the most diverse population in Melbourne, as well as perennial winners like Essendon, which was one of the city's fastest-growing suburbs.

Essendon won the first VFL premiership in 1897 and had six in total by 1924, one more than Collingwood at the time. In 1922, the club moved its home ground from East Melbourne to Windy Hill. That is, from football's home in Yarra Park to its own local area. The suburb of Essendon was middle class, Protestant and expanding. Its population had more than doubled between 1891 and 1921 as those who could afford to leave the inner city moved to the so-called Eden of Melbourne's north-west.

But although Essendon had more people than Richmond or Collingwood, the inner-city clubs still attracted larger home crowds during the 1920s and 1930s. That's because their sense of separation from the rest of the Melbourne forged an identity that drew people to the clubs that represented them. By comparison, Essendon's identity was being remade by the constant influx of people. In time the Bombers would become one of the most popular sporting clubs in the nation, but between the wars they could not keep up with their inner-city rivals.

Collingwood and Richmond had been among the most cosmopolitan suburbs in Melbourne during the 1880s. But that cultural diversity had been erased by the land bust of the 1890s and the introduction of the White Australia Policy. By 1921, Collingwood was whiter than Victoria itself, with 88 per cent of its residents born in Australia. Richmond was right on the state average of 87 per cent. The inner-city clubs thrived because of their monoculture while the middle-class clubs were victims of their relative affluence.

Following these migration shifts, the depression of the 1930s entrenched football's class divide. In this period the most successful clubs came once again from the most damaged suburbs. The most visceral measure of disadvantage was the unemployment rate. In Collingwood, Richmond and Fitzroy it exceeded 25 per cent. In South Melbourne, it ranged between 20 and 25 per cent; in Essendon between 20 and 15 per cent. In St Kilda and Hawthorn it remained below 15 per cent. The remarkable thing about these figures is that football attendance rates mirrored the unemployment rate. In 1933, the suburbs with the highest rates of unemployment also had the highest home attendances. Football was a distraction from the shame of poverty; in a miserable winter, it was the one day of the week people could look forward to celebrating life.

The Great Depression triggered the second big reshuffle of Melbourne's population, after the fallout from the land bust of the 1890s. The seven inner-city suburbs of the VFL – Carlton, Collingwood, Fitzroy, Melbourne, North Melbourne, Richmond and South Melbourne – lost 26 000 people in total. The four VFL suburbs further out – Essendon, Footscray, Hawthorn and St Kilda – added 36 000 between them.

Jack Dyer, the swashbuckling ruckman who became a hero at Punt Road in the depression, described Richmond in this period as a closed shop. 'We were locked in,' he said. 'The Yarra that side. Punt Road that side. North Richmond and Victoria Street the other side.'

The young men of Richmond would patrol the boundary and meet any uninvited visitor with fists, four-by-twos and perhaps even switchblades.

'Anyone come over to us from Collingwood they were out the moment they crossed Victoria Street. [Those] young fellas who had nothing to do, they'd drive them back again. That seemed to be their enjoyment.'

But at the football, the fans were relatively well behaved. Certainly compared to the previous depression. If Alfred Deakin were still alive, he would have beseeched the players to follow the example of the supporters.

The game had become more exciting, and perhaps this allowed it to better relieve the social tensions of the day. Where football had been dour at the turn of the century, the 1930s proved to be a golden decade of goal kicking, in part thanks to a rule change in 1925 that penalised the last team to touch the ball before it went out of bounds. This opened up the play and encouraged teams to kick the ball long to the full forward. No player had scored a century of goals in a season before Collingwood's Gordon Coventry kicked 124 in 1929. By 1940, a total of thirteen centuries had been kicked by six different players, including four by Coventry and three by South Melbourne's Bob Pratt.

In the meanest years of the depression, grand final crowds surged. More than 60 000 in 1931, almost 70 000 in 1932 and over 75 000 in 1933, which exceeded all previous records for sport at the MCG, including test cricket.

'So dense was the crowd that ambulance men were kept busy, and in more than one spot the fence around the arena was in danger of collapsing,' *The Argus* wrote of the 1933 grand final.

The contest itself was a fizzer. South Melbourne thrashed Richmond, the defending premier, by 42 points. But the result was significant in other ways. Seven of South Melbourne's players that day were interstate recruits – five from Western Australia, one from South Australia and one from Tasmania. They had been lured to the Lake Oval with the promise of a game and a job in the grocery empire of South Melbourne councillor Archibald Crofts, who was club vice-president and then later president. The new arrivals were called the 'foreign legion', a subconscious admission of Victoria's isolation.

The people of South Melbourne had no problem identifying with these outsiders. A crowd of 5000 gathered at the town hall for the premiership celebrations in 1933. The players were then loaded onto two charabancs and taken to a victory dinner at Queens Bridge Hotel. In a show of strength, like the boundary-pushing tactics of the gangs, they later resumed their tour with a quick, provocative ride through Richmond.

The economics of football in the depression was complicated by the fame of individual players. From 1930, the VFL capped player payments at three pounds per game, one pound below the basic weekly wage at the time. It was designed to protect the clubs from having to make excessive payments to their stars, but it created a wedge between the wealthy clubs – Carlton, Collingwood and Richmond – and the rest of the competition. The younger VFL clubs such as North Melbourne were so poor that they could only pay their players half the recommended payment. In 1930, South Melbourne could not pay its players at all, instead embarking on a fundraising drive that delivered the premiership in 1933. Melbourne remained an amateur club throughout the decade, although every one of its players and even their coach was compensated with day jobs provided by club officials.

Clubs became informal welfare agencies. In Richmond's premiership year of 1932, the national unemployment rate was 30 per cent, and higher still in the suburb. The club disclosed in its annual report that it had paid 255 pounds in sustenance to the players who could not find work; the equivalent of $24000 in today's terms. Premiership coach Frank Hughes was struggling to make ends meet. When Melbourne approached him for their coaching job with the promise of employment as a sales rep for a printing press owned by the club secretary Percy Page, Richmond could not match the offer and Hughes walked across the park to the MCG.

For the most popular players representing successful clubs in struggling suburbs, the accompanying benefits of football exceeded their match payments. There would be cash bonuses, gifts and most importantly a steady job. These young men might even be free to walk Melbourne's most dangerous streets and back alleys without being beaten up by the gangs that ruled them.

While the big clubs had rich benefactors, individuals from all classes would chip in to support their boys. Richmond's Jack Dyer received around twice as much from fans as he did from match payments. Hats were a common gift to players. Jack Archer, Richmond's treasurer and later club president, had given players 'many substantial presents, and there is hardly a Tiger who has not received a hat from him'.

When Richmond faced South Melbourne again in the grand final of 1934, the Tigers had their revenge sweetened by a cash bonus. At half time, with Richmond leading by 27 points, one of the club's generous supporters, Mr A. Chirnside, told the players that if they won the game, he would give them 100 pounds. By three quarter time, they had extended their lead to 60 points. Victory was assured.

Supporters recognised the game was over, and marked the occasion by souveniring footballs. Four in total disappeared into the crowd after Richmond goals. In the final quarter, the Richmond players relaxed and the final margin in their favour was 39 points. It was the club's second premiership in three seasons, and its fourth since 1920. One would have expected the fans to take another premiership in their stride, but the post-game celebrations in 1934 were the decade's most passionate.

The players were treated like a liberating army, freeing the people from their oppression. After an hour of speeches, the players walked out of the clubroom and into the arms of a thousand-strong honour guard of supporters. Women rushed forward to kiss their heroes.

On their ride through the city streets that evening, the battle cry 'What do we do? Eat 'em alive!' erupted 'every few seconds from the delighted players and their friends in the charabancs'.

At dinner, a cake was cut to commemorate the club's fiftieth birthday, and then the 'triumphal tour' resumed with a ride through South Melbourne, to return the serve of the previous year. They turned for home and the Richmond town hall. From there, they did the rounds of the Richmond movie theatres – the audiences were grateful for the interruption to their feature film and cheered wildly as the players were brought to the front of each house.

> Later the players received a wonderful reception at the Richmond club dance being held at the Richmond ground, and were again showered with kisses and compliments. At midnight they set off for a secret destination, and after a brisk run into the country, found themselves at the Park Orchards dance cabaret, where dancing went on till daylight.

They returned to Punt Road later on Sunday, and had another dinner lined up for the following Saturday. Those breakthrough premierships at the start of the previous decade carried with them the promise of renewal after the Great War. Most supporters would have had to go back to work on the Monday. The depression premierships were cast against years of grinding poverty, and the tangible fear of another world war. Who could blame Richmond people for wanting to extend their celebrations?

The greatest victims of the depression produced the greatest teams.

Like its predecessor in the 1890s, this depression began earlier and lasted longer in Australia than most countries. Reckless government borrowing and restrictions against migrants from Europe were the main culprits and they combined to send our economy into reverse two years before the Wall Street crash in 1929. That first year of economic crisis in 1927 coincided with the first of four premierships in a row won by Collingwood.

In fact, author Sam Walker has made a strong case that this Collingwood team, known as The Machine, was the world's first super team in any sport. He argues there have only been sixteen teams in history that can be considered 'tier one' or 'unambiguously good', by virtue of dominating even other very good teams for years. Collingwood is the first such super team on his chronological list. The next is the New York Yankees team that won five consecutive Major League Baseball titles between 1949 and 1953. Once again, it seems football was ahead of all games.

If Walker had dug a little deeper, he would have discovered that the Collingwood team was also part of the first great suburban rivalry of any football code.

In nineteen of the twenty seasons between the wars, either Collingwood or Richmond was the VFL premier or runner-up. Collingwood won seven premierships in total between 1919 and 1938, and was runner-up on another seven occasions; Richmond won four and was runner-up seven times.

Their falling out was like the worst family break-up. The two neighbouring clubs that once wished each other well redefined themselves by their mutual loathing. The grudges they nursed became fuel for their success. Decades after he had finished playing and coaching Richmond, Jack Dyer would greet new recruits to Punt Road with the fatherly advice to hate Collingwood.

This was the rivalry Australian Rules football had to have, between two evenly matched working-class clubs with loyal followings. It was the biggest story in the decades when football had the greatest engagement, and it gave the game an underdog identity that was in keeping with the times. If the middle-class suburbs had won all the premierships, the game would not have generated the visceral connection with the people of Melbourne it still has today.

A Saturday afternoon spent at Punt Road or Victoria Park was just about the best thing that happened to the residents of Richmond and Collingwood in the 1920s and especially the 1930s. The cost of attending a game was relatively cheap, but even at those prices the large crowds allowed the football clubs to remain financially viable at a time of mass unemployment. They didn't make outrageous profits – in some years they, too, were almost broke. But they had just enough money to attract and retain the best players from their local area and beyond.

The flipside of this story was the working-class clubs of Footscray and North Melbourne. Their local talent pool had been compromised by their late arrival to the VFL. Much of North Melbourne's metropolitan recruitment zone, the area from which the club could draw young players, had already been assigned to Essendon.

These clubs were stuck in a different cycle. Without on-field success, the new entrants could not attract large crowds. And without strong gate revenues and annual membership sales, they could not afford to recruit and retain players of sufficient quality to lift their clubs into the finals.

But once the economy recovered, Richmond and Collingwood lost the advantage of being successful rival clubs in hard times. The post-war boom shifted football's balance of power and middle-class clubs like Melbourne and Essendon grew ascendant.

4

RICHMOND'S FALL AND REBIRTH

The emotional cycle of football is dark and unforgiving. For most supporters, it's one long recession interrupted by the occasional good year. Even the biggest clubs endure premiership droughts that run for decades. Children become parents themselves before they see their side win a flag.

The unlucky ones can barrack for a lifetime and still not experience a premiership. If you were born at the turn of the twentieth century, you had a life expectancy of fifty-five years as a woman and fifty-one years as a man. That means for supporters of a club like St Kilda, whose first (and to date only) grand final victory came in 1966, that first generation of fans would have passed from this earth without seeing their club win a premiership.

An unspoken pact exists between supporter and underachieving club. Supporters are allowed to drift away in the lean years, putting their lives ahead of football, even missing entire seasons if necessary. But they can't change clubs. Football is a lifelong passion. It can be repressed, but not abandoned. The club knows that when they start winning again the supporters will return, and with their own children as witnesses to the miracle.

There is a biblical quality to the Richmond droughts. Decades of famine follow decades of feast. In the twenty-four seasons from 1920 to 1943 the club won five premierships, but then had to wait another twenty-four seasons for its sixth.

In those post-war years, the Tigers reverted to their toothless selves. Defeat was routine and victory had to be double-checked in *The Herald* to be believed. Supporters did not even have the consolation of a regular top-four finish. Richmond played in one losing final, in 1947, and then nothing for the next nineteen seasons. The only other club to miss every single finals series in this period was the Tigers' flamboyant rival of the early 1930s, South Melbourne.

The counterintuitive thing about Richmond's fall is that it occurred in football's most egalitarian era, when the post-war recovery in the economy helped to close the gap between the big clubs and the minnows that had defined the previous era.

Eight of the VFL's twelve clubs won premierships between 1947 and 1966. Footscray, Hawthorn and St Kilda broke their ducks, leaving only North Melbourne without a flag to its name. Yet even this poor club had a relatively successful run, finishing at the top of the ladder in one season and playing in a grand final the next.

Richmond's hard landing was not unavoidable. The system for recruiting players allowed any club to construct a team capable of winning a premiership. All clubs were granted exclusive access to a metropolitan zone from which only they could recruit players. Richmond's zone extended along the south-east suburban growth corridor to Glen Waverley and Mulgrave. Apart from this restriction within Melbourne, clubs were free to compete for players in country Victoria and from interstate. They could also poach players from other VFL teams when their contracts expired.

But Richmond didn't adapt to this more competitive environment. It's hard to believe this was simply down to complacency.

When we look at what was going on in the suburb in that time, it's clear that the premiership drought coincided with the post-war migration wave from Europe. That raises a personal question: can Richmond's failure be explained by the Greeks? Did the arrival of people like my parents to the suburb affect the club's form? At the time that Australia opened the door to blue-collar migration from Europe in 1947, Richmond was one of a cluster of suburbs that had become whiter than the state itself. Across Victoria, 91 per cent of the population was born in Australia; in Richmond and Footscray the figure was 92 per cent; in Collingwood and Essendon 93 per cent. Only one VFL suburb was able to maintain and replenish its diversity during the depression and World War II – St Kilda. The bayside, middle-class suburb had an Australian-born population of 84 per cent, and of the 16 per cent who were born overseas, half were now from Europe, including a significant number of Jewish refugees.

After the war, all of Melbourne followed St Kilda's migration lead. By 1966 every suburb had become significantly more diverse than the rest of the state. So if migration diluted the appeal of football, all the VFL clubs would have felt it – but some more than others.

I've arranged the VFL suburbs into three groups, based on how quickly their ethnic faces changed during Richmond's twenty-year absence from the finals. The first group – Fitzroy, Collingwood, Richmond and St Kilda – were the most diverse, with Australian-born populations below 60 per cent. In the case of Fitzroy, the suburb was approaching a 50–50 split, with the trend showing that migrants would soon outnumber the locals. The second group – Melbourne, Footscray and South Melbourne – were between 60 and 70 per cent Australian-born. And the third – Essendon and Hawthorn – were between 70 and 75 per cent.

If migration remained a predictor of on-field success or failure, as it had been in the inter-war years, the post-war story should have seen supporters and premierships concentrated in the less diverse suburbs. And that is what happened – but only up to a point.

The most successful clubs were middle class, Anglo and Protestant. Melbourne won seven flags between 1947 and 1966, and Essendon won four. Footscray and Hawthorn claimed a premiership each. Geelong, which was whiter than any of the VFL suburbs, won two. In short, sixteen of the twenty premierships were won outside the migrant belt of the inner city.

Of those inner-city clubs, Fitzroy, Richmond and St Kilda were the underachievers. Fitzroy was one of only three clubs to miss out on a grand final in this period. St Kilda did not qualify for the finals until 1961 and its one premiership came at the end of this cycle, in 1966. Carlton and North Melbourne rightly belong in this inner-city group, but there is no comparable data on their ethnicity because they were still being counted as part of the City of Melbourne. Carlton won the first premiership of this era, in 1947, before the first big intake of migrants from Europe, but none thereafter.

So the theory that migration undermines football clubs holds up – except for one notable outlier: Collingwood maintained its status as an elite VFL club despite the diversity of its suburb. The Magpies played in eight of the fifteen grand finals between 1952 and 1966, winning two and losing six.

As a child of Greek migrants, I grew up with two cosmopolitan certainties: Melbourne was the largest Greek city outside Greece and Richmond was the largest Greek suburb in Australia. Both facts are true, but they did not provide the full picture. To my surprise it was Collingwood, not Richmond, that had the highest concentration of Greeks during the wave of European migration.

Both suburbs were transformed, from slums to melting pots. At the peak of the wave in 1971, the Australian-born population of Richmond had fallen to 58 per cent, compared to the state average of 78 per cent. The Greeks were 20 per cent of the suburb, compared to 2 per cent across Victoria.

Yet Collingwood's ethnic face changed even faster than Richmond's, and by 1971 the Australian-born population there was just 53 per cent. The Greeks were now 21 per cent of the entire suburb's population, making Collingwood even woggier than Richmond.

It wasn't just the Greek migrants – the post-war wave made subtle changes to the supporter base of every VFL team. The Italians were the largest migrant community in the inner and middle-ring suburbs to the north of the CBD – Carlton, Fitzroy and Essendon – while the Yugoslavs were the largest to the west, in Footscray. The British clustered to the east and south of the Yarra, in Hawthorn and St Kilda.

However, what these statistical snapshots underestimate is the churn. The newcomers didn't all remain in the inner city. As soon as they could afford to buy a house, many joined the flight to the leafier suburbs. The total migrant population of Richmond began falling after 1966, although the percentage of overseas-born residents kept rising until 1981, because the local-born were leaving at an even greater rate.

My father lived in Richmond in the 1950s. My mother arrived in 1962. Both have fond memories of the people, but not the place. They never looked back once they moved to East Malvern in 1963.

My late aunt Erasmia told me that Dad had an awful time in Richmond. She shared stories he had never revealed to me, about the boozing and the fighting he saw in his neighbourhood. The older Greeks drank as hard as the locals and my father, a shy young man, would have been terrified, although I doubt he would ever concede this.

There is a telling portrait of Richmond's grog economy in Janet McCalman's *Struggletown*. One of the premiership heroes from the 1930s, the full forward Jack Titus, ran a pub with his wife, Ma Titus. 'She was a character,' one local recalled. On Sundays, when the pub was closed, she would keep her customers hydrated at the South Richmond Baby Health Care Centre.

'They used to meet there and sit on the low fence and start a game of cards. That would be about 10 o'clock, then old Ma [Titus] would open up the sly-grog and you'd go in and have a few drinks.'

Richmond's migration boom only partly offset the continued loss of population. In both depression and recovery, the suburb kept shrinking. The Australian-born population almost halved, from 36 000 in 1947 to 19 000 in 1966, while the overseas-born quadrupled, from 3000 to 13 000. Then the migrants also started leaving.

Richmond was at the sharp end of Melbourne's third great reshuffle, which ran from the end of World War II until the start of the twenty-first century. The flight to the outer suburbs was oblivious to the health of the economy. It continued through the full employment of the 1950s and 1960s, the unemployment crisis of the 1970s and 1980s, and the restructure of the 1990s. Between 1947 and 2001, the total population of Richmond halved from 39 000 to 19 000.

The people who lived in the suburb during the post-war boom thrived in a material sense. They had steady jobs. But if they wanted to buy a free-standing house, with a front and back yard and a garage, they had to move out.

Younger Labor people romanticise this post-war era for its supposed stability. They imagine every suburb and town ran like GM Holden's Dandenong and Ford's Geelong, where the men made cars and owned big family homes in the area. But the tariff wall was no friend of the inner city. The factories it propped up continued to dominate the land use, leaving the workers to make do with the pre-war housing stock of tiny cottages or the new indignity of claustrophobic public housing. State governments had cleared the old slums, but they failed the address the underlying poverty, only pushing the problem skyward with high-rise commission flats.

During this transformation, the Richmond Football Club slipped a little too easily into the old habits of victimhood. Even Jack Dyer, who had led the Tigers to their last premiership as captain-coach in 1943, accepted defeat. After retiring from playing in 1949, he coached for three more seasons. Each of those seasons was worse the last. The club sacked him in 1952.

Dyer, the most identifiably Richmond player of them all, had that curious mix of Australian masculinity: violence and deference. When you saw him later in his life on *World of Sport* or *League Teams*, you could have sworn he was the sweetest ex-footballer in the media.

But as a player, Captain Blood thought nothing of running through an opponent. His motto was 'better him than me'. He was tall, quick and skilled; the perfect footballer for any era. In 312 games over 19 seasons, he played in more wins than losses against every team, including Collingwood. But as a coach he had no insights to pass on to the next generation of players beyond macho homilies. Use your brawn. Big kicks down the centre.

'I always thought he was a wonderful leader but I don't think he was a coach,' teammate Bob Wiggins recalled.

'Jack's tactic at three-quarter time on most days was "All up on the backline to save the game." That didn't breed confidence in the side.'

Nevertheless, supporters clung to the memory of Jack Dyer. In the wilderness years of the 1950s Richmond's best player was the ruckman Roy Wright, who won two Brownlow medals. But he was the Gentle Giant – the antithesis of the old Captain Blood. And so the fans' favourites were strongmen like Mopsy Fraser and Max Oppy.

The saddest image of that era of underachievement was Oppy trying to motivate Wright after the ruckman had crashed to earth attempting a mark over an opponent. 'Get up you weak so-and-so,' Oppy yelled. When he got close enough to see Wright was bleeding heavily, and couldn't move, Oppy apologised. 'Oh, you poor bastard, stay there.'

The war stories told from those days are not about the victories, but the injuries inflicted on opponents. Richmond had accidentally adopted the nineteenth-century pose of rugby, where bruises and broken bones had greater social currency than high marks and long, booming goals.

Like the club and the players, the supporters settled for mediocrity. They kept coming to watch their boys fight and fight and lose. Punt Road continued to attract 20 000 people for a typical home game. But in that period of full employment, more people went to see Footscray, Essendon, Carlton, Collingwood and especially Melbourne.

At this point in the game's evolution it's Collingwood that fascinates me the most, because it lifted the shackles of its postcode. By 1954, it was drawing more people to its home games than the entire population of the suburb, making it the first club with a significant supporter base beyond its geographic boundaries.

It's hard to imagine football in its present form if Collingwood had not made this transition. The suburb had become too small to carry the club on its own. In fact, Collingwood lost even more locals than Richmond; the suburb's Australian-born population collapsed by more than half between 1947 and 1966, from 28 000 to just 13 000.

But many of those who left the suburb maintained their faith in the club. These hardened expat supporters raised children and grandchildren to follow the Magpies. The same was true of Richmond but – and it seems such an obvious thing to say – in this period Collingwood became more popular than its larger neighbour by continuing to win. This meant that the second- and third-generation recruits outside the suburb were complemented by the peer group of the schoolyard, where students gravitated towards the successful clubs.

Sport and politics mirrored each other in this era, both mired in the tedium of incumbency. Robert Menzies served as prime minister for just over sixteen years, from December 1949 to January 1966. Menzies was a Carlton man, but the clubs that were most like him – lower middle class and monarchist – were Melbourne in the VFL and St George in rugby league. The St George Dragons, also John Howard's team, won eleven consecutive NSWRL premierships between 1956 and 1966. Melbourne was not quite that dominant; the Demons won five premierships in six years between 1955 and 1960, adding a sixth in 1964.

Collingwood interrupted their streak in 1958, with a triumph that every supporter wishes for their club: against the odds, and with historic significance.

The newsreel of that grand final offers glimpses of the city's class divide. Melbourne's fans were the better dressed. Collingwood fans were more likely to be wearing the club colours of black and white. 'They come from far and wide, and by all modes of transport, and the bad weather makes little difference to their enthusiasm,' the announcer says. 'Per head of population, the Australian Rules game in Melbourne draws greater crowds than any other game in the world.'

Supporters in both camps came expecting to see a whitewash. Melbourne 'looked invincible' that season, according to their captain John Beckwith. The Demons had taken the direct path to the grand final, thrashing Collingwood in the second semi. That put Collingwood in a sudden-death preliminary final against North Melbourne.

To win the premiership from there, Collingwood would have to defy not one but two bogey teams; North Melbourne had already beaten them twice in the regular season. They were favoured to do so again. But Collingwood rediscovered their form, winning the preliminary final by 20 points.

Still, a Collingwood premiership seemed unlikely. Melbourne and Collingwood had met in four previous grand finals and the Demons had won each contest comfortably. The 1958 grand final appeared to be following the script, as Melbourne established a 19-point lead at quarter time.

The Collingwood players, fearing yet another heavy defeat at the hands of their polished rival, decided to go out swinging. As they began targeting Melbourne's stars, the game shifted in Collingwood's favour. There was no honour in king-hitting opponents, but the Collingwood players didn't care. They wanted to prevent Melbourne from equalling their record of four premierships in a row.

At half time, Collingwood were in front by 2 points. At three-quarter time, their lead had blown out to 33 points. The element of surprise was not the violence but how controlled it was. Collingwood had split itself into two units: one group attacked the man, the other kept their eye on the ball. Melbourne was baited into retaliation and, for those two quarters, the champions lost their composure.

The Demons staged a fightback in the final quarter, but it was too late. Collingwood won by 18 points.

It is possible to read the result as a fairytale, the underdog beating the odds. But truth be told, Collingwood had simply bashed their way to a premiership. There was no higher social meaning to the game. It had not been played as a war of class or religion. The Melbourne players were not seen as toffs at the time, and their supporters would not be burdened unfairly with that label until much later. Their captain Ron Barassi was a third-generation Italian Australian. And Collingwood's fan base, which stretched across the city, had its share of lower-middle-class Protestants.

As Collingwood celebrated in the rooms after the game, Melbourne coach Norm Smith and Barassi entered to offer their congratulations. 'I hate you bastards,' Smith said, 'but by God I admire you.'

Later that evening, at a function at Melbourne's Royal Exhibition Building, Collingwood supporters dug into their pockets and gave their heroes 1500 pounds (the equivalent of $45 000 today).

The accounts of that grand final remind me of the ploy the Western Suburbs rugby league coach Roy Masters used in the 1970s. 'There would always be an initial period of pretty heavy confrontation,' he tells me. 'But then we found that when we started to play football we were being skilful and had forgotten about the biff. Whereas the opposition were still desperate to get square.'

For Melbourne, defeat was a blessing of sorts because it became the motivation for the thumping grand final victories of 1959 and 1960, against Essendon and Collingwood respectively. The Demons won one more premiership against the Magpies, in 1964, by four points.

Collingwood's bluff had been called, and every other club noticed. 'The Machine' lost its aura of invincibility. In the next era, as football found a new audience through television, Collingwood assumed the role of whipping boy. They were still good enough to reach the grand final a number of times, but three torturous decades would pass before they won another premiership.

The baton of working-class champion would have to be handed to its neighbour.

Richmond finally stopped losing at about the same time as Carlton. The Tigers had fallen into a deeper hole than the Blues after the war. Neither its playing list nor its home ground were up to VFL standard. Carlton, on the other hand, had a reasonable team and Princes Park was the second-best venue after the MCG. The Blues made the grand final in 1962, but then missed the finals the following season. In 1964 they dropped to tenth, one place below Richmond.

That year, both clubs elected new presidents, the lawyer Ray Dunn at Richmond and the dentist George Harris at Carlton. Both were prepared to spend money. The very first deal each man cut on behalf of their club marked a new era for the game. Dunn negotiated Richmond's move to become the second tenant of the MCG, while Harris lured Melbourne's premiership captain Ron Barassi to Princes Park. Announced two days before Christmas 1964, supporters and pundits cried that Barassi's defection to Carlton had debased football. But club loyalty had been a self-delusion of the game ever since war hero Dan Minogue had crossed from Collingwood to Richmond in 1920.

Richmond's upgrade to the MCG was made possible by the club's friendly ties with Melbourne. Frank Hughes had been a premiership coach at both clubs. And when the ground was requisitioned for the war effort from 1942 to 1945, serving as a rest and recovery barracks for the US Air Force, Marines and the RAAF, Richmond welcomed Melbourne to Punt Road.

The immediate effect of Melbourne returning the favour was a near doubling of attendances at home games, from an average of 20 000 at Punt Road Oval in 1964 to almost 36 000 at the MCG in 1965. Like Collingwood before it, Richmond was now bringing more people to the football than lived in the suburb.

The move to the MCG was a factor in the team's improved form. The superior playing surface and a new game plan combined to lift Richmond to fifth on the ladder in 1965, its best result since 1954.

Two other clubs changed address that season, but without Richmond's spectator windfall. St Kilda upgraded from Junction Oval to Moorabbin Oval, laying claim to the expanding bayside suburbs in Melbourne's south east. North Melbourne left inner-city Arden Street for Coburg, which was then Melbourne's northernmost suburb. St Kilda added just 1500 fans per game, while North Melbourne lost 3000, or 19 per cent of their average home crowd. The Kangaroos went straight back to Arden Street.

The season following these moves provides an important lesson in the demography of football loyalty. Even though St Kilda won the premiership, in 1966 the club saw its home crowd slip back to 27 000, right where it had been before the shift. The club became no more popular on their march to the top than they were when they missed the finals two years earlier in 1964, playing at Junction Oval.

By contrast Richmond, in its second season at the MCG, finished fifth again (their record of thirteen wins and a draw would have been good enough to make the finals any other year). But even on that middling form, that year they passed Melbourne to become the most watched club in the competition, with an average attendance of 42 000.

A cynic would read Richmond's popularity surge as the bandwagon effect. Richmond people, according to their detractors, are fairweather followers. They only hop on the train when the Tigers are roaring. While that may be the case, it was true of any club at the time, not just Richmond. It was normal for attendances to shrivel during a sustained period of failure and then spike when success returned.

Between its last finals appearance in 1947 and the wooden spoon year of 1960, Richmond lost 31 per cent of its audience. Footscray were defending premiers in 1955 and finished third from the bottom in 1960, and in that time their support collapsed by 40 per cent. Later Essendon saw their home crowd contract by 29 per cent as they fell from the premiership in 1965 to second last on the ladder in 1971.

Richmond's popularity surge in the mid-1960s was built on the pillars of its five premierships between 1920 and 1943, and the recruitment of a new guard of young, exciting players.

The recruitment drive was being led by club secretary Graeme Richmond. A workaholic with a network of contacts across Victoria and interstate, Richmond could charm any family to hand over their son to the club. But he was Aussie quick with an insult when rejected. When one young man he met for an interview told him he had already signed with South Melbourne, Richmond replied: 'Well, I'll tell you what, when you play your first game, I hope you break your fucking leg.'

In its weakened state in the 1950s and early 1960s, the Tigers had lacked the ambition to chase the best young talent outside their local area. The club had money, but wouldn't spend it. That attitude changed when Ray Dunn became president in 1964, and Graeme Richmond began spending it.

The first recruit of note was Barry Richardson, a schoolboy champion from St Patrick's College in Ballarat. All the big clubs made their pitch, but Graeme Richmond beat them with the personal touch, bringing Jack Dyer with him when he visited the teenager at his family property near Wodonga. Richmond heaped praised on the family – the mother's hibiscus plants and scones, the father's herd of cattle. Dyer closed the deal by telling Richardson he could wear his old number 17.

Richardson played in his first senior game in 1965, the same year the club moved to the MCG. Another young man who made his debut that season was a local boy named Kevin Bartlett. He had grown up in a boarding house on Lennox Street, and Bartlett walked into Punt Road in 1962 asking to play for its junior team. He won best and fairest first in the under 17s, then in the under 19s.

Each season brought a fresh synthesis of talent from Richmond's metropolitan zone and the country. The class of 1966 included Michael Green, who played amateur football in Richmond's zone, and Dick Clay, who had kicked a century of goals in the Goulburn Valley League. Clay had signed with North Melbourne in 1964, but Richmond convinced him to delay his arrival to Melbourne until that contract had lapsed. A brand-new Holden car was left in the driveway of the Clay family home as an incentive; Clay signed with the Tigers the day after his existing contract expired.

While impressing for Prahran in the VFA, Kevin Sheedy moved to Armadale with his family, meaning he'd shifted from Melbourne's metropolitan zone to Richmond's; Graeme Richmond seized the opportunity. Sheedy made his debut for Richmond in

1967 alongside Francis Bourke, who grew up in Nathalia in northern Victoria.

Joining them on the field that year was the Tasmanian teenager Royce Hart, whose contract included a kickback for the local Richmond economy. Hart's mother told Graeme Richmond that her son did not have enough clothes for a move to Melbourne. So Richmond had Hart fitted out by a tailor on Lennox Street for a grey suit, six white shirts and pair of shoes. Perfect for his job as a teller at the Commonwealth Bank.

By today's standards it seems cheap, but it reflected the moderation of the era. The wages explosions for football and the general economy were still a few years away.

By 1967, all the young talent Richmond had assembled had grown into a team ready to challenge for a premiership. But they seemed to sneak up on the competition. Newspaper reports of their early victories carried the condescending assumption that they were still too immature. Yet they kept winning, and finished the home and away season on top of the ladder, half a game ahead of Barassi's Carlton.

None of the Richmond players had been in a finals game before. The trio of nineteen-year-olds in the side – Hart, Green and Graham Burgin – hadn't been born when the Tigers last played a final, in 1947.

Richmond overwhelmed Carlton in the semi-final and won by 40 points. Asked when he thought he had the game won, coach Tom Hafey replied: 'At the first bounce of the first quarter.'

Carlton did not get a second chance, losing the preliminary final to Geelong. The Cats were playing in their sixth consecutive finals series, and had been premiers in 1963. But the Tigers went into the grand final as favourites.

Previewing the game for *The Age*, St Kilda player Ian Stewart wrote a prescient column. When his Saints had played Richmond earlier in the year, 'the Tigers were much cruder in technique and less versatile than they are now. They would strong-arm the ball from the centre bounce and hope to scramble goals out of a fairly congested attack.' But now they were moving the ball with purpose, and their forward line had a 'cleaner edge'. Many goals were being scored 'with apparent ease through smart teamwork leaving the last player in the chain well clear of any opposition'.

That article could easily have been written about Damien Hardwick's premiership-winning class of 2017.

The reality is that Richmond's new core of young players didn't know any other way. They did not wear the burden of the club's history. Ten of the twenty who played in the 1967 grand final began their senior careers with the MCG as their home ground. They had no experience of Richmond as easy beats. And they had always played together – five of those ten youngsters made their debut in 1965, two in 1966 and three in 1967. The competition was open enough for a side to rise to the top in three years, from reconstruction to premiership.

The VFL thought it had unleashed a monster. On the eve of the 1967 grand final it closed the free-trade market that had allowed Graeme Richmond to assemble this grand final team. From the following season, each club would be restricted to recruiting from a designated country zone in Victoria and in the Riverina district of southern New South Wales, where football was still more popular than rugby league.

In the week of the grand final against Geelong, Richmond people walked a little taller. From the town hall down to Punt Road, the suburb was 'bedecked in bunting and flags' in yellow and black. 'The city had one thing to say,' *The Age* reported. '"Come on the Tigers."'

Forty-five miles down the road, at Geelong, the mayor Sir Roy Fidge said the players would be welcomed at city hall after the game 'win, lose or draw'.

No Victorian would have been unaware of the 1967 grand final. It attracted 109 000 people to the MCG, the second highest grand final attendance to date. Three of the four television stations – GTV9, HSV7 and ABC2 – replayed the match from 6 p.m. that evening. The ABC interrupted its broadcast at 7 p.m. for an eighteen-minute news and weather bulletin before resuming its replay. The delay simply meant Tigers fans could watch the happy ending twice.

If you wanted to avoid football on the tele that evening, ATV0 was showing *Petticoat Junction*.

Like many Richmond fans through the years, I've watched the replay with fascination. What strikes me about that grand final is its manic energy. Kicks were sprayed. Tackles missed. Players set off on grandiose runs, bouncing the ball once, twice, thrice, only to pass it to a stationary opponent, who blasted it back, where another error was made.

The disorder has the effect of exaggerating the game's individual highlights. Late in the final quarter, when the scores were level, Royce Hart took the first great screamer of the television age. The ball was kicked out by the Geelong fullback to his teammate at centre halfback. It was a booming drop kick, and if the Geelong player marked it, he would surely send it further forward. Hart was slightly to the side of his opponent and running into the camera's view. He leaped into the air, catching the right shoulder of the Geelong player with his leg and pushing off him, reaching up and securing the ball. The movement was improvised but perfect in its execution. He reacted a second quicker than everyone else. The other players look bewildered, out of place.

Hart was not the best on ground, that was the Richmond centreman Bill Barrot. But every time Hart went near the ball he looked as if he was playing a different game. I imagine this was how Essendon people felt watching John Coleman in the 1950s.

For three quarters, Geelong was the more efficient team, kicking 13 goals 7 behinds to Richmond's 12 goals 15. The Tigers led by just 2 points. In the final quarter, Geelong had 10 scoring shots to Richmond's 7. If the Cats had maintained their accuracy, they would have won. But their older players were tiring, while the young Tigers rose to the occasion. Richmond kicked 4 goals from their 7 attempts, while Geelong managed just 2 from their 10.

The final minutes of the game were unbearably tense. Geelong were surging. The ball was hurtling towards the Punt Road End like a space rocket when the Tigers captain Fred Swift juggled a mark on the goal line. He kicked the ball straight back into play and a Geelong player swooped on his kick, immediately firing it back at the goal. He missed. A split second later the siren sounded and the players and crowd exploded in celebration. Richmond was victorious by 9 points, with both teams contributing to the highest-scoring grand final for twenty seasons.

It was the perfect game for the new medium of television. Two other grand finals in this era match it for excitement, St Kilda's 1-point win over Collingwood in 1966 and Carlton's frenzied comeback against Collingwood in 1970. In those games the crowd didn't roar, it screamed. It sounds like the adolescent squall that greeted the Beatles at the Melbourne Town Hall.

On that night in 1967 when Richmond ended its premiership drought, a small but boisterous crowd gathered at the town hall on Bridge Road to revive an old tradition. But something was missing. The town hall was closed for a private function – it had been booked for a wedding reception, the mayor Tom Peluso explained – and the players, officials, wives and girlfriends were dining at a restaurant in St Kilda that evening. It did not occur to them to return to Richmond at the end of their celebration.

Robert McGaw, who had lived all his eighty-one years in Richmond, waited to see his heroes for two hours, in vain. 'The locals seem to have been forgotten in the big business of football today,' he told *The Age*. 'When Richmond won in 1943, thousands were cheering in the streets here.'

What had changed was Richmond's fan base had been scattered into the outer suburbs. This new generation of supporters didn't hang around after the game to join a street party in a suburb they didn't know, they went home to watch the replay.

PART TWO

POLITICAL FOOTBALL

1970s–2000s

5

THE OLD RICHMOND MODEL

I was born into Richmond even though I never lived there. I follow the club because my mother began her Australian journey in the migrant suburb in the early 1960s. As a young man, my father also lived in Richmond, but his first night on Australian soil was spent at an aunt's house in Fitzroy, and so he barracked for the Lions.

Dad liked football, although he wasn't quite as enthusiastic as Mum. He would pull out his maroon and blue Fitzroy beanie and sing his special Hellenic version of the club song, which he renamed 'Oi Fitzroydes', whenever the Lions beat the Tigers.

His first love was soccer: AEK Athens in Greece's national competition, South Melbourne Hellas in the Victorian State League. He'd follow the results of the Greek games on his short-wave radio, while he read the match reports of the local games in the Greek-Australian newspapers. My father's favourite player at Hellas was the Scottish-born striker Jimmy Armstrong. Neither AEK nor Hellas grabbed me as a child. I was a mummy's boy, and she was a Tiger. Mum had me converted by the time she dropped me off on my first day at kindergarten, in 1969.

'Where did you learn to speak English?' the odd politician has asked me, and I pretend not to remember. The correct answer is, 'The same place you did mate: at home.' Mum's English was broken, but Dad's was excellent. He came to Australia as a sixteen-year-old and I was born just before his thirtieth birthday. The radio was always on in our house, and the kitchen table was overrun with his newspapers. The tabloid *Sun*, the afternoon broadsheet *The Herald* and *The Sporting Globe* provided the raw material for my scrapbooks on footy and the Apollo missions. I skipped his Greek papers because I couldn't read them.

Like many migrants of his generation, my father followed the horses, and this pastime accidentally sparked another of my obsessions. It brought music into our house through the Melbourne racing station 3UZ, which he listened to. Their playlist in the early 1970s was drenched in melancholy. Even now, when I hear Elvis Presley's 'In the Ghetto' or Johnny Cash's version of 'Sunday Morning Coming Down', I picture Dad cursing a losing bet. It was in those formative years of passive listening that I latched on to the Beatles.

Later, when I owned my own radio and cassette recorder, I built a small library of Beatles compilation tapes, collated over many hours of diligent surveillance of every station on the AM dial. I would press record whenever the DJ announced a Beatles track, which meant the sequencing was left to chance. On one tape, 'Dizzy, Miss Lizzy' segued into the mini opera of *Abbey Road*. On another, taken from our black and white Pye television, the closing credits of *A Hard Day's Night* were followed by the final two minutes of Richmond's victory in the 1967 VFL grand final and then the opening theme for *Lost in Space*. Today, I'd happily swap some of the rarest albums in my collection to hear those recordings again.

Football and music were the twin shields of my childhood identity. I wasn't Greek or Australian, but a Richmond supporter and a Beatles fan. My boyhood heroes were pairings of contemporary

Tigers and rock stars from other eras. Royce Hart and John Lennon. Michael Roach and Jim Morrison. Maurice Rioli and Bruce Springsteen.

'Miss, who do you barrack for?' The first teacher I recall asking that question of was Miss Cook, the benign ruler of our grade two class at Tooronga Road Primary School. That year, 1971, at age seven, somewhere between the arrival of our first black and white television and discovering Miss Cook was a Hawthorn supporter, I realised that I needed to go to a game of football.

How I nagged my poor parents. First I wanted a Richmond jumper. I sensed that it would consume a disproportionate share of our family income, but kept asking anyway. When Mum finally relented I took the woollen guernsey to school to show off to my buddies, even though the day was too warm to wear it. During recess, I left it on a hook in my classroom. I never saw it again. Someone had pinched it while I was outside. Miss Cook searched every bag for me, but couldn't find the thief. That afternoon, in tears, I returned home to the full Mediterranean symphony of blame.

Losing the jumper was a setback, but I would not be deterred. I wanted to see Richmond play and once the shouting had subsided, I resumed my campaign. Eventually it was agreed that Mum would take me and my younger sister to a Richmond game at the MCG. But Dad had two non-negotiable rules for our engagement: we were to sit in the dry area to the right of the Punt Road End goals, and as close as possible to the police on horseback. They would protect us if mob violence erupted in our section. His fear was based on the contemporary examples of British and European soccer, where rioting was common.

Mum could not have chosen a better induction than that game between Richmond and Hawthorn. Round eighteen, the Hawks were on an eleven-match winning streak, and Peter Hudson was on course to break Bob Pratt's record of 150 goals in a season.

Almost 48 000 people were there, a mass of humanity beyond my comprehension. Before that day, the largest collection of people I had seen in the one place was at the wedding of my Collingwood-supporting uncle, Dad's brother James. Now, in one place, I was confronted with 2 per cent of the entire population of Melbourne. Still, that was on the low side for a Richmond blockbuster. In round two, 82 000 people had filled the MCG for the game against Collingwood.

Looking back on the crowd numbers for my first day at the football, it's striking how dependent the competition was on its big three at the time, Richmond, Carlton and Collingwood. Spectators at those games accounted for 87 per cent of the round's total attendance of 116 000.

I was in awe of the noise. The sonic boom that greeted a Richmond goal was life-affirming. But when the Hawthorn fans celebrated one of theirs, I was crushed. To be fair to the Hawks, our supporters were the more feral. Hudson had six goals from six kicks, and the Richmond cheer squad booed him for each. Early in the last quarter, he left the field with a minor injury. I don't recall this detail but *The Age* reported that Hudson 'was subjected to jeers and abuse' as he walked off. A beer can was thrown at him. It missed, and a Hawthorn trainer retrieved the missile and hurled it back into the crowd.

Mum's favourite player was the Tigers' captain, Roger Dean, but I navigated the play via the star of Royce Hart. Counting each goal, mark and kick. It was his number four that had been sewn onto the jumper I had lost earlier in the year.

The game was close for three quarters but I doubt that I ever contemplated the possibility of defeat. Hudson's departure was the turning point. Once the Hawks lost their target forward, the Tigers ran amok. In the last quarter, we kicked 5 goals to their 1, to win by 32 points. Each goal was exhilarating, making victory more certain. Back home that evening, watching the replay, I bored my parents by pointing out the moment when Hawthorn stopped scoring. I suspect it was an early warning of the data nerd that I would become.

Football for kids of my age was a voluntary course in arithmetic; the first lesson was our six times table. A month before the Hawthorn game, I was mesmerised by Collingwood's final score against Essendon – 30 goals and 20 behinds for a total of 200 points. A monumental round number that was beyond most clubs, mine included. Later came the pure and applied maths of recording every run, dot ball and wicket of a cricket test, following Lillee and Thomson, the Chappell brothers and Doug Walters.

That first season, we saw two further Richmond victories at the MCG, against Melbourne and Geelong. Late in the last quarter of the Melbourne game, I waited for the lull after a behind and yelled, 'C'mon the Tigers.' When we watched the replay that evening we heard my pipsqueak voice ring out across the MCG.

A parental nudge into the schoolyard, a footy-loving teacher and a cameo on the replay – I was hooked. I followed the finals series on Dad's radio. My confidence in a premiership was, I thought, grounded in careful analysis. We won the semi-final against Collingwood, a team that had beaten us twice during the regular season. Our next opponent was St Kilda, a team we had defeated twice. A pessimist would spot the trap, but I had not yet graduated to superstition. My seven-year-old self was spoiled by success. Richmond had won premierships in 1967 and 1969. Another in 1971 made perfect sense. I was already thinking ahead to the grand final against Hawthorn, and the earnest conversations I would have with the two Hawks that I knew, Miss Cook and my aunt, Erasmia.

I wasn't prepared for the trauma of that preliminary final against St Kilda. My dad's uncle Apostolos had paid us a visit that miserable Saturday as we were listening to the game. When the final siren tolled the end of our season, I melted into tears. Apostolos tried to cheer me up but my grief had already crossed the threshold to tantrum and I kicked the poor fellow. Mum should have given me the *koutala* – the wooden spoon she threatened me with whenever I acted up. But she felt our defeat as keenly as I did and shepherded me to the milk bar to buy me a bag of marbles. The sporting gods administered their punishment within a week as I lost every one of those marbles playing against mates at school.

The following season was the most difficult of all. We saw two early games in person, for one win and one loss. Then we moved house from the Greek end of Malvern to leafy Caulfield, from a quiet side street that had more children than cars to a main road that woke us with the rattling alarm of the first tram of the morning. I wanted us to buy a house in Richmond, but my parents told me I was stupid; Richmond was the suburb people left.

Mum fell ill during the move and couldn't take us to another game that season. Dad was preoccupied with shift work and the mortgage. I followed the Tigers on the radio, on the TV replay and in the sports pages. We had finished the regular season second on the ladder and by all accounts the coach and players were as sure as I was that we would win the premiership. The semi-final against minor premiers Carlton ended in a draw, but we crushed them in the replay. We were favourites to beat them again in the grand final.

But on the day, Carlton had nothing to lose, adopting what was apparently a surprise strategy of all-out attack. They had a 10-goal lead by half time. I was speechless. Our final score of 22 goals and 18 behinds, for 150 points, would have won any previous grand final. But the Blues still beat us by 27 points.

My pain was compounded by the 10-cent bet I had made with a Carlton-supporting school friend. I was still relatively new to Caulfield North Central School and did not want to lose face. But I had no pocket money; that was a privilege reserved for Aussie kids. All weekend I calculated the options before settling on the most shameful. I lifted the 10 cents from my mother's purse and hid it in my school sock. Football had pushed me from sook to thief.

Football's grip on my imagination tightened with those childhood humiliations. Now I really needed a premiership to validate my belief system, and my prayers were answered with back-to-back grand final victories in 1973 and '74. Those two seasons were our busiest as a spectating family. We went to virtually every home game at the MCG, and, now that my father no longer held fears for our safety, even ventured to some of the smaller suburban grounds where we stood with the mob.

A trip to Windy Hill for the opening round of the 1973 season took us into another time. The older Essendon men were in mourning because John Coleman had passed away that week. I didn't pick up their conversations, but felt the sorrow that hung over the start of the match.

Mum's homing mechanism took us to a section near the Richmond cheer squad behind the goals. When the play was at our end, my heroes loomed like giants. But the other end of the ground could have been on Alpha Centauri for all I could tell. I kept losing the Richmond jumpers against the swirl of colours in the crowd. I squinted, but could not follow the play. So I let the crowd guide me. When the Essendon supporters fell silent, I joined our cheer squad in singing out. 'One, two, three, four, who do you think we barrack for? Five, six, seven, eight, who do you think we appreciate? R-I-C-H-M-O-N-D Richmond. Whada we do? Eat 'em alive. Richmond!' *Clap, clap, clap.*

No more than 5000 of the almost 29 000 people in attendance would have been Tigers. I was too young to be intimidated, and too small for any Essendon supporter to need to take me on. I had no sense then of the menace of an away game at a suburban ground. As a kid, I wasn't aware of the pervasive standing-room stench of beer, smoke and piss. Seated at the MCG all I could smell were the Chiko Rolls, and those deep-fried donuts injected with lava-hot jam.

If we had gone to Windy Hill a year later, we would have witnessed the infamous half-time brawl involving players and officials from both teams. My father might have declared a state of emergency and suspended our travel rights.

But in 1973, I rode every goal like the roller-coaster at Luna Park. I thought that the Bombers would win and, late in the final quarter when they stole the lead, their supporters began screaming for the siren to sound. I remember the clock had moved well past thirty minutes, which usually signalled a game was about to end. But then Kevin Sheedy kicked a goal for Richmond and suddenly it was our turn to plead to the timekeeper. 'Siren, siren.' When it finally rang out, we were ecstatic. Richmond had won by 2 points.

It's chicken and egg who was lobbying in 1973 and '74. Mum had slipped easily into the fanatic's skin and would tell us we were going to a game before we had even asked. My barracking form changed in response to hers. She was a nervous watcher; I tried to be the cool one. We'd have an argument when she gave up a game as lost and dragged us away from the MCG to catch an early train home. There was dishonour in leaving before the final siren, I thought. You felt the eyes of your fellow supporters on your back as you trudged towards the exit. How I dreamed that we would win one of those games she had us abandon. But her instincts never failed her.

I can't speak for others of my generation, but footy in the 1970s served as the week's big adventure. We didn't eat out as a family. The only non-Greek meal we allowed ourselves was Chinese takeaway. Dad didn't drive, so there were no trips to the beach or the bush. Football was day release from the house arrest of migrant life.

In the early years I went to Greek school on Saturday mornings, reciting the alpha beta and practising my Greek script. Those lessons were sadly wasted on me – my brain was already running an hour ahead, to the commute to the game. The Frankston train was usually packed by the time it reached our stop. We'd squeeze on and I'd scan the carriage to see if the Tigers supporters outnumbered the opposition. The yellow and black scarves, the beanies and the long black duffle coats with their pinboards of badges, all of it reassured me that we were among our people. We'd pour out at Richmond station and march to the MCG in a column of anticipation.

The trip home after a win was never boring, there was always a bloke yelling 'Carn'a Tigers' as the train pulled away from each station. But we didn't talk much after the losses. I'd count the stops home, reading the graffiti along the bricked embankments of the Frankston line. After 1975, I would look forward to pithy commentary on the dismissal. 'Remember, Remember, 11 November, Day of Vice-Regal Treason and Plot' and 'Kerr for Governor General is like Barassi for Umpire'. I didn't really understand the first one, but it always meant our stop was next, and we could depart the funeral carriage of grieving Tigers.

September was the exception to our footy routine. It was the most insular month of our season because we couldn't afford finals tickets. Mum tells me now that even if we'd had the cash to spare, she didn't know how to buy them. You couldn't just walk up to the MCG on game day.

We listened to the live coverage on my new Philips transistor radio. At half time I would retreat to the backyard, where I played out the game with my plastic football, then dash back inside for the second half. When the game ended, I would rush out to the backyard again before being called back inside for dinner.

Dad had his radio on throughout the day, following the races. There was a clear dividing line across the house. Dad's territory was the front bedroom and the lounge. He would pace between the two, then, if he was ahead on the day, make a return trip to the

TAB to collect. Mum, my sister and I listened to the football in her domain, the kitchen. In the evening our family would unite in the lounge room for the TV replay.

Then every Sunday morning, we all watched the *World of Sport* panel show. I was fixated by the mark and goal of the week, the review of the game with the two coaches and the handball competition. I'd zone out when Dad's segments came on, the racing roundup with Bill Collins and the soccer with Fred Villiers.

On the Monday after every grand final I would offer to pick up his copy of the *Herald* so I could get my hands on the eight-page souvenir insert. I read and re-read the articles over the summer, and memorised the statistical table on page six, which listed every game of the season. Not the scores – I wasn't in as deep as some of my friends – but the sequence of Richmond's wins and losses.

Football's hegemony was reinforced in the schoolyard with recess and lunchtime games of kick-to-kick. The taller kids usually took the marks, while the shorter kids would swoop whenever the football spilled from the tangle of arms. To ensure no individual player dominated, we would pick a partner to share our kicks with, which we called waxing. The practice regulated the asphalt battleground of Caulfield North to ensure that none of our mates went without a kick. If one of our group took too many marks, he'd be banished to the other end where, presumably, he'd face stiffer competition.

The high mark – the hanger, the screamer, the speccie – is football's enchanted element. It allows a child to re-create the game at home. You don't need a mate to play with or even a proper football. My parents didn't trust me with a real one. There were too many things I could destroy with a stray Sherrin: Mum's tomato patch, a window, Mr Jenkins' greenhouse next door.

When I lost my plastic football, I invented a minimalist form of the game for the backyard using the lemons that had fallen from

Mum's tree. They would only be good for one or two kicks before disintegrating, so the play had to be special. I'd start off with a speccie, climbing a stepladder of teammates and opponents. Then I'd land, cat-like, and sidestep the Hills hoist before punting the lemon between two fence posts for the winning goal. Indoors, I followed the tradition of rolling up a pair of socks to kick and mark along the corridor; my parents yelling at me to shut up, always in Greek, whenever I added commentary and crowd noises to my fictional grand final.

As a child of Richmond's glory days, I had no conception of the old rivalry with Collingwood. The Magpies were not a serious threat in 1970s. The teams that beat us in finals were John Nicholls' Carlton and Ron Barassi's North Melbourne, and I was obliged to hate them. The irony is that the Blues were more representative of the world I knew.

Despite the Greekness of the suburb, the Richmond team did not look like the people I grew up with. There were no southern Europeans on our playing list. It was Carlton who happened to be diversity's glamour club at the time, with Sergio Silvagni, the local-born son of Italian migrants, and Alex Jesaulenko, born in Austria to a Ukrainian father and Russian mother, among their very best players.

I did have a soft spot for Jesaulenko. It was his nickname I invoked whenever I leaped over school mates in games of kick-to-kick. We didn't take screamers at Caulfield North, we took Jezzas. I was too young to appreciate the richness of my own club's Australian working-class roots, or football's ability to unite warring tribes from the old world – the Greeks and Turks who followed Collingwood together; the Serbs and Croats who barracked for Footscray. Interestingly, the wrestling on GTV9 was closer to the world I knew. The Golden Greek, Spiros Arion, and the Italian Stallion, Mario Milano, were heroes to the migrants who couldn't relate to Aussie Rules.

But the memory plays tricks. My child's-eye view of the culture had football at the centre of Victorian life when, in fact, it was still safely contained on the back page.

The Age covered our 1973 premiership seriously in its sports section, with an avalanche of words, statistical tables and action shots. But in contrast to today's excessive coverage of the game, the front page saw football as human interest, not news. The lead story was Gough Whitlam's referendum proposal to give the Commonwealth power over prices. The second story dealt with a shocking road crash that killed four and left a three-year-old boy orphaned. Wedged between those two reports was a stage-managed photo of the two Kevins, Bartlett and Sheedy, dressed in daggy shirts and daggier slacks. The camera catches them with arms linked, leaping above the premiership cup. A short caption explained: 'It was late on Saturday night, the celebrations were hours old, but there was plenty of life in the Tigers.'

The next year, Richmond's premiership did not even warrant an image. The front-page picture was of former prime minister Billy McMahon denying claims that the CIA had helped fund the Liberal Party's election campaigns. On the top right-hand corner of the page was a two-line summary, pointing to the sports section, where the grand final was chronicled in thrilling detail.

The separation between sport and politics held throughout the 1970s. There was so much politics in that decade that Malcolm Fraser declared his mission as prime minister was to put sport back on the front page, a gag which no one outside Victoria understood, and which I now assume referred to his own childhood in the 1930s when sport had featured more prominently in the news.

Football did not become political, that is, it did not become front-page news for the serious press, until the summer of 1981–82, when Bob Hawke's club, the South Melbourne Swans, were sent to

Sydney. The notion that football had to take sides on social issues would not occur to the game's officials until the mid-1990s, after Indigenous players Nicky Winmar and Michael Long forced them to confront on-field racism.

But football has always been about power. Big clubs versus impoverished ones. Head office versus ordinary supporters. For children of the 1970s, the game simultaneously extended our innocence and prepared us for the cynicism of adulthood.

I grew up in one of football's most violent decades. Without replays from earlier eras to compare, it is impossible to know if the brawling and the sniping that we witnessed on the field was the worst the game has seen. But I suspect that might be the case.

In wider society, the 1970s was Australia's most conflicted decade of the twentieth century. We set records for industrial disputation and alcohol consumption. For the only time in history, our economy suffered a sustained period of rising inflation and unemployment. And the political system was in crisis at every level, from the chaos of the Whitlam years and the bastardy of the dismissal, to the crooked premiers and corrupt police forces. Not surprisingly, respect for democracy was at a then all-time record low. It was a polarised, uncivil decade.

Following Richmond, the era's most ruthless club, meant pretending you were a victim even as you won premiership after premiership. I knew that our success inspired a fury of jealousy, and that the rules could be changed to bring us back to the pack. For instance, Kevin Bartlett was the game's quickest player. Even when an opponent caught up with him, he would outsmart his pursuer. Bartlett would throw the ball out in front as if to bounce it, then surrender to an illegal tackle, earning a free kick. It was no better than diving in soccer. But I sincerely felt that he was being picked on when his tactic was finally outlawed.

I had the zealot's habit of lumping imagined and real outrages into the same basket of grievance. The scariest part of football in the 1970s was the risk that your hero would be knocked out. The creative bravery of Royce Hart's play invited retaliation from lesser men. He flew for marks from all angles and his stationary opponents would feign an attempt to punch the ball, miss, and whack him in the back of the head.

I also felt for the players at other clubs who were targeted. The incident that affected me most was the assault on Collingwood's John Greening in 1972. Very early in the game, he was felled by a St Kilda player, putting him into a coma. For days I checked the newspapers for updates on his condition. Beyond the simple life lessons of winning and losing, football gave my generation the first intimation that cruelty was life's default setting.

Greening made his comeback two years later, against Richmond. He had 24 disposals and they beat us by 69 points. It was the first heavy defeat I remember not being troubled by. Collingwood had a favourite son back from the dead.

But I didn't have the same degree of empathy for the Carlton players my boys flattened in the 1973 grand final. I have to admit I enjoyed the theatre of the first brutal act of the game when we watched the replay that evening. Little Laurie Fowler leaped into the path of big bad John Nicholls. I watch it now and see that it was a cheap shot. But my nine-year-old self cheered. Big Nick had hurt our players in the past. Served him right, I thought then.

Nevertheless, I did wince a little later when in the same game I saw Neil Balme take his eye off the football and, with a round-arm punch, break the jaw of Carlton's stylish fullback Geoff Southby. Balme, with his wildman hairdo of mop top and Medusa mullet, was playing a real-life wrestling villain. A few minutes later, he whacked Carlton's enforcer, Vin Waite. Now he was being ridiculous. As he comically protested his innocence, the Carlton players rushed in. But you could sense their reticence. *Who will he belt next?*

Balme regained his composure in the final quarter. He kicked the goal that put the game beyond Carlton's reach. That's my strongest memory, listening to the grand final on the radio. Carlton had rallied at the start of that quarter and I was worried sick – Balme's goal calmed me down.

To be honest, I didn't really enjoy the 1974 grand final, even though it was the cleaner and more decisive of the two victories. I listened to part of the game perched halfway up the giant maple tree that blanketed the front of our house. My gangly ten-year-old world was collapsing as I climbed; branch in one hand, transistor radio in the other. Richmond had just surrendered the lead to North Melbourne and I couldn't bear the anxiety in the kitchen. I left Mum with Dad's radio and took mine outside.

The Tigers scored the next goal, a sure sign from up above that I had changed our luck from my new vantage point. I remained in my sanctuary long enough to be sure that we wouldn't lose.

But the stone of worthlessness returned to my stomach soon after the final siren. I knew that a schoolyard kicking awaited me, win or lose. Grade five was the worst year of my childhood because it was the year I first heard the word 'wog'. At my previous school, we were too young to notice the differences in our group. At Caulfield North, I stood out as one of the few Greek-Australian boys in the classroom. It hadn't seemed to matter in grades three or four. But in grade five, at the age of ten, I experienced the full force of the 1970s in the schoolyard.

I endured some terrible beatings. My parents pleaded with the school to look after me, but my grade five teacher was out of his depth. I suspect that I annoyed him.

Our schoolyard race war, in so far as it affected me, ended without casualties in the autumn of 1975. The ceasefire was negotiated by our grade six teacher. He micromanaged our games of kick-to-kick. At the start of each week, he would hand the class football to one of the students. It was a simple job: you walked out with the ball and you brought it back when the bell rang. When my turn came, our teacher was effectively ordering the boys in the class to let me play with them. They were happy to allow me back into the group because I had the footy. That game of kick-to-kick helped me to rediscover the lost art of making friends, while my tormentors found another wog to pick on.

Not once in my youth did it occur to me that the Richmond football club personified some of the worst aspects of public life in Australia in the 1970s. The club bent the rules and behaved as a bully. It posed as anti-establishment while bragging about its connections to the top end of town. Richmond president Ian Wilson would walk guests to the club's corporate luncheon via the MCG members stand and a section of the public area 'to show we weren't some hick club from the slums of Richmond'.

The Tigers were always provoking fights with the game's officials and with the eleven other clubs in the VFL. If an umpire made a call the Tigers didn't agree with, the club's officials didn't just protest, they punched on. At the 1974 Bronwlow medal count, the Richmond table was incensed that Kevin Bartlett didn't win. They heckled, and should have left it at that. But the club secretary Alan Schwab and his colleague Charles Priestley decided they would fight all 500 guests at the Southern Cross Hotel. 'I think the count was that by that stage I'd had twenty-five clarets and Charlie had had twenty-six,' Schwab recalled.

The Richmond model was win at all costs and whinge at every opportunity. With the hindsight of three decades covering politics and economics, here's what I missed then that makes me laugh now: Richmond was half ACTU Bob Hawke – gifted, media savvy and self-destructive – and half Malcolm Fraser – willing to break every convention in the pursuit of power.

Richmond's story reads like a counter history of Australia. Multiple premierships for its working-class supporters in hard times; long, pitiful droughts during periods of political stability. Five flags between 1920 and 1943, when the nation was beset by depression and war. Then nothing for twenty-four years. Another five premierships between 1967 and 1980, when the old protected economic order was crumbling. And then nothing again for the next thirty-seven years, during which time the game went national and the economy entered its longest winning streak since the gold rush.

6

REMOVING BARRIERS

For the first eight decades of the Australian federation, football and rugby league observed a strict separation of powers. Football did not send clubs north, while rugby league did not need to look south. The characters of the nation's two largest cities were reflected in their respective codes. In sheltered Melbourne, the VFL was in stasis, relying on its twelve established clubs to compete for the loyalty of the people who moved to the outer suburbs after World War II. Sydney was more fickle. The NSWRL operated in a more divided capital; the inner-city clubs did not have a constituancy that spanned Sydney, like Richmond and Collingwood did throughout Melbourne. So rugby league made its post-war play with new clubs to the north, south and west of the CBD. The competition expanded from eight to ten clubs in 1947 with the addition of Manly and Parramatta, and to twelve in 1967 when Cronulla and Penrith joined.

The first time the geographic boundary between football and rugby was breached was in 1982, a year before the Hawke government kicked open the door to economic reform with the floating of the dollar. The South Melbourne Swans relocated to Sydney and, in the same year, rugby league extended its reach to Canberra and Wollongong.

The first season outside the cocoons of the capital cities reaffirmed football's power to grab an audience. The Swans immediately became the most popular club of any code in Sydney. Almost 16 000 people saw a typical home game at the SCG, although many of those tickets were giveaways. By comparison, rugby league's leading club that season was Manly, which averaged 12 500 per game at Brookvale Oval.

But these numbers are deceptive, because the Swans had entered a city that didn't have a habit of mass attendance. Even in rugby league's salad days in the late 1960s, when South Sydney and Balmain dominated the competition, the crowds at suburban grounds were only half the size of their equivalent in the VFL.

The Swans were football's least popular club in 1982. They were actually seen by more people at their away games in Melbourne than at their new home at the SCG. For the VFL, this was no great concern because the venture was not a realistic challenge to rugby league. The goal, instead, was to create a new audience through television, following the lead of its forgotten local sparring partner, the Victorian Football Association.

Since the earliest years of television, the VFL prohibited the live broadcast of games in Melbourne, fearing it would reduce attendances. The VFA, which scheduled its games on Sundays, saw an opening and allowed its match of the day to be televised live into Melbourne. With South Melbourne in Sydney, the VFL could do the same without breaking its own rules. Every second Sunday afternoon the game played at the SCG was broadcast live, from opening bounce to final siren, to all parts of the country outside Sydney.

But the relative strength of football's debut in Sydney said more about rugby league's failure to engage the inner city than it did about the appeal of the invader. Rugby league attendances had been in freefall since the late 1960s. It's tempting to conclude that on-field violence was turning people away from the game. But the biff, as Sydneysiders called it, was also a central part of football, and it didn't hurt attendances in Melbourne and Geelong. Football crowds increased by 15 per cent from 1971 to 1981, while the numbers at rugby league games fell by 16 per cent over the same period.

The other possible explanation is that Sydneysiders have better things to do in winter than watch rugby league. It's what my Sydney friends keep telling me, that they don't need the contrivance of sport when they can go to the beach. But the data doesn't support this urban myth either. In summer, when presumably the surf issues its strongest call, there were football-sized crowds at the SCG to watch one-day cricket.

The difference was not in the quality of the codes, or even the temperament of the people, but in the physical layout of the two capitals. After people left for the suburbs, Sydney didn't have the transport network to sustain rugby league in the inner city. The game was easier to follow on the television – at home, in a pub or in a rugby leagues club. Melbourne kept bringing people back to watch Richmond, Collingwood and Carlton at the MCG, Victoria Park and Princes Park because the trains and the trams all pointed in the same direction: to the footy.

When the VFL built a stadium of its own in the outer suburb of Waverley in 1970, it ran an accidental trial in Sydney logistics. Waverley Park rose like a Soviet-era mausoleum along the South-Eastern Freeway (now the Monash). Situated in a suburban growth corridor, but separated from the metropolitan train and tram networks, it was the stadium you drove to. Fans turned up as individuals, united in the stands, then returned home alone. The ground itself lacked the intimacy of the MCG; the seats were set too far back and in the winter the meanest chill wind would blow through the place. Waverley Park was the closest ground to Richmond's metropolitan recruiting zone, yet the crowds for the home games the Tigers played there were 36 per cent lower than their equivalent at the MCG.

Rugby league found larger audiences outside Sydney, where a city or town could identify with a single club. Canberra and Illawarra fielded the two weakest teams in the expansion season of 1982, finishing last and second last respectively. But in terms of home attendance, they were ranked fourth and sixth out of the fourteen clubs. Canberra's home crowds at Sieffert Oval in Queanbeyan beat the attendances of each of the six inner-city Sydney clubs. (One of the inner-city foundation clubs, Newtown, was struggling to remain financially viable and was thrown out of the competition at the end of the following season.)

When Brisbane and Newcastle joined the NSWRL in 1988, they immediately drew the most spectators in the league. Newcastle had the largest home crowd, while Brisbane was the most-watched team across all home and away games. The Broncos also won the first head-to-head with VFL in Queensland, attracting 3000 more people per home game than the Brisbane Bears football club, which had entered the VFL along with the Perth-based West Coast Eagles a year earlier (16 000 compared to 13 000).

For the VFL, expansion revealed two awkward truths. The first was that the game was barely credible in New South Wales and Queensland. Support for the Sydney Swans, as they were known from 1983, was especially mercurial. By 1985, the typical home crowd at the SCG had slumped to just 10 000, but the following season, when the Swans made the finals for the first time as a Sydney-based outfit, it rebounded to almost 26 000. A further finals appearance in 1987 was rewarded with an audience of almost 22 000 per game. But then the party ended. By 1990, the Swans were watched by just 9000 people per game.

Sydneysiders were behaving no differently to the fans of Melbourne-based clubs. The problem was the Swans had a much smaller base level of support because they were new to the city.

In other words, they drew football-like crowds in the good years and rugby league–like crowds in the lean.

The second uncomfortable truth revealed by the VFL's expansion was that the Victorian clubs would struggle to adapt to a national competition. The volatility in Sydney coincided with an extraordinary collapse in support for the big clubs. Between 1982 and 1987, total attendances fell by 22 per cent. I can safely blame my club for the game-wide recession, because Richmond suffered a prolonged depression. And it served us right.

At its zenith in 1980, Richmond became the first club of any code in Australia to attract an average of more than 50 000 people to its home games. The Tigers had found a sweet spot between youth and experience that conjured a style of play that made each game flow like a highlight reel of the best marks and goals of the week. The 21-year-old full forward Michael Roach took screamer after screamer. Old man Kevin Bartlett, aged thirty-three, still ran rings around his opponents. The telepathic midfield of Raines, Rowlings, Weightman and Wiley moved the ball with a precision I had not seen from a Richmond team before. They would stream out of the centre with one simple choice to make: pass to Roach or shoot for goal.

The games were one-sided, but never boring. Richmond's average winning margin was 55 points during the home and away season, and 49 points during the finals series. A record-breaking grand final victory against Collingwood had the pundits predicting another decade of dominance for Richmond.

According to *The Age*'s chief football writer, Ron Carter, Richmond had 'everything a premiership side should have – the perfect blending of team effort, strength, skill, pace and quick thinking'. *The Sun*'s Tom Prior said the Tigers' 'direct, straight-ahead football' signalled a new era for the game. 'In the eighties we'll see much less of the complicated handball and pretty play which Ron Barassi and North Melbourne had made a feature of the seventies.'

History suggested that this team would win at least one more premiership. The young drought breakers of 1967 had won a second flag in 1969. The mature, more aggressive team they became won two more premierships in 1973 and 1974.

There was also a structural reason to expect further success in the 1980s. The allocation of exclusive country recruitment zones, which the VFL had thought would make the competition more even, had achieved the opposite. It concentrated the talent among a handful of clubs.

When the VFL originally designed the system it recognised there were disparities between the zones, and it planned to rotate them between the clubs every season to ensure a fair go for all. But the clubs that received the most productive zones in the first lottery refused to give them up. The VFL blinked, compromising the system by leaving each club with that first country zone.

Carlton and Hawthorn were the main beneficiaries, winning eleven of the nineteen premierships decided in this uneven market between 1968 and 1986. At the other end of the ladder were South Melbourne and St Kilda, who won nine wooden spoons between them in the same period.

Although Richmond's country zone around Mildura was weak, the club still thrived in this regulated environment. The Tigers retained the advantages of a big supporter base, the MCG as a home ground and an established playing list that was used to winning.

But the club was only one angry decision away from implosion. How Richmond went from premiership to wooden spoon is a parable of the 1980s: a sorry tale of greed, vendetta and insolvency.

The warning signs were there. For years the club had been treating its coaches and players badly.

Club powerbroker Graeme Richmond, the man who had begun the revolution of young talent at the club two decades earlier, believed that the Tigers could only maintain their hunger in an austere setting. The training facilities at Punt Road were left as they had been in the 1950s. Most players were paid modestly, but there was no consistency. If Graeme Richmond wanted a champion from another club, he was prepared to offer whatever it took to secure his signature.

In the real economy, workers enjoyed full employment and wage justice. In Richmond's brutal football economy, job insecurity was used as a motivational tool. In its treatment of coaches, players, and even captains and star players, the club that identified as working class was behaving like the most bloody-minded boss.

The early years of success under this approach seemed to justify the behaviour. There had been a push to sack coach Tom Hafey midway through the 1969 season, when the club was struggling to make the finals. Even the man who had helped the club break its premiership drought was seen as expendable. The players made a pact to save their coach and surprised everyone by winning their second flag in three years.

I'm always amazed by this detail of Richmond's modern history. The officials who had plotted against Hafey might have been humbled by their misreading of his ability, but instead they viewed his success as a result of their backroom genius. They thought that if they hadn't threatened his position, he might have succumbed to complacency.

Hafey came under pressure again in 1971, but two more premierships in 1973 and 1974 should have settled the question of whether he was an elite coach. But after a disappointing 1976 season, Graeme Richmond withdrew his support for Hafey. It turns out he opened the gates of hell. Hafey went to Collingwood and took them to the grand final in his first year, sowing an immediate seed of regret at Punt Road.

A Richmond player at the time, Neil Balme has reflected on this period. He says it's only now that he sees Hafey was decades ahead of his time in his relationship with the players. 'He wasn't really the yeller. He had his moments when he had to yell, because otherwise we would have thought he wasn't doing his job. But essentially he was different to that stereotype of coach.'

The accepted coaching method hadn't changed all that much in the first eight decades of the VFL. Coaches behaved like military officers, punishing their players at training and shouting at them on game day.

Balme cites the examples of two of the most successful coaches of the post-war era, Norm Smith and Ron Barassi. They saw the spittle of abuse as the mortar that built team unity. 'They picked on their best players and demanded something exceptional out of them all the time so that maybe the other blokes would come along for the ride.'

Hafey, by contrast, didn't humiliate his players. He trained them hard, but he didn't bombard them with advice. He trusted them to take responsibility on the field.

'I wouldn't have been his favourite,' Balme says, explaining the corners he cut at training and the beers he enjoyed after a game. 'He had his devotees, like Sheeds, KB and Bourkey [Kevin Sheedy, Kevin Bartlett and Francis Bourke], who were just mad and trained all the time. I was a bit naughty. But I don't remember him being anything but encouraging and positive. He was still honest. If you weren't working quite hard enough he would tell you. But it wasn't in a derogatory kind of way.'

Balme says at the time the players 'accepted the inevitability' of Hafey's departure. 'I thought he was resistant to change. But that made sense because we had been pretty successful. It was just his way, there was only one way for him. He went to Collingwood, arguably never a grand final side in terms of their personnel, but he got them there regularly.'

Hafey's successor Barry Richardson had a reasonable first season, lifting the club to fourth place. But he was dumped after missing the finals in 1978. This precedent became impossible to set aside. One disappointing season was grounds for dismissal, regardless of past achievement. By this logic, Tony Jewell should have been removed after his first season in 1979, when Richmond won just nine games, its worst return since 1964. But the club gave him a reprieve and he rewarded their temporary patience with a premiership in 1980. But then the team just failed to make the finals in 1981 and Jewell was shown the door.

Neil Balme shakes his head. 'How can you win one and not quite make the finals the next year and say the bloke is no good? They made rash decisions year after year.'

Graeme Richmond did offer Hafey his old job back as the replacement for Jewell, but Hafey remained loyal to Collingwood. Unfortunately, the courtesy wasn't returned, and Hafey was himself sacked by the Magpies midway through the 1982 season. The decade of madness that followed for both clubs might have been avoided if Hafey had returned home when he had the chance.

Richmond was trapped by the logic of its *Eat 'em alive!* marketing. When it was winning, the club picked fights to create a magic circle of paranoia, binding players and supporters together. At the start of each season the club president, Ian Wilson, would manufacture an argument with the VFL to encourage people to come to the game in solidarity.

But once the team started slipping down the ladder, the club responded to every setback with an execution. The sackings were meant to reassure supporters that the Tigers would never tolerate failure, but all they accomplished was to make Richmond an unpleasant club to work for.

In 1982, Tony Jewell was replaced by Francis Bourke and the team returned to the top of the ladder.

I was a little detached that season. I was eighteen now, and at university; old enough to make the spectating transition from my first love to my second, from the Ponsford and Southern stands at the MCG to the sweaty pubs and sardine-tin clubs of Melbourne's independent music scene.

I also worked most Saturdays as a cleaner at a suburban cinema. On the day of Richmond's semi-final against Carlton, we screened three sessions of *Rocky III*, at 2 p.m., 5 p.m., and 8 p.m. My shift ended at 3.30 p.m., so I missed the first half of the game on the radio. By the time I got home and checked the score, the Tigers were cruising to victory. Another premiership would be nice, I thought, and arranged to have the day off on grand final day so I could watch the live telecast at home.

I think I can speak for every Richmond supporter of my generation when I say that the 1982 grand final defeat to Carlton didn't feel like the end of the world. It was reasonable to assume that the Tigers would retaliate with another premiership or two. But internally the loss divided the club. The recriminations triggered the walkout of three of our best players, with six premierships' worth of experience between them.

The team captain, David Cloke, was the first to vent after the defeat, complaining that Bourke had treated the players like children. For his part, Bourke had an uncomplicated view of the relationships between club, coach and player. He had listened to everything Hafey had told him, and was happy to accept whatever the club could afford to pay him.

'The coach lays down the law for all players to adhere to,' he said in response to Cloke. 'If that is treating someone like a schoolboy . . . then I don't know.'

But most of the players had been his teammates just a year before he was appointed coach, and many resented his new authority over them.

Enter Collingwood. The Magpies saw Richmond's disunity as a lifeline, offering the disgruntled Cloke a substantial pay rise to move across to Victoria Park. Collingwood wanted Cloke to cover the loss of Peter Moore, the Brownlow medal–winning ruckman who had just defected to Melbourne.

Collingwood also pursued Geoff Raines, a three-time best and fairest winner at Richmond. Raines asked the Tigers for a substantial pay rise, to match what he thought they were giving star recruit Maurice Rioli, but he was knocked back. The Magpies made their own offer, and although Richmond belatedly tried to match it, it was too late. Raines was determined to leave.

The other big name to depart after the grand final was Bryan Wood, a former captain and three-time premiership player, who went to Essendon.

Michael Roach was the game's most prolific goal kicker at the time, but he said his own game suffered without Cloke and Raines alongside him. 'I don't think I played as well without those two boys being around the club.'

Richmond's emotional response to these departures accelerated its decline. The club sought to retaliate against Collingwood by poaching two of its best young players. But when the very best player at Victoria Park, Peter Daicos, didn't take the bait, Richmond should have paused. The club should have looked elsewhere to fill the void left by Cloke, Raines and Wood. Instead it kept working its way down the Magpies playing list, grabbing whomever it could, just to show the neighbour that it still had the more desirable address. Collingwood returned fire and captured the young Richmond full forward Brian Taylor. The Magpies had won the battle, but at a crippling cost to the balance sheets of both clubs.

Virtually every VFL club lost its mind in this early 1980s, spending money it didn't have in a futile attempt to buy a premiership. The splurge occurred before the new Labor federal government had opened the banking system to competition from overseas, so the VFL could at least be grateful that the clubs did not have full access to the decade's easy credit. Nonetheless, as many as six of the twelve clubs were broke by 1983. St Kilda, for instance, still owed back pay to its 1966 premiership coach, Alan Jeans, and senior players, including the grand final hero Barry Breen. They would eventually agree to accept 22.5 cents in every dollar owed.

Football's financial crisis was compounded by a challenge to its player-trading laws. The wages explosions of the 1970s and early 1980s had seen an increasing number of players bought and sold without their consent. Sooner or later, someone would object to being told who to play for. In 1982, Silvio Foschini did not want to move from South Melbourne to Sydney with the Swans, and he sought a transfer to St Kilda. The Swans denied his request. He took them to court, claiming a restraint of trade. The Victorian Supreme Court found in his favour in 1983, and the VFL was forced to redraft its rules.

These own goals prompted an unusual concession from the clubs. They realised that their player-poaching wars, left unchecked, would destroy them financially, and thereby the game. In 1984 they agreed to establish an independent commission to oversee the competition. The first significant reform of this new VFL commission was to introduce a salary cap in 1985, setting the same limit for each team's total player payments.

The salary cap was football's version of the Hawke–Keating program of wage restraint, which had been national policy since 1983. The Labor government offered workers increased spending on social benefits such as Medicare in exchange for a reduction in real wages to help improve the profitability of businesses. The formula varied from year to year, but essentially the trade unions agreed to ask for wage rises below the inflation rate – hence the cut in real wages.

The salary cap worked on a similar principle. The clubs gave up the right to buy a premiership in order to improve the profitability of the game. The VFL had a system of maximum wages between 1930 and 1961, but it had progressively deregulated the market in response to pressure from players and clubs. Even before the poaching wars between Richmond and Collingwood, player payments had exploded, rising seven times faster than the average wage in the 1970s.

Following the salary cap, the next phase of football's re-regulation was the national draft, which replaced the country zones in Victoria, but not the Riverina, in 1986. The draft gave the bottom teams on the ladder preferred access to the best young talent across Australia, to rebuild their playing lists and close the gap with the teams above them.

The salary cap and the draft were designed not just to restore the game's financial stability, but to reduce the inequality between clubs. In the twenty seasons between 1967 and 1986, only five clubs had won premierships, compared to eight in the twenty before that.

However, the commission, the salary cap and the draft all came too late to spare Collingwood and Richmond the embarrassment of asking their supporters for a bailout.

Collingwood had been the most decadent in the trading wars. The reported transfer fee for Geoff Raines in 1983 was $180 000, which would have bought three workers cottages in Collingwood at the time – plus a new Holden Commodore to park in the front of each of them. That same year, almost twice that amount was paid to secure Western Australian player Gary Shaw.

By 1986, with more than $3 million owing to the bank, the Magpies were on the verge of bankruptcy. The club was ordered by its lender to come up with a plan to slash the debt or face liquidation. The new club president Allan McAlister, and nineteen other cashed-up supporters, kicked in $10 000 each. A general appeal was launched, and the rank and file of the club donated another $300 000, for a total of $500 000.

The players were asked to accept a 20 per cent pay cut. Raines was one of two players who wouldn't agree and he was traded to Essendon early in the 1986 season, which then passed him to Brisbane in 1987. Shaw joined him at Brisbane in 1987. The bank was satisfied with the debt retirement and the player cull, and extended Collingwood's line of credit.

Richmond were just as deep in debt but took longer to accept the need for restructure, preferring the quick fix of another public execution. Francis Bourke was dumped as coach at the end of a disappointing 1983 season. His replacement Mike Patterson was sacked after one unsuccessful season, as was his successor Paul Sproule. In total six coaches were removed between 1976 and 1985. Every one of the departed had been a loyal son of Punt Road. Hafey coached four premierships, Bourke played in five, Richardson in three, Sproule in two. Jewell and Patterson had been teammates before the move to the MCG and were members of the breakthrough premiership team in 1967.

The most frustrating part of the coaching turnover was that three former players who didn't get to coach Richmond were Kevin Sheedy, Neil Balme and Mick Malthouse. By 1985, Sheedy had already secured two of his four premierships at Essendon. Balme had coached Norwood to two premierships in the South Australia National Football League. Malthouse had coached Footscray to a preliminary final and there were premierships to come with the West Coast Eagles and Collingwood.

Exhausted by the revolving door of leadership, Richmond asked Tony Jewell to return in 1986. Later that year, the club pressed the ejector button on its credibility, accepting Alan Bond as its financial saviour by appointing him president. The America's Cup hero and corporate raider had a master plan to reinvent Richmond for the national competition. We would be football's first fly-in fly-out club, playing our home games in Brisbane and away games at the MCG. A supporter revolt killed the idea before the VFL could seriously consider it. Bond then relinquished the club presidency after just three months in the post, without overseeing a single game.

When Jewell was coach from 1979 to 1981, Richmond had won 59 per cent of the games it played. In his two-season encore in 1986 and 1987, Richmond won just 27 per cent of its games. It felt like the 1987 fixture was designed to humiliate the Tigers. The final round saw Richmond host the Brisbane Bears at the MCG before a rugby league-sized crowd of 12 000. Going into that last round, the bottom three teams were Collingwood with six wins, then Richmond and Brisbane with five wins each. There was a simple path to avoiding the club's first wooden spoon since 1960: beat Brisbane. But the Tigers were disinterested observers at their own wake. The team was outscored in each quarter and the final margin of defeat – 56 points – probably flattered them. Geoff Raines was one of the best for the Bears and received two Brownlow votes.

I don't doubt that fans of rival clubs laughed at us. But the result contained a warning for the VFL. A dirty secret of the game is that big clubs aren't easily replaced when they falter. Behemoths like Richmond need to be near the top of the game not just to fill their own home ground and coffers, but those of their opponents as well. Ideally, at least two big clubs rise together, preferably three, so their rivalries become the game's dramatic plotline for a number of seasons. That rule can be seen in effect across eras.

The modern game had two significant periods of booming suburban attendances. The first, after World War II, was led by the supporters of Melbourne, Collingwood and Essendon. It ended when Melbourne and Essendon stopped winning premierships in the mid-1960s. Attendances fell sharply, then plateaued as Richmond and Carlton became the destination clubs for young fans, positions previously held by the Demons and Bombers.

Richmond, Collingwood and Carlton were responsible for the game's second popularity surge, in the 1970s.

Once Richmond stopped making the finals, the MCG was reduced to just another suburban ground. By 1987, Richmond was being watched by just 18 000 people per game, the lowest figure since 1960, back when the Tigers were still playing at Punt Road Oval. On its own, the Richmond downturn might not have hurt the game. But Collingwood was also in trouble in the grandstands, to go with its financial difficulties. The typical crowd at Victoria Park had fallen to 22 000 by 1987, the lowest since 1950. The combination of the two underachieving neighbours gave the VFL its worst attendance figures since 1953.

Fortunately for the VFL, Collingwood used its time near the bottom of the ladder productively. The Magpies renewed their playing list, attendances rebounded, and by 1990 they had finally broken their premiership drought.

An example for Richmond to follow, one would have thought. But instead the Tigers had blundered into the eye of an economic storm.

The best time to restructure would have been in 1986, a year before the competition expanded to fourteen clubs, or at the latest 1988, before Paul Keating and the Reserve Bank began driving up interest rates to recession-inducing levels. But Richmond didn't face up to its financial problems until the spring of 1990, when the recession was already underway and two of the big four banks were at risk of collapsing.

In October that year, as Collingwood celebrated its first premiership in thirty-two years, Richmond launched an appeal to raise $1 million and save the club.

I cringed when I saw the television campaign. The ad is framed through the telescopic sight of a high-power hunting rifle. First a bear is shot, then a rhino, then an elephant. Finally, the target focuses on a group of Richmond players.

'The Richmond Tigers are facing extinction,' the voiceover warns. 'Liquidators have us in their sights. If we don't pay our million-dollar debt by October 31st, they fire, we're dead. Please donate now. Save our skin.'

While I don't deny the romance of digging into one's pocket to prop up a football club, at the time the exercise struck me as a little cynical. I had moved to Canberra by then, to work in the federal parliament press gallery. Strange how one's perspective changes once you shed the partisan certainty of childhood.

Obviously I didn't want Richmond to fail, but I couldn't separate the club's scare campaign from those I was covering in politics. I even saw the telescopic sight again in a 1993 Liberal ad attacking Paul Keating.

The options for Richmond were said to be relocation, merger or being kicked out of the competition. Whether any of these were really on the table doesn't matter now; the appeal exceeded its target.

It's counterintuitive, but rugby league had the better first decade of national competition because it had nothing to lose, while football began its expansion beyond Victoria with its two biggest clubs in financial freefall.

Although Collingwood recovered to win a premiership by 1990, Richmond had dropped so far behind the rest of the competition that the league's overall attendances suffered. The average game of football was watched by 23 000 people in 1991, compared to 25 500 in 1981. While its crowds were still lower, rugby league could see its glass as half full. The game's average attendance had jumped from 9000 in 1981 to 12 500 in 1991.

The danger for rugby league was the disconnection between its headquarters and the supporters. The game was run out of Sydney, but its viability depended on the clubs beyond the capital. Sydney had to accommodate the shift in power to Canberra and Brisbane.

The VFL had anticipated this dilemma when it established an independent commission to govern the game. The proof is in what *didn't* happen in the 1990s. The West Coast Eagles, Adelaide Crows, Brisbane Lions, Sydney Swans and Port Adelaide shared ten of the fifteen premierships between 1992 and 2006, but without dividing the code.

Rugby league, on the other hand, could not manage the conflicting interests of the expansion clubs and the old Sydney clubs. Canberra and Brisbane had won five of the six rugby league premierships between 1989 and 1994, yet neither was happy with their position in the competition. They were ripe for poaching by commercial interests, and the Raiders and Broncos were among the first to sign with the rebel Super League competition. A century after the big football clubs left the VFA to form the VFL over questions of money and control, rugby league split for the same reasons.

Australia's sporting landscape would be radically different today if Rupert Murdoch's News Corporation had not disrupted rugby league. Murdoch was only after a share of the television rights for the competition, and although he got what he asked for in the end, the fight cost his company more than $100 million.

Rugby league, meanwhile, lost a large part of its identity. The Super League wars ultimately claimed three Sydney clubs – Balmain, North Sydney and Western Suburbs – as well as five expansion clubs, including Illawarra. Some merged, others were wound up. A fourth Sydney club, Souths, was kicked out of the competition under the terms of the peace treaty with Super League but was welcomed back after a sustained community protest.

In football's long argument with modernity in the 1980s and 1990s, only two Melbourne-based clubs were sacrificed – South Melbourne in 1982 and Fitzroy in 1996. Others flirted with the near-death of merger, notably Footscray, Hawthorn and Melbourne.

Ironically, the pressure for these clubs to amalgamate was relieved by the closure of the old suburban grounds. This allowed the most popular Melbourne clubs to play their home games at the MCG, while the others moved to a new stadium in the Docklands precinct, next to the CBD. Waverley Park was demolished and sold off for property development.

I think football got lucky because this consolidation occurred just before people moved back to the inner city, in the fourth big reshuffle of Melbourne's population. After nearly a century of decline, at the start of the new millenium the population of Richmond and its neighbours began growing again. Young professionals who were raised in the outer suburbs moved to Richmond to be near their work in the city. They were joined by a new wave of skilled migrants, which turned the former slum into high-income postcode within a decade. The Tigers were now a poor team in a rich suburb.

It was also football's good fortune that attendances recovered by the mid-1990s. There were multiple drivers for the improvements: the big Melbourne clubs moving to the MCG, as well as Adelaide, Brisbane, Sydney and West Coast climbing the ladder at the same time. This made the game too big even for Murdoch to take over.

While in 1995 News Corporation was dreaming of a twelve-team national rugby league competition with just four clubs from Sydney, football already had a glimpse of its gentrified future. Richmond was briefly back in the finals, after an absence of thirteen years, and sitting alongside were old rivals Carlton and Collingwood, and the new superpower Essendon.

The last time these four clubs had played in a finals series together was in 1972, when the home crowds at Princes Park, Victoria Park and Windy Hill averaged 27 000 per game, and Richmond was seen by 37 000 per game at the MCG. But in 1995, on the common ground of the MCG, each club drew old Richmond-like crowds in excess of 40 000. The two biggest interstate clubs were also enjoying bumper home attendances – 39 000 per game for the Adelaide Crows and 32 000 for the West Coast Eagles.

Football's second decade of expansion went better than the first because it returned to the inner city of Melbourne, and added three interstate clubs with strong inner-city bases, Adelaide, Fremantle and Port Adelaide. In the ten years to 2001, the average attendance jumped by 46 per cent, to 33 500 per game. In the same period rugby league increased its average attendance by just 7 per cent, to 13 500 per game, ending whatever dream it might have had of usurping football as the game that runs the nation.

7

A LATE CONVERT TO THE GAME

I first met Bob Hawke in the non-members' bar of Parliament House in the winter of 1989. The prime minister wanted to discuss my footy tipping record. The season was almost over and I was eight games clear in the press gallery competition. Barrie Cassidy, the PM's senior press secretary, had told his boss that this was an extraordinary feat. With that lead, I would probably win any footy tipping competition in the country.

'What's your secret?' Hawke asked.

I mumbled something about how I was a recent arrival from Melbourne and I guessed that gave me a little more insight. But then I confessed. I'd been tipping against my own team.

My colleagues assumed I didn't care for Richmond. If I were a loyal supporter, I should have picked the Tigers every week, no matter whom they played. I could then shrug when they lost or, if they caused an upset, I'd be entitled to say, 'I told you so.' I explained to them that, as an economics correspondent, I had to be rational. Why start each round one tip behind the rest of the pack? My first winter in Canberra coincided with Richmond's second wooden spoon of the 1980s. After the beginner's luck of the first season, my form deteriorated, and in direct proportion to the years I was away from Melbourne.

I took over the administration of the competition in the early 1990s and let the power go to my head. The competition was open to politicians, their staffers and to the public service. The system I inherited had a flat $60 fee for all tipsters. It funded a weekly jackpot for those who picked every winner and end-of-season prizes for the top three. At close of business on Friday night I would lock up the handwritten tips that had been deposited in the box on my desk. Monday morning, I manually marked off each set of tips and added them to the ladder.

My predecessor Lindsay Olney would write a pithy weekly report on the round of tipping and pin it up on a board in the News Limited bureau. A copy was faxed to a privileged few, including the offices of the prime minister, opposition leader and treasurer. Lindsay's reports were invariably hilarious. Mine were not in his league.

These reports were the platform for some of the silliest things I wrote in my time in the press gallery. I was young, and could not resist the temptation to rib the politicians who had tipped poorly. They loved the notoriety.

Following the 1993 election, I decided to introduce a poll tax, as a collective punishment for the GST debate. Journalists and staffers would still pay $60 to join the competition, but politicians would be charged $70. They couldn't say no, and I kept sneaking up the fee, until it reached $90. My successor decided I had been too cruel and restored parity between journo and pollie at the old rate of $60.

I'm not sure that the poll tax was worth the trouble anyway, because it inflated the payouts for politicians. Labor minister Simon Crean was the first to win the competition on my watch. Later Liberal treasurer Peter Costello finished on top. Both men were good sports and reinvested their winnings in an end-of-season office party for all tipsters.

I had arrived in the press gallery in the spring of 1988, just after democracy had located to the new Parliament House on the hill, where politician and journalist were physically separated for the first time. I hadn't experienced the boarding-house familiarity of the old house, but it was easy to detect its echo in the boozy corridor parties that ministers threw to baptise their suites in the new house.

The informality should not be mistaken for complicity. Back then the press gallery was allowed to be a brutal inquisitor and politicians felt an obligation to explain themselves. Newspapers still directed the rhythm and direction of public debate. The printed word fed morning radio, politicians competed throughout the day for a place on the television news bulletins, and everyone went to bed knowing that the newspaper reporter had the final word, because what we filed that evening would set the agenda the following morning.

I returned home to Melbourne at the end of 1999. Print was still in command, but political power had shifted to Sydney, and the culture had coarsened.

Bob Hawke's government sat at the crossroads between two ways of looking at Australia, between the broad-mindedness of the south and the polarisation of the north, between an age when leaders promoted multiculturalism and one where leaders encouraged race debates.

Hawke's was the last truly Victorian government of Australia, which means it was the last to be preoccupied with football. His ministers and advisers were among the most zealous supporters that politics has seen. John Button, the industry minister, wrote how he once dropped the name of Gary Ablett (the father, not the son) in a conversation with Margaret Thatcher. 'In Geelong, I told Gary Ablett about Margaret Thatcher. I gained the impression that neither had heard of the other.' He and his good friend Michael Duffy, the communications minister and later attorney-general, would distract one another in cabinet meetings by drawing up their all-time best Geelong and Essendon sides and arguing over who would win their hypothetical grand final.

It was ever thus with Victorian politicians. Football would divert the course of a discussion for the simple reason that the mind wandered to that scared place. There was no filter because football is the one passion Victorians don't repress. Every other part of one's private self: the school you went to, the work you do, the places you've travelled to, the books and records you collect, the rent you pay or the capital you've gained on your property, it all carries an implied transactional cost if you reveal it in the wrong context. It's safer to wait to be asked about those things, and then you can choose which truth to conceal. With football, that's not necessary because the game is so firmly entrenched in the culture that no one will judge you for your zealotry.

The parliamentary prize for gratuitous tribalism belongs to Country Party minister Peter Nixon. He put Richmond's 1967 premiership into the Hansard record with an amusing game of word association in question time. He was answering a question without notice from his colleague Donald Jessop, the member for the rural South Australian electorate of Grey.

Jessop asked:

> Is the Minister for the Interior aware that recently two honourable members have been attacked by marauding magpies in the vicinity of Parliament House? As back bench members of the Parliament are not afforded the protection of Commonwealth cars, will he issue safety helmets to those members who require them?

Nixon replied:

> As a supporter of the Richmond Football Club, which won this year's Melbourne premiership, I have frequently been attacked by

> a certain Magpie supporter who sits in a corner of this chamber. However, in view of the request, I will confer with the Minister for Works [Senator John Gorton] to see whether his Department can design some suitable form of protection for honourable members from this pest.

Robert Menzies, too, could not hide his love for the game. Earlier that same year, the former prime minister dropped football into his final lecture as scholar-in-residence at the University of Virginia. 'The 72-year-old statesman, giving his last lecture here, turned from international problems and Australian constitutional law to give an illustrated discourse on football,' the Associated Press reported.

> He screened for the 200 present a 55-minute film of the last half of last season's VFL championship final in which St Kilda downed Collingwood by one point. The movie showed football, Aussie style, to be an exciting, non-stop, rough-and-tumble exercise in organised mayhem that makes the American college game pale by comparison.

I am torn between admiring his cheek and shaking my head at his provincialism. But I don't doubt his sincerity. Following a serious stroke Menzies suffered late in 1971, Carlton installed a ramp behind the northern-end goals at Princes Park so he could watch his beloved Blues from the passenger seat of his Bentley.

Malcolm Fraser was heir to the Menzies throne at Carlton. He was a prominent visitor to the dressing rooms, offering encouragement before big games and delivering an awkward prime ministerial back slap afterwards. Before Carlton's grand final against Collingwood in 1981, he told the players that if they won, he would host them and their partners at The Lodge. When they dispatched the Magpies by 20 points – Collingwood's eighth grand final defeat since 1958 – he was as good as his word. He repeated the invitation before Carlton's 1982 grand final against Richmond, and again the Blues won.

They were wild parties. For my ABC documentary *Making Australia Great* I asked Fraser if he wanted to recall the incident of players souveniring The Lodge's cutlery. It was a long bow, I guess, but I had in mind an extended scene on Australia's rorting culture in the 1970s. The trade unions had been on a decade-long industrial disputes bender. The top end of town cheated on their tax. And here were the stars of the dominant VFL club stealing the prime ministerial silver.

Fraser offered that there were 'a couple of other stories' but I let it go. We were too far off the topic of stagflation. Fraser was not a man's man, or even a Melburnian, yet he always felt at home at Carlton. It was the one place where this polarising prime minister could be himself, because football had been happily mixing with politicians for more than 100 years. He didn't go as far as the Geelong-following politicians who elbowed their way to the front of the premiership celebrations in 1925, but he didn't need to. His presence would be noted by the newspaper photographers and television cameras.

Rugby league was more wary of politicians, as Fraser himself discovered when he visited the Western Suburbs leagues club at Ashfield in 1978. 'He was invited there by the president of our club, Bill Carson, who owned a big trucking business,' says Roy Masters, the Magpies coach at the time. 'Bill was a card-carrying Liberal. Menzies was his hero. He encouraged me to get the players to come along to welcome Malcolm to our club. Not one turned up.'

These days federal parliament is rugby league territory, even though Canberra is actually a rugby union town. I have it on reliable authority that when one particular Senate committee was in session during state of origin games, the committee chairman asked that he and his colleagues be given regular updates of the score. You won't find those interruptions to the hearing in the

Hansard because they were left off the public record. A Victorian would never be so coy about their fanaticism.

I had assumed from my first meeting with Bob Hawke that he was a footy tragic. But I realised later that his interest was not the football, but the tipping. He loved a punt. This is not to suggest that he didn't obsess about sports. He was a handy cricketer, and told the nation to take a day off when we won the America's Cup. But his most senior advisers, who played and watched sport with Hawke, tell me that football wasn't a passion of his. He might have been number-one ticket holder for the old South Melbourne, but he didn't follow the club that closely. That is, he wasn't Victorian in the way many of his ministers and adviser were. Which made him more like Paul Keating – a supporter of political convenience – than either man might concede.

The expectation that the prime minister must barrack for a football club carried treasurer Paul Keating to Victoria Park on the eve of the 1990 federal election. By Keating's reckoning, Bob Hawke still intended to honour his promise to hand over the leadership in the next term. So he was willing to accept the indignity of offering himself as a convert to footy in the year that the VFL became the Australian Football League.

Keating did not pretend to understand the game, but he could relate to its tribalism. Collingwood was the club he wanted to barrack for, he said, because they were his people: working class and anti-establishment. 'I've found a show that sees everything in black and white, which is a one-eyed outfit, which is an underdog outfit and it just hates losing. I thought, "That's the club for me because I just bloody well hate losing, I hate it."'

I had heard a version of the speech a week before, at a luncheon for the Canterbury-Bankstown rugby league club. Here in his local area, the treasurer read the room perfectly. He confessed that all politicians, himself included, were simply 'frustrated entertainers'. He had loved playing sport when he was younger, but wasn't good at it. He was 'too light for heavy work and too heavy for light work' to succeed at rugby league, and a little too slow to make it as a swimmer.

Sydney's economy was booming and Keating's message of reform did not yield any hostile questions. But at Victoria Park, he stepped into the parallel universe of Melbourne's decaying inner-city. It was still Labor territory, but it was seething. Collingwood people preferred the world as it had been, behind the tariff wall, before Keating tore it down.

The first question from the floor summed up the mood: 'We heard about this need for Australia to become part of the global scene. I am a Labor supporter and will be voting for the Labor Party on Saturday. However, the logical extension of your economic policies means we won't be seeing Collingwood's first match of the season here at Victoria Park, we'll be seeing it played in Tokyo in ten years.'

As the economics correspondent for the News Limited bureau, my coverage of that election campaign was published in the group's five morning newspapers – the Melbourne *Sun*, Sydney's *Daily Telegraph*, Brisbane's *Courier Mail*, the *Adelaide Advertiser* and the *Hobart Mercury*. The hard news from the Collingwood event was Keating's pledge that housing interest rates would 'fall well below 17 per cent' after the election. Every masthead gave it a prominent run the next day, with the *Courier* placing it on the front page. But Melbourne's *Sun* buried it on page four, because its front page carried the scoop of Keating becoming a Collingwood supporter.

I use the term scoop loosely. No one else in the group wanted the piece. The words were beside the point. The story made it to page one because of the photo I had set up between the treasurer and the *Sun*'s best-known footy columnist, Lou Richards, the captain of Collingwood's 1953 premiership team.

Richards and I had history. Four years earlier, the reporters of the *Sun* and *Herald* had arranged a social game of football. It was of no importance. Thousands of these social games are played each year. But ours earned a mention on *League Teams*.

Richards read out the players for the *Sun* and when he got to mine, he complained, 'I can't pronounce that fella's name.'

'Megalenis,' Bob Davis offered. Jack Dyer said nothing.

Richards regained his composure and told the viewers that 'Megalomaniac' was playing in the ruck. He should have known better. Lou Richards was a fourth-generation Greek Australian, the grandson of Charlie Pannam.

Actually, do you see what happened there? Before a football anecdote can be concluded, the Victorian mind can't help but navigate the full course of each tributary.

For the photograph in question, I suggested to Keating and Richards that they pose with the Collingwood jumper, each tugging at one of its sleeves – the treasurer usurping 'Louie the Lip' as the loudest mouth at Victoria Park. They went along with the stunt. The picture would fit the line I had already jotted in my notebook: 'Move over Lou Richards, the Mighty Magpies have found a new head-kicker.'

For political balance, there was a second, smaller photo on the front page, placed alongside the main news story of Liberal leader Andrew Peacock on the campaign trail with his daughters. Good clean tabloid fun, and it did not move a single vote. The Labor government lost nine seats in Victoria but managed to hold on to office by picking up seats in the rugby league states of New South Wales and Queensland.

The mistake Keating made was to think he could get closer to Victorians by adopting their sport. Instead it made him look like a phony. Victorians preferred the other Keating, the one who supported the arts, engagement with Asia, multiculturalism, reconciliation and an Australian republic. At the two elections

Keating contested as prime minister, in 1993 and 1996, Victoria was his strongest state. And in 1999, when John Howard put the question of a republic to a referendum, Victoria recorded the highest yes vote.

Keating went to Victoria Park in 1990 on the false assumption that because football defined the state it must be the only thing the people cared for. Football is central to Victorian life, but not to the exclusion of all other things. For example, more people go the National Gallery of Victoria than the MCG. Many Victorians do both. That is the point outsiders miss. The best analogy I can think of is religion; you don't need to convert to someone else's faith to relate to them.

Collingwood made the grand final the very year Keating joined the club, and it was fascinating to watch Hawke circle back into the limelight. That season, Hawke revealed that he had switched his allegiance to Hawthorn, because their seven consecutive grand final appearances from 1983 to 1989 aligned with his first seven years in The Lodge. But on the eve of the 1990 grand final, he declared an affinity with the Magpies, who were looking to win their first premiership in thirty-two years.

This was my only other football scoop for *The Sun*. I asked Hawke's office for his tip, and a deeper thought on the game, to feed into our grand final–day edition of the newspaper. The word that came back was all about Bob: 'Today is a special game for me because I first went to live in Melbourne in 1958 – the year of their last win – and I actually went to the game.' Translation: Hawke would always be more Collingwood than Keating.

Rupert Murdoch's media empire was in a spot of bother at the time and his morning and afternoon mastheads in Australia were being combined to cut costs. *The Sun* and *The Herald* became the *Herald-Sun* (the hyphen was later dropped) and *The Daily Telegraph* and *The Daily Mirror* in Sydney became *The Daily Telegraph-Mirror* (both the hyphen and the *Mirror* were eventually discarded).

The company delayed the mergers until the first week of October, after the end of the footy and rugby league seasons. But while God might have barracked for Collingwood that year, she also had a sense of humour. Collingwood drew its first qualifying final against the West Coast Eagles, meaning the game had to be replayed. All other finals games were pushed back a week. The grand final would now be played on Saturday October 4, which placed it in the jurisdiction of the new *Herald-Sun*. But in 1990 the collective wisdom of the *Herald-Sun* editors was to treat Collingwood's first premiership in thirty-two years as a two-day-old human-interest story, with a picture-story on the front. The back page had a full write-up.

The first edition of the new Melbourne tabloid led, instead, with news from Sydney: media magnate Kerry Packer was fighting for his life after suffering a massive heart attack during a weekend game of polo. Murdoch looked at the front page and counselled that Victorians would still be talking about Collingwood's premiership on the Monday after the grand final. The second edition of the paper was respectfully reworked to bring the back-page lead to the front, while Packer was relegated to the second story.

Inside the news pages, the coverage of the post-game celebrations revealed a shift in Victorian sensibility. Ordinary Collingwood fans were treated as throwbacks, while the late convert Keating was given star treatment. Looking back over it now, I'd forgotten how class-based our coverage was.

The lead story on page five was written by the police reporters. 'More than 85 footy fans were arrested as grand final victory celebrations kicked on until the early hours,' the opening paragraph screamed. The report carried a picture of mounted police clearing Collingwood supporters off the street and back onto the footpath. It was a beat-up. You had to read halfway through the article to see that police described the 20 000-strong crowd at Victoria Park as well behaved. 'People just wanted to party on,' Senior Sergeant

Greg Hillier told the paper. 'It was a bit silly. They had a gutful of grog and didn't want to move on.'

On the left-hand page, it was all about Paul. Keating was pictured lifting singer Marcie Jones during a dance routine at Collingwood's pre-game breakfast at Victoria Park. The treasurer had been booed on his arrival at the event, but they cheered him when the singer invited him on stage. And at the grand final celebrations at the Southern Cross Hotel, Keating had the guests eating out of his hand, leading them in a stirring rendition of the club song, 'Good Old Collingwood Forever'. According to the *Herald-Sun*'s Tattler gossip column, the treasurer signed more autographs that evening than Magpies captain Tony Shaw.

Keating and Collingwood were weirdly compatible as treasurer and premier. But the politician and the club grew apart; by the time Keating was prime minister, Collingwood was an embarrassment to him.

You'd think it would have been the other way around, that the politician would make a fool of himself by mispronouncing a player's name or congratulating them for scoring a try, but that wasn't the case. Collingwood kept drawing attention to the bigots in its ranks at the same time as Keating was pushing the cause of reconciliation. I doubt that Keating minded, because the misdeeds of his adopted club gave him an unlikely platform to argue for his own agenda. But the relationship between football and politics was forever changed by the shared controversy of Keating's final term – race.

8

WHEN FOOTBALL AND POLITICS COLLIDE

It didn't have to be Collingwood. In the early 1990s, every club had a section of its supporter base that racially abused the Indigenous players in the game. But once an Indigenous player forced the game to confront the bigots in the stands, and on the field, the poor reputation of the Magpie cheer squad made it easier for white Australia to hear his demand for a fair go.

Before a game at Victoria Park in April 1993, Nicky Winmar and his St Kilda teammate Gilbert McAdam were familiarising themselves with the layout of the ground. Members of the Collingwood cheer squad spotted them and began hurling racial abuse.

'We just looked at each other and, whether it was me or him, just basically said to each other, "We're not going to put up with this crap! Let's get out there today and run amok. Let's get first and second best on ground,"' McAdam recalled. 'And it was funny. It turned out that way and we won the game, which was the most important thing.'

At the game's end, Winmar blew kisses to the crowd, then lifted his jumper and pointed to his skin and declared: 'I'm black – and

I'm proud to be black!' The photo of that moment, taken by Wayne Ludbey, ran on the front page of the *Sunday Age*.

Winmar had grown up in an Australia that promised equal treatment to its first people. In 1966, the year of Winmar's first birthday, Vincent Lingiari led the strike for equal pay at the Wave Hill cattle station in the Northern Territory. The referendum to count Aboriginal people in the census was passed before his second birthday. Through the governments of Holt, Whitlam, Fraser, Hawke and now Keating, both sides of politics had talked up the cause of reconciliation. Winmar need not have known any of the detail to absorb the cultural signal that he should be able to speak up. He drew his line in the sand one month after Paul Keating won the 1993 federal election with a mandate for Indigenous empowerment.

Keating was into his fourth season as a member of the Collingwood football club, and his second year as prime minister. He had already delivered his Redfern address, the first by a prime minister to admit that 'it was we who did the dispossessing, took the traditional lands and smashed the traditional way of life'. He devoted 1993, the International Year of the World's Indigenous People, to legislating for native title.

Keating need not have taken Winmar's side against his own club. If the Magpies had issued a prompt apology to Winmar, the story might have remained outside the world of politics. But Collingwood president Allan McAlister kept the issue alive by offering paternal advice from another age. 'As long as they [Indigenous Australians] conduct themselves like white people, well, off the field, everyone will admire and respect them,' he said. 'As long as they conduct themselves like human beings, they will be alright. That's the key.'

Collingwood went into damage control and the club arranged a goodwill tour of Indigenous communities for the new year. A game was organised in Darwin between the Magpies and an Aboriginal all-star team, and Keating was the special guest.

Football was now being played on the prime minister's terms. At a dinner before the game Keating singled out Winmar for praise. 'Nicky Winmar's gesture of defiance at Collingwood is destined to be legendary,' he said. 'In my view it was a great gesture. Think of what one gesture of defiance triggered – a national debate on racism in sport and a new recognition of the role Aboriginals play in Australian sport.'

Keating was careful not to embarrass his club and congratulated Collingwood on organising the game with the all-stars. But there was a hint that his loyalty was swinging to Essendon, a club that would previously have offended the prime minister's working-class Catholic upbringing.

These role reversals are part of football's enduring charm. Essendon, middle class and Protestant, had been the tired old bully that capitulated to Collingwood in the 1990 grand final. Three seasons later, the club was reborn as the glamorous Baby Bombers, with a playing list that Keating could more easily weave into his political storyline than Collingwood's.

'There were other gestures in last year's football season which were, in a sense, just as significant [as Winmar's] because they spoke of success,' the prime minister went on. 'There was Gavin Wanganeen with the Brownlow medal in his hand. There was Michael Long with the Norm Smith medal – and the premiership cup above his head.'

Coincidentally it was Essendon's Michael Long who drew the next line in the sand, after Collingwood player Damien Monkhorst racially abused him in the first Anzac Day game between the clubs in 1995.

What I think football people miss when they look back on this period is the role Keating played. They prefer to believe that the game took a stand against racism without outside help. In this rendering of history, Winmar and Long are the American athletes Tommie Smith and John Carlos, who gave the black power salute at the Mexico Olympics in 1968, and the AFL is Peter Norman, the white Australian offering moral support alongside them on the dais.

But Keating deserves a share of the credit. With his Redfern address and native title legislation, he created an environment where Winmar and Long could speak out.

Not that they needed the endorsement of politicians. The photo of Winmar would have been committed to the national memory regardless of what was said after it was published. But Keating made it easier for people to hear and understand a footballer's demand for equality.

Football's isolation in Victoria had protected it from the politicisation of international sport in the 1970s and 1980s. Bob Hawke, the casual footy fan, led the trade union campaign against the Springbok rugby union tour in 1971, and as prime minister tried to stop the rebel Australian cricket tour of South Africa in 1985. Malcolm Fraser called for an Australian boycott of the 1980 Moscow Olympics. Football wasn't in this league. It wasn't played in apartheid South Africa or the Soviet Union, so it never crossed the prime minister's desk as a dilemma of foreign affairs.

If Keating had been born into supporting Collingwood, he might have observed the convention that football should remain separate from political debate. But as an outsider, he could see beyond the fog of club loyalty.

Football was slow to follow the prime minister's lead on reconciliation. When Michael Long challenged the AFL to make racial abuse a reportable offence, a rift opened between present and past players, while the bureaucrats who ran the game tried to sit on the fence. The players' association issued a joint statement with independent MP Phil Cleary that was written with keen awareness of the eggshell fragility of the male footballing ego:

> There's nothing wrong with sledging and we're not saying that a player who makes a remark with racist overtones is necessarily racist.

> However, it is our view that society's expectations have changed and that Aboriginal players such as Michael Long and Nicky Winmar have every right to expect 'white fella footballers' like the rest of Australia, post-Mabo, to be committed to the reconciliation process.

Note the political context. The statement acknowledged that football had to take account of Keating's agenda.

Tony Shaw, the former Collingwood premiership captain, thought Long was being precious. He should have followed the example of the previous generation and kept smiling. 'All I can really say to Michael is to have a chat with Glenn James, the Aboriginal umpire. To me, "Jamesy" was a sensational man, and Michael might learn a lot from talking to him.'

Former Richmond player Mal Brown revealed that in his day in the early 1970s, it was common to sledge an Aboriginal opponent with the phrase 'n——, n——, pull the trigger'.

The AFL commission struggled with the issue. It asked Long and Monkhorst to sit down for a private meeting. There the players agreed not to take any further action, which the AFL misread as a resolution. Long thought the AFL was trying to put words into his mouth. He said he had stood up for what he believed in, 'but I've been made a fool of'.

Long wanted a sincere apology from Monkhorst, and he finally got one after a second private meeting, two weeks after the original incident. As Patrick Smith wrote at the time, 'The AFL Commission has fumbled its way to the most honourable outcome possible.' The tin ear is forgotten in the applause the AFL gives itself for being the first sporting code in Australia to make racial abuse a reportable offence.

On the fringe of the debate in 1995 was Australia's original cultural warrior, B.A. Santamaria. That he bothered to write about this issue at all showed that both sides of politics had now decided football was fair game. Santamaria dismissed the government's new racial vilification laws as 'tripe' and took a pot shot at the media consensus that Long had been treated appallingly.

> If Michael Long had had an Italian name and Monkhorst had called him a 'wog', would we have had the columns of hypocritical breast-beating which has been served up because Michael Long, one of the most brilliant, effervescent and effective players in the AFL, is an Aborigine? If he had had an Irish name, and had been called a 'Catholic b . . .' would the media have gone into such paroxysms of indignation?

What is clear is that the debate helped to enlarge the audience for football.

I witnessed an early example of the effect Long had on the game when Richmond played Essendon before a crowd of almost 77000 people at the MCG on a cool Friday evening in July 1995. Seated behind the Punt Road End goals, I kept checking the stands to absorb all the new faces. The black, yellow and red of the Australian Aboriginal flag flew proudly alongside the Bombers' red and black. I had never seen so many young Indigenous fans at the football before.

Essendon became the most popular club in the AFL in 1996, and from 1997 to 1999 it set a new attendance record each season, eclipsing Collingwood and Richmond's previous benchmarks.

The examples of Winmar and Long should have affirmed the game's social conscience and provided the AFL with a template to handle future cases of racial abuse. But when Adam Goodes was booed two decades later, the AFL was powerless to stop it.

Adams Goodes came of age in the backlash against Indigenous empowerment. He joined the Sydney Swans as a teenager in 1998, the year John Howard wound back Paul Keating's native title legislation. At the federal election that year, just over one million people voted for Pauline Hanson's One Nation Party in the Senate.

Early in his career, one of the game's most high-profile players called Goodes 'a fucking monkey-looking cunt'. Goodes mentioned the incident in a heartfelt essay for the AFL's official history of the game, published in 2008, in which he celebrates the connection between football and marngrook. 'I know that when Aborigines play Australian Football with a clear mind and total focus, we are born to play it.' By then he had won two Brownlow medals and played in the first of his two premierships for the Swans.

The political climate was less hostile in 2008. Kevin Rudd had apologised to the Stolen Generations, raising hopes for a new era of reconciliation. But the backlash had not receded. Another of the writers who contributed to the AFL book, Gillian Hibbins, wanted to kill the 'seductive myth' that football borrowed from marngrook. Football, she argued, derived 'solely from a colonial dependence upon the British background'.

Hibbins took particular exception to the claim by her fellow essayist Goodes that Indigenous people were born to play football. That was racism, she told the *Marngrook Footy Show*. 'If you define racism as believing a race is superior in something, this is what he was doing,' she said. He was doing no such thing, but her comment was a warning of the coming political storm.

No one ever contested Nicky Winmar and Michael Long's right to speak as Indigenous men. Goodes was treated differently. What had changed was the politics of the nation around him.

The Swans were the reigning premiers when they faced Collingwood in the first match of the Indigenous Round in May 2013. Goodes was best on ground that night, but he lost interest in the game when a Magpie fan called him an 'ape'. He pointed her out to security guards, who escorted her from the stands. Collingwood ruckman Darren Jolly had also alerted security. After the game,

Collingwood president Eddie McGuire went to the Swans dressing room to apologise to Goodes on behalf of the club.

'It felt like I was in high school again being bullied,' Goodes told the media the following day. 'I don't think I've ever been more hurt by someone calling me a name. Not just by what was said, but who it came from.'

The girl was only thirteen, and Goodes emphasised that she needed help. He did not want people to go after her. 'I've got no doubt in my mind she's got no idea what she was calling me last night.'

She rang later that day and apologised.

Football crowds did not boo Goodes after that episode. In fact, the empathy he had shown the girl was one of the reasons he was named Australian of the Year in January 2014.

Eight Indigenous Australians had won the award before him. Three of the eight were sporting heroes, the boxer Lionel Rose, the tennis player Evonne Goolagong and the Olympic athlete Cathy Freeman; the five who didn't play sport had been champions for Indigenous rights. Goodes was both. He was neither an exceptional nor provocative choice at the time. Tony Abbott, the newly elected prime minister, presented the Australia Day award and said the footballer's stance against racism on and off the field had won the admiration and respect of people around the nation.

Goodes told the audience at Parliament House that it was an honour to receive an award for playing the game he loved and for doing what he believed in. He wanted to use his platform as Australian of the Year to tackle racism.

> My hope is that we, as a nation, can break down the silos between races. Break down those stereotypes of minority populations, Indigenous populations and all the other minority groups. I hope that we can be proud of our heritage, regardless of the colour of our skin, and be proud to be Australian.

In a short video profile aired as part of the awards coverage, Goodes explained that a life in football had 'made it easier for me to assimilate'.

Over the course of the 2014 season, a small section of supporters from opposing clubs booed Goodes whenever he touched the football. It didn't happen in every game, but it was painfully obvious on grand final day, when the Swans played the Hawks. The timing is important to bear in mind – the booing only started after he was named Australian of the Year.

There was another factor. As prime minister Tony Abbott had taken up the cause, first promoted by B. A. Santamaria, to amend the Racial Discrimination Act. He would not have intended for Goodes to be sacrificed as part of this campaign, but once his government reawakened the race debate of the Howard era, it was inevitable someone like Goodes would be caught in the crosshairs.

The attorney-general George Brandis made the case for change in March 2014, just weeks into the new football season. 'People do have a right to be bigots, you know,' he told parliament. He wasn't one himself, of course. The bigots were on the other side of the chamber. Responding to an interjection from Labor senator Penny Wong, Brandis continued:

> Well, you know, Senator Wong, a lot of the things I have heard you say in this chamber over the years are, to my way of thinking, extraordinarily bigoted and extraordinarily ignorant. But I would defend your right to say things that I consider to be bigoted and ignorant. That is what freedom of speech means.

The spectators who first booed Goodes may have been unaware of the government's campaign, or that a legislative right to bigotry lacked the numbers to pass through both houses of parliament. But they need not have known any of the detail to absorb the cultural signal that they were now free to speak out.

It is hard to imagine this level of hostility towards a sportsman under any previous prime minister. Abbott scratched the itch of vulgar nationalism and anticipated the governing model of Donald Trump, in which polarisation was both the means and the ends of politics. He would provoke an argument, the conservative press would escalate it by repeating his talking points, and he, in turn, would recite their attacks to keep the debate going.

Abbott demonised the ABC and Muslim Australians for political gain. He accused the national broadcaster of not barracking for Team Australia in its reporting of the government's asylum seeker policies. He demanded that Muslim leaders condemn terrorism and mean it, implying that so far they hadn't and didn't. He coined the phrase 'death cult' to describe the Islamic State terrorist group and could not stop repeating it. In one press conference, he used it seventeen times. All these attacks were meant to assure his conservative base that he was protecting Australian culture from the tyranny of political correctness. Every week of the Abbott government felt like White Pride Round.

Goodes did not make conservative commentators' list of enemies in 2014, because they hadn't yet noticed the booing. But they were onto the story in 2015. They were almost willing Goodes to offend them, so they could continue to write and talk about him. At the Indigenous Round in May that year, Goodes celebrated a goal he scored against Carlton by hurling an imaginary spear into the crowd. He said he had learned the 'war cry' from young Indigenous players and used it as a form of tribute to them. But it could also be misread as a champion player taunting the supporters of a lowly club.

The conservative press accused Goodes of provoking the crowd. They advised Goodes that he was being booed because people didn't like him. Stop accusing Australia of racism, they said. 'Adam Goodes can fix all this by changing his behaviour,' as prominent Sydney-based opinion maker Alan Jones put it, in an uncanny reprise of the argument used by the Collingwood president two decades earlier.

Here, another aspect of the Trump method was being predicted: black athletes being told to stick to sport and stay out of politics. 'Wouldn't you love to see one of these NFL owners, when somebody disrespects our flag, to say, "Get that son of a bitch off the field right now, out, he's fired,"' the president said of the footballers protesting racism in America.

Abbott did not want Goodes to be booed, and made a belated plea for respect. But he could not stop his supporters in the media from making an example of one of the most prominent Indigenous voices at the time.

The AFL did not wish for Goodes to be booed either, but its commissioners were split between those who thought Goodes was being racially abused, those who thought he was just the latest in a long line of players, white or black, to attract the ire of fans, and a minority who thought Goodes had provoked the crowd with his conduct on and off the field. There was also a fear that naming the abuse as racism would have upset footy fans, who did not see themselves as racists.

Unable to make a clear statement in defence of Goodes, the AFL re-created the dynamic of 1995, when present players supported Michael Long while past players thought he should have copped it sweet. Adam Goodes was defended by his peers but criticised by an old guard, led by former test cricketer Shane Warne, who said the booing had nothing to do with racism. Warne claimed there was a simpler explanation: footy fans didn't like to see Goodes exaggerating contact to win free kicks.

The difference in the 2015 debate compared with the one twenty years earlier was the pile-on by conservative commentators and the addition of social media, which amplified what public opinion there was against Goodes. Many of the participants were not even footy fans. They had co-opted the game to make a political point.

It was only after Goodes had had enough, and took a week off from the game, that the AFL finally spoke out. But it was too late. The time to act was a year earlier, before Goodes had been taken hostage in the culture war.

The AFL's chief executive, Gillon McLachlan, issued a belated apology to Goodes in the league's annual report, released in May 2016. 'Adam stood up to represent indigenous people and he took a stand on racism, and for this, I believe he was subject to hostility from some in our crowds,' McLachlan wrote. 'As a game, we should have acted sooner and I am sorry we acted too slowly.'

But even if the AFL had acted decisively, there is a question that still troubles me. Why would Victorians, the nation's most cosmopolitan people, boo Goodes in the first place? Surely the Hawthorn supporters who could afford a grand final ticket in 2014 were more evolved than the members of Collingwood cheer squad of 1993? Yet they booed Adam Goodes as their team thrashed the Swans. Not many of them, of course. In football's long history as a mass spectator sport, it's only ever been a minority that misbehaves in the grandstand. But rugby league did not have an equivalent race row in 2014 and 2015, or even in 1995 or 1993. The problem is peculiar to football.

One possible explanation is the absence of contact between white and black Australians in the southern states. Football may have been inspired by marngrook, but the free migrants who first played the game in Victoria had overrun the local population within a decade of arrival. It took half a century of colonisation in New South Wales and Queensland for the settler population to become the overwhelming majority. This meant that while blood was spilled across the continent, in the rugby league states it was also mixed.

NRL commissioner Professor Megan Davis explains that the largest urban populations of Aboriginal and Torres Strait Islander people today live in rugby league territory. And in the working-class and underclass regions of Western Sydney and South East Queensland, 'rugby league's core fan base live alongside the mob'.

'Having grown up in Eagleby in Logan City, it's always been my belief that these urban populations are the worker bees of successful multiculturalism in this country. Along with the welfare net it is these peoples who keep a lid on any racial tension. It's not that there isn't racism or flare-ups, but there's a practical co-existence.'

Unlike football in Victoria, rugby league has an unbroken link to the Aboriginal people of New South Wales and Queensland because the game became an immediate tool of inclusion for the men who were forced into racially segregated missions and reserves at federation.

'This is often how Aboriginal men were able to leave the reserves and missions: with permission to play in local rugby league games, alongside white Australians. Rugby league played an emancipatory role for many men during the brutal era of Australia's own apartheid, and it facilitated a fellowship between many Indigenous and non-Indigenous rugby league players.'

Professor Davis says another factor is the example of generations of Aboriginal players who represented Australia in rugby league. Arthur Beetson was captain of the national team, the Kangaroos, in the 1970s, at a time when only a handful of Aboriginal people played VFL.

She notes that in the year Adam Goodes retired from football, rugby league had a counterstory of unity between black and white Australia, in the example of the North Queensland Cowboys. The club's territory covers the sites of some of the most brutal frontier wars between the locals and settlers, and simultaneously has 'the richest native-title footprint in the nation'.

The Cowboys captain, Jonathan Thurston, a proud Aboriginal man, is regarded as one of the greatest players in the game's history. On grand final day, he won the game for his team with a thrilling field goal kicked in extra time. Professor Davis says the photo of him after the game, 'exhausted, with his daughter Frankie and her black Aboriginal doll', is destined to be remembered as one of rugby league's iconic images.

The game and the people should not be confused. Rugby league has the more tolerant crowds, but it was the voters of New South Wales and especially Queensland who first resisted Keating's reconciliation agenda. And while Victorians were the ones who booed Goodes, they've also given Pauline Hanson's One Nation the lowest vote in each federal election it's contested.

The interests of football and politics diverge on the question of race. While parliamentary majorities can still be built around policies of exclusion – stopping asylum seeker boats, military intervention in Indigenous communities, tougher citizenship tests for migrants – the game can no longer afford the perception that it thinks white.

Almost half the Australian population (49 per cent) is either a migrant themselves or has at least one parent who was born overseas. In Victoria, the figure is 53 per cent. In Melbourne, where the largest migrant community is from India and the second-largest from China, first- and second-generation migrants account for 60 per cent of the city's total population. In this real world, where football's home base is already Eurasian, the booing of Adam Goodes was just about the last thing the AFL needed. It sent a discouraging message of parochialism to the new Australians who will determine football's future: the skilled migrants from Asia.

To maintain its status as the nation's most-watched winter sport, football needs to convert these new arrivals at a faster rate than it did the Greeks, Italians and Vietnamese of previous migration waves. In the past, football and indeed rugby suffered no penalty to their market share if they ignored the low-skilled migrants, because they could get to their local-born children with the old tools of integration: media monopoly in the living room and peer-group pressure at school. The children of my generation were force-fed Australian culture – the footy replay on Saturday night, *Countdown* on Sunday night.

Today new arrivals have access to the media of their mother country and of third countries such as the United States and Britain. Tribal loyalties are harder to secure in a global information age when Collingwood or Richmond or the Sydney Swans are pitted against multiple codes, teams and individual players from soccer, basketball and American football. Australian Rules football was the only winter sport on the TV in the 1970s and it would have taken a wilful act of social disobedience to choose another pastime. Now a new arrival brings their team with them on their smart phone.

Critically, the new arrival today is younger, better educated and with a higher earning potential than the general population. This consumer will ultimately decide what sports will remain financially viable through the cash cow of broadcasting rights.

The migrants of my parents' generation started at the bottom, and indeed every wave from the end of World War II carried a majority of low-skilled workers. These migrant groups came from the war-ravaged countries of Europe and Indochina. But since the turn of the twenty-first century migrants have come from rising countries like China and India, and around 70 per cent of these new arrivals are skilled workers. Those earlier waves averaged between 80 000 and 100 000 new settlers per year; in the new century the intake has doubled, to 190 000.

But the challenge for football, indeed all national codes, is not just the scale and composition of the migration program. It's the differences it's created between cities and regions.

In the past, migration waves tended to flow uniformly across the country so that the largest overseas-born communities in each city and region were similar. Today the only place where the top-five migrant groups match that of the nation as a whole is the rugby league town of Newcastle. That is, the English-born are most common, New Zealanders second, Chinese third, Indians fourth and those born in the Philippines ranked fifth.

To the north, on the Gold Coast and in Brisbane, the New Zealand–born are the largest migrant group, but in Sydney it's the Chinese. When I mention this statistic to rugby league officials, they say, only half joking, 'That explains why Queensland always wins the state of origin.'

In Melbourne, the Indian-born are more likely to adopt football than the Chinese, based on what I've gleaned from private discussions with AFL officials. Nevertheless, it is difficult to see how the AFL can maintain nine Melbourne-based clubs in the long run. A newly arrived Eurasian-Australian need not become a soccer fanatic to hurt football, the danger lies in them not choosing any local sport at all. Football won't notice their absence at the grounds, because the local-born and their children will still fill the stadiums. Instead the loss will be felt in the television rating numbers.

Consider how quickly the nation's ethnic face has changed. In 1976, when football and rugby league were still provincial games, 80 per cent of the Australian population was local-born. Of the 20 per cent who were born overseas, more than half were English speakers. Europeans like my parents were 8 per cent of the total population and those born in Asia were just 1 per cent.

By 1996, the overseas-born had increased their share of the total population to 26 per cent and migrants from non-English speaking countries accounted for almost half of that – the Europeans were 6 per cent of the total population, Asians 5 per cent and those from the Middle East and North Africa 1 per cent. The AFL had a stable national game, while rugby league was in the middle of the Super League wars.

Another twenty years later, the overseas born are now 28 per cent of the population. Eleven per cent of the population were born in Asia, 5 per cent in Europe and 2 per cent in the Middle East and North Africa.

In this more disparate country, football can no longer rely on its aesthetic appeal. It needs a fresh story of inclusion to appeal to the new arrival, but it won't find one if it continues to deny the most unique aspect of the game – the bond between black and white, between traditional and migrant Australia.

On the weekend that Adam Goodes did not play for the Sydney Swans, the Western Bulldogs and Richmond showed their support for him by again wearing the special jumpers that had been made for the Indigenous Round earlier in the season. A third club, Melbourne, took the field with players wearing wristbands in the Indigenous colours of red, yellow and black.

The Western Bulldogs said it was taking 'a strong stand against all forms of abuse'. Richmond coach Damien Hardwick said, 'We have all had enough, and I'm pleased our club will make an important statement.' Goodes, he said, 'has been a wonderful ambassador for our game and his people'.

I had not seen this side of my club before. Richmond – my mighty, flawed Tigers – had made a timely intervention in a public controversy. The club didn't overplay its hand, nor lose itself in self-importance. It simply did the right thing.

Richmond's gesture was also pitch perfect because their Dreamtime jumper would be worn against Hawthorn – the club whose supporters had first booed Goodes, in the previous year's grand final.

The Tigers brought their best defensive game to the MCG that Friday evening, restricting the Hawks to their lowest score of the season. The winning margin was 18 points; not a thrashing, but decisive enough to have the pundits talking up Richmond's chances of winning the premiership.

But the season refused to deliver a moral victory for Goodes or the players who stuck up for him. The nice guys, Richmond and the Western Bulldogs, were knocked out in the first weekend of the finals series. The two clubs' collective premiership drought now reached ninety-six years – sixty-one for the Bulldogs and thirty-five for the Tigers. The Swans were themselves defeated in the second weekend of the finals, and Goodes retired after seventeen seasons and 372 games of senior football. He walked off the SCG without a guard of honour because he didn't want the fuss.

Hawthorn went on to win the premiership, its third in a row. Between the first and second weekend of the finals, Tony Abbott was sacked by his own party.

If I were still working for *The Australian*, I might have written a column explaining how sport had nothing to teach politics, because political culture will defeat even the most earnest of sports, football. National leadership sets the tone. The difference between the Keating and Abbott prime ministerships can be seen in the game's response to Nicky Winmar and Michael Long on the one hand, and Adam Goodes on the other. One leader extended the bandwidth for debate by welcoming Indigenous voices, while the other added the static of backlash.

I might have added a smaller footballing moral for my own amusement: Richmond will always tease during the home and away season, before capitulating in September.

I would have been wonderfully wrong. The nice guys won the next two AFL premierships – the Western Bulldogs in 2016 and Richmond in 2017 – and in a manner that lifted the national spirit.

The Richmond premiership, in particular, carried two unexpected lessons for politics.

First, it demonstrated the power of diversity. On grand final day 2017 the six Richmond players who polled votes in the Norm Smith medal for best on ground were the son of a Maori, Dustin Martin;

a Muslim Australian, Bachar Houli; an Indigenous Australian, Shane Edwards; a Jehovah's Witness, Alex Rance; an Italian Australian, Dion Prestia; and a teenager from the northern suburbs of Adelaide, Jack Graham. Has any successful sporting team looked more Australian?

The second lesson is about leadership. Richmond realised it could not become a premiership club again until it taught itself how to govern well. I can think of two struggling sides who would benefit from the new Richmond model – Labor and the Liberals.

Football looks like no other game in the world except marngrook. This is the only surviving image of the Indigenous game, from a drawing by William Blandowski in 1857, before the settlers invented football.

Early games of football were mostly played along the ground, without high marks or long kicks, as seen in this spirited encounter in Yarra Park in 1874.

(Oswald Rose Campbell/State Library of Victoria)

ABOVE: Football as it looked in the first decade of the twentieth century, when it lost the contest for the loyalty of Sydney's working class to rugby league. *(State Library of Victoria)*

BELOW: Almost 54 000 people saw Richmond win the 1920 grand final against Collingwood. The Tigers' first VFL premiership kicked off football's greatest decade of attendance.

(Table Talk, 7 October 1920/Trove)

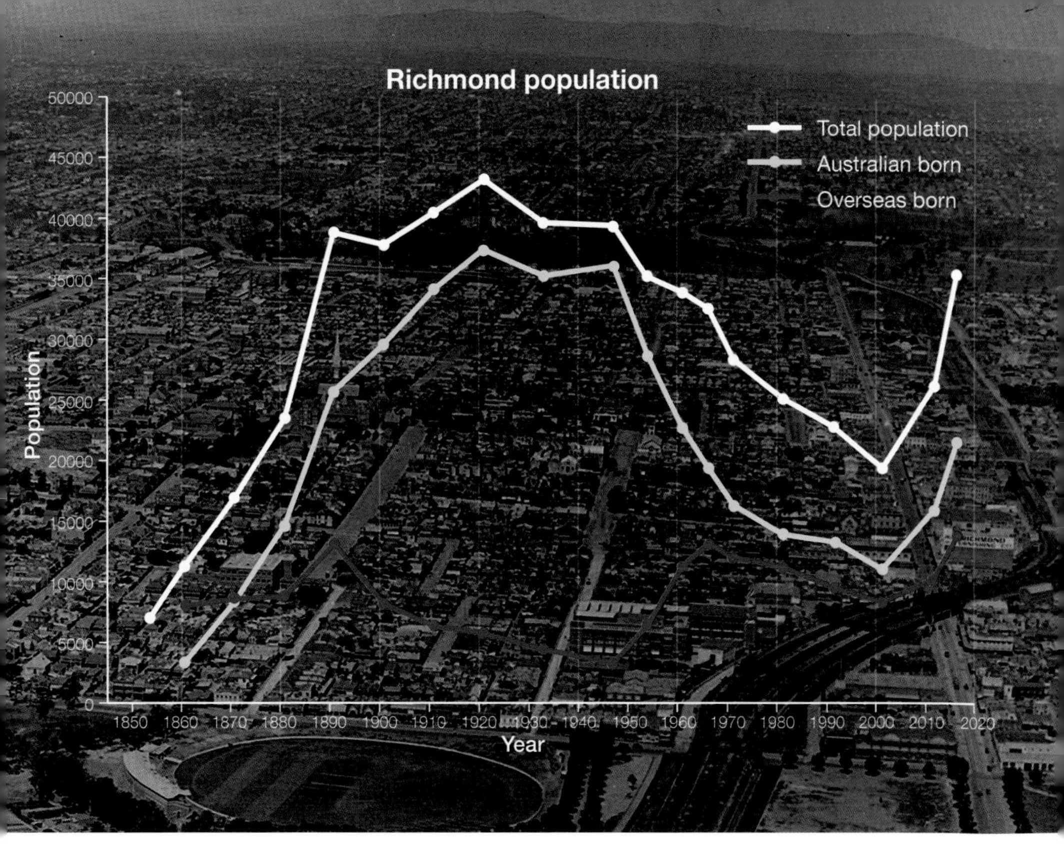

Tracking the boom and bust cycles of Richmond's population, from the gold rush to the present day. This graph is set against an aerial shot of Richmond c. 1930. *(State Library of Victoria)*

The inner-city slum c. 1920–26.
(Algernon Darge/State Library of Victoria)

ABOVE: Former prime minister Robert Menzies watches his beloved Carlton at Princes Park from the passenger seat of his Bentley. *(News Ltd/Newspix)*

RIGHT: Treasurer Paul Keating converted to football, and Collingwood, on the eve of the 1990 election. Following his speech to a club function I arranged a photo with Lou Richards for the front page of the Melbourne *Sun*. *(John Casamento/Newspix)*

BELOW: Queen Elizabeth is introduced to Fitzroy player Bob Hodgkin at the half-time break in their game against Richmond at the MCG, 5 April 1970. It was first VFL game to be played on a Sunday. The Lions defeated the reigning premier by 20 points. *(Fairfax)*

The final decades of the old VFL were dominated by the supporters of three clubs: Richmond, Collingwood and Carlton.

TOP: Fans queue for tickets to the 1966 grand final between St Kilda and Collingwood. *(John Lamb/Fairfax)*

LEFT: Magpie fans at Victoria Park in 1980. *(Fairfax)*

BOTTOM: The MCG on the day of the 1973 grand final between Richmond and Carlton, which drew a crowd of 116 956. *(Peter Mayoh/Fairfax)*

LEFT: The line in the sand. St Kilda's Nicky Winmar blows a kiss to the Collingwood cheer squad after a fiery game at Victoria Park in April 1993. What he did next, lifting his jumper and pointing proudly to his black skin, triggered a national debate on racism in sport.

(Wayne Ludbey/Fairfax)

BELOW: The calm before the blowback. Sydney's dual Brownlow medalist Adam Goodes at the peak of his powers, flying for a mark in 2010. After Goodes was named Australian of the Year in 2014, some supporters of opposing teams began booing him. By 2015, the booing had become a full-blown crisis for the game. The AFL admitted later that it was too slow to respond, and finally apologised to Goodes after he had retired.

(Sean Garnsworthy/AFL Media)

The new Richmond – proving that nice guys and women can win a premiership. Captain Trent Cotchin above and, from left to right, the three key off-field leaders who rebuilt the club from laughing stock to role model: CEO Brendon Gale, president Peggy O'Neal and coach Damien Hardwick. *(Michael Wilson/AFL Media; Adam Trafford/AFL Media)*

ABOVE LEFT: The bad hair 1970s. My nine-year-old self with Mum and my sister, watching Richmond play Hawthorn at Glenferrie Oval in 1973. ABOVE RIGHT: Mum and me on grand final day 2017. It was our first grand final together after five decades of watching footy. BELOW: The Tiger Army celebrate at Punt Road Oval the day after the grand final. *(Quinn Rooney/ Getty Images)* INSET: The players share the premiership with their adoring fans. *(Scott Barbour/AFL Media)*

PART THREE

A NEW WAY TO WIN

2010–2017

9

THE CHIEF AND THE PRESIDENT

Brendon Gale played senior football for Richmond in the decade of false hope from 1990 to 2001. In those twelve seasons, two moments stood out that have informed his work as the club's chief executive. Both moments came at the end of a season, when the premiership had been won by someone else and Punt Road was consumed by a financial or political crisis.

The first lesson was an easy one to grasp. In September and October 1990, after playing all twenty-two games in his debut season, Gale hit the road with teammates and past players to help raise $1 million for the Save Our Skins campaign. 'You can't compete for flags if you're insolvent and players are shaking collection tins,' Gale tells me.

The second lesson took years to reveal itself, as Gale continued to reflect on the lost opportunity of 1995. Speaking to him about the club's history, our conversations often drift back to that season and its aftermath, because it was the most Richmond season of all. The club had just played a cracking finals series, its first since 1982. 'We were a young committed team building towards a premiership,' he says. But then the coach who had taken them to a preliminary final suddenly quit. 'Now who takes responsibility for an environment where he feels the need to walk?'

Gale didn't have the answer at the time. He was twenty-seven, with a law degree, but no real understanding of what a successful football club looked like from the inside. All he knew was Richmond.

His perspective changed when, after a brief period in commercial law, he began working for the AFL Players' Association. First as its president, then as its chief executive after he retired from the game. Those positions gave him an insight into how every other club in the competition operated. He saw how various club bosses led, how they ran their business and managed their teams. He also saw how they responded to wins and losses: the meetings held on a Monday after a bad defeat were the most revealing. He observed the clubs that were reactive and those that sailed through setbacks; the clubs that got ahead of themselves and those that were patiently building towards a premiership.

Gale realised that Richmond's serial underachievement on the field was in part linked to the way the club was run off the field.

When he returned to Punt Road as its chief executive in 2009, he was determined not to repeat the mistakes of his axe-wielding predecessors, who executed coaches too soon, and who made decisions based on vendetta. He did not believe in quick fixes, silver bullets or messiahs.

Gale grew up in a big family with six sisters and a brother. Football was in his genes. His grandfather Jack had played three games for Richmond in 1924, his father Donald was an accomplished local footballer in Tasmania and his brother Michael was already playing with Fitzroy.

Richmond drafted Gale at the end of the 1987 season, after he had played a year of senior football for the Burnie Hawks in the Tasmanian State League. He says he didn't really covet a VFL career at first. Growing up in northwest Tasmania, his football heroes were local and the mainland seemed too remote. He was nineteen when he put his name in the draft and, after discussions with Fitzroy, he had expected to join Michael at the Lions. Unexpectedly, Richmond called out his name before Fitzroy. His father told him not to worry – Richmond was a superpower of the competition.

'My old man said to me, "Don't ever tell your brother, but if you are good enough – and that's a big if – if you're good enough, you are every chance of playing in a grand final and a premiership with Richmond, as opposed to Fitzroy. Because that's what they do." It was only six years after their last grand final.'

Gale thought he had joined a sophisticated organisation, but his employer was broke. Our first interview is conducted jointly with Richmond president Peggy O'Neal. She asks Gale if he always got paid on time. 'No.'

Back then, recruits were allowed to grow into young men before they were selected in the senior team. Gale served a two-year apprenticeship in the reserves before his senior debut in 1990. He joined a team that was carrying the wooden spoon and an eight-game losing streak from the previous season.

Few players in the game's history have suffered a more desolate introduction to the big league. In Gale's first match against Brisbane, on the Gold Coast, the Tigers were belted by 59 points. The following week against North Melbourne, at the MCG, the losing margin of 141 points was a new club-record defeat. There was a brief rally in the middle of that season as the young team won six games between rounds five and fourteen, but the Tigers could not sustain their run. They lost their next seven by an average of 57 points.

The sword of insolvency hung over Punt Road, and in the final round of the season, against fellow battlers the Sydney Swans, the players donated their match payments to kickstart the Save Our Skins campaign.

Based on the precedent at Collingwood and Footscray, the camaraderie of fundraising between players, club officials and the fans should have lifted Richmond to the finals within two or three seasons. The Magpies had rattled the collection tin in 1986 and then played in three consecutive finals series between 1988 and 1990, culminating in a premiership. Following their 'Fightback' campaign in 1989, the Bulldogs took a year longer to return to the finals, making a preliminary final in 1992. They played finals again in 1994 and 1995.

But not Richmond. Having raised the funds to save the club, the shared sense of purpose disappeared as soon as the team resumed losing, the very next year. At the end of the 1991 season the club revived one bloody tradition and broke with another. Kevin Bartlett was sacked as coach and his replacement was chosen from outside the Richmond family.

The club thought it had found the perfect man to mentor its young team. Alan Jeans had taken St Kilda to its only premiership in 1966 and had won three more with Hawthorn in the 1980s. But unfortunately health issues meant that he was forced to leave after just one season. The club returned to its roots and appointed former player John Northey as its coach for 1993.

For Gale, the first of the patterns of instability had identified itself. Three coaches in three seasons, and the team went backwards each time. Seven wins under Bartlett in 1991, five wins with Jeans in 1992 and four wins under Northey in 1993.

Looking back, Gale says the club wasn't run well. 'It's a tough thing to say and it's not about individuals, because many fine people served so selflessly, but so often over a long period the various elements of the club just didn't seem to be on the same page. There appeared to be a lack of trust and the club was never able to operate near its full capacity.'

But even a poorly run club should eventually make the finals, because the national draft is designed to give weak teams a leg up. Picks are assigned in reverse order to ladder position, the bottom team getting the first choice of player, and so on. A few years on the lower rungs should see the team improve.

The AFL tilted the playing field further in favour of the underdogs by expanding the finals from six to eight teams in 1994. To finish ninth in these circumstances was neither a pass nor an abject failure, but it was memorable, and Richmond had the misfortune to be the first club to finish ninth.

The 1994 season began with a familiar acquiescence. Three losses from the opening four games were followed by a boardroom coup, instigated by former player Mal Brown. Halfway through the season, the Tigers sat twelfth on the ladder, three places from the bottom. Then, without warning, the team embarked on a rollicking six-game winning streak.

The first scalp was Collingwood's. I was caught in a traffic jam on the road back to Canberra after a long weekend on the South Coast. I doubt I will ever spend a more entertaining hour in gridlock, with the window down and the radio turned up to catch the roar from the MCG. I hadn't been to a Richmond game since joining the press gallery six years earlier, but I hadn't forgotten the noise that captivated me as a child.

The broadcast of that 11-goal victory felt like a message from home. A fortnight later, I was on a plane to Melbourne to catch up with friends and to take Mum to the footy for our first game together since 1985. Under a Mondrian grey sky, with the MCG floodlights switched on in the daytime, we watched Richmond overrun Melbourne in the final quarter to win by 16 points.

At the end of the season Melbourne, Collingwood and Richmond had each won twelve games, but the Tigers finished behind both, and outside the finals, on percentage.

The sudden improvement in form was due to two factors. The first was that Richmond had, in fact, recruited well. Matthew Richardson, destined to be the club's best player for the next decade and half, was drafted in 1993, while six new players joined in 1994 – the experienced premiership ruckman Greg Dear from Hawthorn, Paul Broderick and Michael Gale from Fitzroy, and Paul Bulluss, Matthew Rogers and Jamie Tape from South Australia. Meanwhile, Matthew Knights, Brendon Gale and Wayne Campbell, who had been nurtured under Kevin Bartlett before his dismissal, were maturing into elite players.

The second factor was the coach, John Northey. 'There was no sophistication,' Gale says of his tactics. 'But it was always about team and we wanted to play for him.'

Early in the 1995 season, captain Tony Free and young gun forward Matthew Richardson were both felled by knee injuries. Yet this Richmond team wouldn't die wondering. They found ways to keep winning without them, and with a little luck might have played for a premiership. One more win during the home and away season would have secured second spot on the ladder, giving them a clear run to the grand final.

Instead Richmond finished third, which effectively gave them a double chance, guaranteeing at least two finals. I had long promised Mum that I would take her to a final if we ever made one, but I picked the wrong one to honour that commitment.

I flew down from Canberra for the first game, against North Melbourne on a Friday night. It was the strangest commute to the footy Mum and I had ever experienced. The train carriage was crowded, and tense. There was very little conversation. Just as we were coming into Richmond station one fan yelled 'Come on the Tigers!' more in anguish than expectation and we erupted in laughter.

I don't recall much of the game, other than that North Melbourne appeared to be the better team. They beat us by 30 points. I didn't see the point in flying back for the following final, against Essendon. Two weekends in Melbourne watching the footy was a step back into the fanaticism of childhood that I was not prepared to take. I regretted that decision for the next twenty-two years.

I was at the beach, without access to a television, for that second final. So I missed the game that sustained a generation of

Richmond supporters during the ordeal that was the Walls–Gieschen–Frawley–Wallace era.

Researching this chapter, I watched the replay again for the first time in ages. I still can't work out how we won.

Richmond scored just 4 goals in the first half, 3 of which came from the centreman Matthew Knights. His goals were of such individual brilliance that they look like the highlight reel from another game.

In general play, when Knights wasn't involved, Richmond was purposeful but sloppy. The tall forwards were having trouble marking the ball. For Gale in particular it was a rotten day at the office, but he tells me the players never doubted that they could beat Essendon.

At half time Richmond was 5 goals behind. Essendon dominated play early in the third quarter, but couldn't conjure an extra goal to put the game beyond reach. Meanwhile John Northey made the move that would change the course of the game: he sent Gale to the backline and brought Scott Turner forward.

With ten minutes left in the third quarter, Richmond's Nick Daffy was awarded a free kick. He secured the team's first goal in almost half an hour of play. Half a minute later, Turner grabbed the ball from a boundary throw-in and snapped another goal. The supporters behind the Punt Road End goals rose like a monster wave. A piercing primal roar erupted across the stadium.

The momentum was suddenly with the Tigers. One minute the game was meandering to a dull victory for Kevin Sheedy's Bombers, the next, a sleeping giant had awoken.

Gale tells me that once a final turns like that, it's difficult for the side that was in front to restore its authority. He remembers the same thing happened to Richmond against North Melbourne in the previous game, when the Kangaroos' centre half-forward Wayne Carey inspired a rush of goals in the last quarter.

Against Essendon, the Richmond wave kept building. Another pair of goals followed late in the quarter, from Chris Naish and Daffy.

Turner had a hand in each. Just before three-quarter time, Naish kicked a further goal. Amazingly, Richmond was 1 point in front.

Gale says there was an element of retribution in the comeback. The players wanted to atone for the game against Essendon during the home and away season, which had ended in a draw.

The final quarter was a celebration. The television cameras kept catching Richmond supporters in a state of delirium. After thirteen years out of the finals, the Tigers finally won one. The Richmond theme song, 'We're from Tigerland', was belted out with a quasi-religious fervour. The refrain 'Yellow and black!' was shouted, not sung.

Something had changed while I was being distracted by politics in Canberra. I remembered the song in the 1970s, but not the crowd participation. Now it was part of the game itself, like the encore of 'Born to Run' at a Bruce Springsteen concert.

When the siren sounded, Northey, a two-time premiership player with Richmond in the 1960s, leaped out of the coach's box like the most demented fan of all, swinging his jacket over his head. He was imitating his former teammate Sheedy, who made the gesture famous when the Baby Bombers took the competition by surprise in 1993.

The following week, for the preliminary final against Geelong, there was nothing left in the tank. The Tigers were thrashed by 89 points. But the supporters could start dreaming again.

More than 1.1 million people attended Richmond games in 1995, breaking the previous club record, set in 1980. It is easy to see now why this particular season was so popular with Richmond fans: the players. They were a charismatic mix of traditional footballing tradesmen and long-haired trendies. In the former camp were the short back and sides of Matthew Knights and Paul Broderick, although both were exceedingly talented. The surfies and grunge rockers included the Gale brothers, Brendon and Michael, Wayne Campbell and Nick Daffy. In a category of his own was Stuart Maxfield, with his long blond mullet and trusty left foot.

And then there was Matthew Richardson. All arms and legs, Richo could fly, but he did not know how to land. He could kick the most majestic goal from an implausible part on the ground, but freeze when confronted with a simple set shot.

Northey's game plan suited this team. Long kicks to a forward line with three tall beacons, led by Brendon Gale the reliable and Richo the spectacular. The third beacon that year was Stuart Edwards. What could possibly go wrong? The answer, as a new generation of players and supporters would learn, is ego.

At the end of a successful season, a club's attention should turn to what changes are required – to the game plan, to the playing list – in order to take the next step to a grand final. But the Tigers got ahead of themselves. They canvassed replacing Northey with Sheedy, even though Northey had just been voted coach of the year by the AFL Players' Association and Sheedy was tied to Essendon.

'My understanding, rightly or wrongly, is that there were some elements of the board who didn't believe he had the credentials to coach a premiership team,' Gale explains.

After the 1995 season, Northey still had a year to run on his contract. But he wanted job security. He asked for an extension, and a pay rise. In so doing, he forced a confrontation he could not win. The club knocked back his request and, in the week after the grand final, Northey quit to take up a better offer at Brisbane.

The TV news in Melbourne carried the farce from every angle. The players had been summoned to a secret meeting at the Hilton Hotel, where a television camera was waiting for them. There was a quick comment on behalf of the team from captain Tony Free, declaring their support for the ex-coach. Northey himself was interviewed leaving Punt Road. He said he didn't think he had asked for too much. The identity of the official who he thought was against him was left for the viewer to decode.

The report concluded with a slanging match between Northey's partner, Pam Shearer, and a consultant to the Richmond board, former player Mal Brown. It was like a scene out of the *Sylvania Waters* reality TV show. She accused him of being a bully; he said she didn't conduct herself in the best interests of the club.

I had thought I understood leadership challenges. There were three easily identifiable acts: tension, showdown, catharsis. In the first act, the incumbent is undermined by whispers and leaks. In the second, the rival launches the challenge. In the final act, the fallen leader gives a more human press conference than they ever did in office, while the new leader is humbled and a little awed by the responsibility.

To that point I had covered the Peacock–Howard, Keating–Hawke, Howard–Hewson, Downer–Hewson and Howard–Downer challenges. Every one of them had been triggered by the fear of election defeat, the breakdown in relations between the leader and his colleagues, or a combination of both.

The Richmond coup of 1995 violated these simple rules of self-interest. Northey had the party room onside and the polls were in his favour. That is, he had the support of the players, and the form line was pointing up. But the club was governed by a fractured board, and in a choice between division and unity the Tigers of old would always seek the path of self-sabotage.

To be fair to the old board, Gale concedes that Northey's long-kicking game wasn't the most innovative in the AFL. But he thinks that the team was young, building on the right trajectory and that Northey should have served the final year of his contract.

Northey's departure sent a message of insecurity to the playing group. The bond of trust between the club's administration and the team was broken. 'There was no commitment to each other.' Gale thinks back to the effect on the emerging stars in the team. Knights had just turned twenty-five, Campbell twenty-three and Richardson was twenty. 'Constant change – instability – means underlying issues aren't addressed. They may be player-related issues, or club-related issues.'

Each new coach needs time to establish their authority, and the players have to adjust to a new game plan.

Once they let Northey go after a successful season, Richmond talked itself back into the corner of firing any coach after a poor season. Northey's successor Robert Walls returned Richmond to ninth in 1996 and was sacked before the end of the following season. His replacement Jeff Gieschen repeated the cycle: ninth in 1998, terminated in 1999.

You could almost set your calendar by Richmond's near misses. There would be six ninth-place finishes in total: 1994, 1996 1998, 2000, 2006 and 2008. Ninthmond became the club's nickname, and one enterprising footy fan rewrote the lyrics to the theme song and uploaded the result to YouTube. At the time of writing, it has more than 300 000 views.

'We finished ninth again, the Richmond Tigers finished ninth again. In any season you will see it is our fate, to miss out on the eight . . .'

Gale believes that Richmond had the talent in the 1990s, but did not know how to harness it. The club was still operating under the assumptions of the old semi-professional model, where football boards saw themselves as executioners. 'When the coach comes in and they don't get the success they want, the instant sugar hit, they cook the coach and get a new one in, instead of addressing the underlying issue. Looking back and knowing what I know now, I believe that the underlying issue was the club hadn't modernised.'

The quality of the administration helped determine on-field performance, but Richmond was the last of the big Victorian clubs to grasp this new reality of the national competition. The addition of the interstate clubs in the 1980s and 1990s expanded the market for football, delivering a windfall to all clubs through television broadcasting rights. But the player draft and salary cap meant that the richest clubs could no longer hoard all the talent, although poorer clubs like Richmond still had to build their playing lists carefully to remain competitive.

'You can't get a suitcase full of cash and Pelaco shirts and drive around the countryside plundering and pillaging,' Gale says. 'You get a few chances to improve your playing list, and you've got to make those decisions good ones.'

In this dual world of corporatisation and managed competition, of big money and salary caps, clubs were bound to fail if they were run by part-timers, time-servers, ex-players or middle-aged businessmen attracted to sport's reflected glory.

'As the game modernised, you needed a strong, capable board governing the enterprise,' Gale says. 'And you needed increasingly sophisticated management who make consistent, rational decisions by consensus, not through messianic-type zeal and decisions often based on vengeance, tribal warfare.

'And you need to make sure all those elements are focused and aligned, that the board, management, staff, coaches and players are all on the same page. So when the shitstorm comes, you can weather it. And you need a business that can make money.'

Gale reached these conclusions slowly. Richmond had provided the raw material; the perspective to interpret all that experience came from his time at the AFL Players' Association, between 2000 and 2008. There he built a model in his head of what separated the successful clubs from the one he had played for.

'It takes a whole club to get a team to a grand final,' he says. However, on grand final day, 'the responsibility [lies with] the players, the coach and his assistants' and the team has a fifty-fifty chance of winning. 'Getting there is the hardest part.'

He is careful not to reflect on any individual. The board had already made some tough decisions and committed the club to change, which smoothed the path for his reform program, once he became Richmond's chief executive. But Gale needed a decade away from Punt Road – and the club needed another decade of repeating its mistakes – before he could apply the lessons he had learned.

Richmond had known just two types of backroom operators before Peggy O'Neal arrived at Punt Road: the manipulator and the benefactor. Two types of men, sourced from the narrowest of gene pools: ex-players and local businesses.

O'Neal was neither. She was a skilled migrant, a lawyer, in an era when the majority of new arrivals to Australia still wore blue collars. She worked in an area of law in which negotiation and compromise were routine, and contracts were honoured. If O'Neal ever had an ego, she had laid it to rest before she walked into Punt Road at the end of the 2005 season.

She had been approached to join the board earlier in the decade, but had been denied by her employer. As a senior partner at a national law firm, O'Neal needed permission from her firm's board before she could join Richmond's. The law firm's board was very Sydney-centric at the time, and told her that they didn't want their partners associated with football clubs.

'I remember someone saying, "Well, no one would want to join a rugby league board, there is no prestige in that, and they're always in trouble."' As a colleague of O'Neal's explained to me later, Sydney just didn't appreciate the importance of football in Victoria.

The next time Richmond approached her, the same colleague tells me, people from Melbourne and Perth held the balance of power on the firm's board. Her request was approved, and she took up the position at Richmond in November 2005.

One of the things that had first attracted O'Neal to the Tigers was the community spirit of the Save Our Skins campaign. Fifteen years on, the first thing she noticed as a board member was that the club's financial position had not really improved. 'There was no strategic plan,' she says. 'The strategic plan was "get us out of debt".'

By 2005, Richmond arguably owed more money to its creditors than it was worth. The annual report revealed 'a net asset deficiency of $704000'. That was the gap between the club's $10 million debt and other liabilities, and the cash, property, plant and equipment that it held.

Locals would tell O'Neal that she should have been there in the 1970s. 'Others would say "Oh, you don't want to go on the Richmond board because they always end up fighting."'

Peggy O'Neal landed in Richmond in 1989, a wooden spoon year, and a time when the suburb was still losing people. She had grown up in West Virginia. As a young girl, she had been obsessed with sports and wanted to be sports journalist. But her calling was the law, and she earned her degree from the University of Virginia, where, coincidentally, Robert Menzies had lectured about footy two decades earlier.

The big difference O'Neal saw between the US and Australia was the level at which fans engaged with sports. In the US, most people identified with teams at the local level, through the college system. The big pro teams were inaccessible 'unless you lived in a big city, and then had the money to spend [to attend games], and I never did'.

In Melbourne, suburban teams operated at the scale of those big city teams, but with the accessibility of college teams. The MCG was walking distance from her home, 'and it was $10 to get into a game'.

She came to Richmond via a backpacking holiday in Greece, where she met and fell in love with a Melburnian. He didn't want to live in a small US town, so they settled in Richmond. He barracked for Hawthorn, but O'Neal thought that club was too white-bread. She picked the Tigers with the same unerring logic as generations of migrants before her, because 'Richmond is where I live'.

O'Neal kept a diary in her early years in Australia, and noted the quirks of her new home. In the US, she had advised employers on how to package wages and benefits for their staff. There the most sought-after perk was health insurance. In Australia, it was a company car. Australia had universal health care but expensive cars. In the US, capitalism had determined a price for everything, and an automobile was cheaper than health care.

She was struck by the city's obsession with sport. She wrote that on grand final day the streets were empty. 'It was like there was a tomb around Melbourne.'

O'Neal went to the University of Melbourne to requalify, so she could practise law in Australia. Brendon Gale went to Monash law school at the same time, in the early 1990s. Although they did not cross paths, I like to think that the footy gods had registered the rich narrative potential, guiding the two of them to Punt Road to become 21st-century saviours.

What made O'Neal unique, first as a board member and then as president, went beyond gender. She specialised in superannuation law, which meant she could think long-term. She also understood corporate governance, which had been a blind spot not just at Richmond but at most sporting clubs.

When she joined the board at the end of 2005, there were often no clear lines of authority between the board, management and the football department. 'The change from being a board of management to being a board of governance was underway but not complete,' she says. 'Richmond was not unusual in that regard, as many football club board members find it difficult to cease being a footy fan and, instead, remember that they are a director of a company and must act in the long-term interests of the club.'

O'Neal had a simple piece of advice for her fellow directors. 'If you really want to know what's going on in football maybe you should get a job in football.'

She would extend the analogy, at her own expense, to reinforce the policy: 'Why are we paying people who we think are experts at various aspects of football and I – with no experience in these fields – go down and tell them how to do that job. Why don't we just pay someone as bad as me?'

She understood why people wanted to get involved. Their friends loved to hear the insider gossip from the club. 'You know, "I was just talking to Dustin Martin the other day." "I was just playing golf with Damien [Hardwick],"' she says.

'But you can't have this job [on the board] if you want that job. How would you feel if you had the coach's job and these people kept coming in asking stupid questions? And they assumed that it was permissible to drop in and take ten minutes of the coach's time. "Why did you play so and so?" "Why did you recruit so and so?"'

She says if a board member is discussing footy with the coach, the coach may think the director's individual opinion is the official position of the board.

The best use of a director's time is to set the strategy and keep an eye on the big picture. Any question they might have for the coach, or the head of the football department, or the CEO, could be put forward at the regular meeting each of those people would have with the board. 'Don't go to their office, we'll get to talk to them here [in the boardroom].' Rule one, she says, was 'stay away from the football people during the season'.

'Maybe for me, being an outsider and a woman, it was a bit easier to stay away from it, much as I was interested in the game. I didn't need to ask the coach who was going to be picked in the team.'

The addition of a woman to the board signalled Richmond's willingness to change. But the club had to endure one more cycle of false hope under coach Terry Wallace between 2005 and 2009 before it was finally prepared to blow up the old model for good.

Brendon Gale did not covet the chief executive's job at Richmond before it came up in 2009. But when the then Richmond president

Gary March invited him to apply for the vacant position, his competitive instinct kicked in. 'I thought *there* was a real challenge.'

Gale wasn't filled with regret about missing out on a premiership as a player. That didn't define him as a person. 'There have been a lot of wonderful, deserving players who have missed out on premierships – they are bloody hard to win.' But there was a sense of unfinished business. An itch, he calls it.

The challenge confronting him in 2009 was both financial and cultural. The club had $4 million in debt it needed to clear. That meant the collection tin would have to come out again.

But the equation was no longer just about solvency. In the decade since he had been away from Punt Road, the competition had been polarised. There were now two classes of clubs: those that could afford to invest in their football departments and those that were still cutting costs.

At the 2004 end-of-season draft, Richmond had five picks inside the top twenty. But at the same time the club cut $2 million out of its football budget, so it was missing the assistant coaches required to adequately develop the new intake.

Gale did not want to repeat that mistake. 'There was a correlation between the teams that won premierships and their football department expenditure,' he says. That meant he had to somehow address both sides of the budget at once, reduce debt and increase spending in the same cycle.

But as difficult as that might prove, a bigger headache for Gale was reforming the club's culture. A club's finances can be repaired, but how does a club change its identity? Gale admits that it took time to appreciate this aspect of the challenge.

Generations of supporters had been raised to believe that Richmond only succeeded when it was ruthless. Play the game on the field and in the boardroom like the late Jack Dyer and the late Graeme Richmond. That is, run through the opponent. Eat your own if they let the team down. The ghosts of those men still haunted the club, because there was no other model of success to point to.

Gale says the urge for retribution was part of the club's DNA. 'There wouldn't be a week that went by that I wouldn't receive some correspondence, via social media or email, [that said] "Mate, grow a pair, just like GR. Grow a pair, stop pussyfooting around, and sack the lot of them, just like GR."'

The expectations of members had to be managed just as carefully as he balanced the budget. The first step was to acknowledge that despite the best endeavours of many selfless officials, coaches and players, the club had 'failed to perform on-field over the previous thirty years because over that time it had been poorly run as a collective unit'.

He told members they would rebuild 'the organisational effectiveness and financial strength of our football club, in order to support the needs of our football department'. That would establish 'a very solid platform or base camp from which we could ultimately become contenders'.

The supporters did not need to be reminded of the pitiful record. Between 1983 and 2009, from the player mutiny against Francis Bourke to the club's belated acceptance of off-field responsibility, Richmond had made the finals just twice, 'won' four wooden spoons and finished ninth on six occasions. It was the only Victorian club not to play in a grand final during that period.

Richmond no longer had the loudest voice in the competition, either. In 1983, it was still the most popular club in the VFL. By 2009, it could not even pretend to be in the top tier. Collingwood, Essendon and Adelaide were now the big three. Richmond was in the second tier, along with the West Coast Eagles and Carlton.

Gale announced an aggressive five-year plan to create a new Richmond model. It stipulated that by 2014 the club would have played in three finals series, cleared all its debts and signed up

75 000 members. The digital slogan was 3-0-75. Unstated was the number of premierships Gale was aiming for.

As part of the program, Richmond established a second, standalone team in the state-based VFL competition, which combined the old VFL reserves and the VFA. The idea was to give the coaches more control over the coaching and development of young talent and fast-track their progress into the AFL.

Gale says the targets had to be ambitious if the club was to return to the top tier. The early returns were mixed.

The debt was cleared ahead of schedule, thanks to supporters delivering $6 million in donations in eighteen months. That was more than three times the equivalent raised by Save Our Skins ($1.7 million in 2010's dollars). This reflected the relative affluence of Richmond's member and corporate base in the twenty-first century, but also the more sophisticated fundraising techniques employed, using email and social media to target existing and lapsed members.

The most controversial part of Gale's plan was the selling of home games. Between 2011 and 2013, three games scheduled to be played at the MCG were transferred to Queensland. We talked about it at the time and Gale admitted that he wasn't comfortable with the move. But the club's financial position left him with no choice. The extra money it generated for the football department was worth ceding the home-ground advantage. Peggy O'Neal says, 'We had no sponsors when we made that decision. Without selling those games we were in danger of becoming insolvent.'

The club lost the first two of those three games against Gold Coast. The supporter backlash provided the first serious test of Gale's leadership temperament – and of the board's unity.

The second of those defeats, on a sticky July evening in Cairns in 2012, would have reminded Gale of his playing days, when Richmond would terrorise the very best teams in the competition and inexplicably surrender to the worst.

The comic nature of the loss infuriated fans because it suggested a fragility in the playing group. The Tigers were 10 points in front with less than a minute remaining in the game. All they had to do was get their hands on the football and reliably pass it between teammates a few times until the clock ran out. But the Suns were gifted a goal after a Richmond player spilled an easy mark near the middle of the ground.

At the next centre bounce there were 20 seconds left to play. Just enough time to snatch defeat from the jaws of victory.

It started with a Richmond fumble, which released a Gold Coast player to boot the ball forward. Young Richmond defender Alex Rance tried to punch the ball back towards the boundary line but another Gold Coast player swooped and, with a short kick over his shoulder, found the least likely hero on the ground, Karmichael Hunt.

The AFL would have loved the sheer implausibility of this play. Hunt was in the team as an experiment. He was recruited from the Brisbane Broncos rugby league team with a view to converting fans from the English game to the Australian. Hunt kicked the goal after the siren and Richmond hearts broke. 'The worst 47 seconds in footy,' was how former Sydney premiership coach Paul Roos described the end of the game.

Gale fielded questions from a provocative media and irate fans on the following Monday. He told them that while he shared their disappointment with the result, 'it doesn't change the confidence we have in the path we are taking'.

What was so galling about this particular loss was that Richmond had already beaten the top two teams in the competition, Sydney and Hawthorn, while Gold Coast had lost their first fourteen games. The defeat was compounded by narrow defeats the following two weeks, by 4 points against North Melbourne and by 4 points against Carlton.

The first finals appearance of the new era was achieved a year later than promised, in 2013, and it followed the old Richmond script of heartbreak – but with a new twist.

The Tigers had finished fifth on the ladder, one rung short of a double chance. In a normal season they would have played an elimination final against the team that finished eighth. But this finals series had to be reconfigured after Essendon was penalised in the fallout from its supplements program. The Bombers were demoted to ninth and instead the ninth-placed Carlton was given a free ticket to the finals.

Ordinarily this would be viewed as a gift for the team that finished fifth – they would get to play a weaker team. But Carlton had beaten Richmond in ten of the previous eleven games between the two clubs. Damien Hardwick, in his first final as coach, was pitted against Mick Malthouse, who had coached in fifty finals and won three premierships.

The game was a reverse of the 1995 final against the Bombers. Richmond were 32 points in front early in the third quarter and looked set for a thumping victory. Then Carlton, inspired by their best player, Chris Judd, kicked the next five goals. You could hear the collective gulp from the Tiger fans. Richmond rallied briefly, but the Blues, growing in confidence, kicked 6 of the last 7 goals in the final quarter. They won by 20 points.

Defeat is a reliable teacher in football, and all successful teams endure some sort of humiliation before they graduate to grand finals and premierships. But this Richmond side kept flunking the same elimination-final class, again falling at that hurdle against Port Adelaide in 2014 and North Melbourne in 2015.

At the end of the 2015 season, Gale and the board faced their most consequential decision yet. The five-year plan had been completed only a year late: three finals appearances, zero debt and an engaged but impatient membership of 70 000. But they could not be satisfied with the way the team played in those three finals.

The question that confronted Gale and the board was what to do with the coach, Damien Hardwick. After six years in the job, his record showed three years of progress followed by three losing finals. Six wins out of the twenty-two rounds in the first season of the reform program in 2010, eight wins and a draw in 2011, and ten wins and a draw in 2012. The three finals were secured with fifteen wins in 2013, twelve wins in 2014 and another fifteen wins in 2015.

His current contract had one more year to run. Would the club extend it by a year, to 2017, and see if the team could win a final in that time? Or would they give him an extra two years and risk supporter backlash if the team's form stalled or went backwards?

Writing in *The Age*, Jake Niall warned that 'any deal that stretches beyond 2017 would be a show of excessive faith'.

This is when Gale thought about John Northey, whom he'd seen walk away from the job after reaching the finals because he felt he'd lost the backing of the club. Gale shared his insights with the board through a detailed evaluation, including the use of a particular graph. He had plotted out Richmond's ladder position at the end of every season, starting with its last premiership in 1980 and going all the way to the season just ended, 2015. A red dot marked the sacking of each coach.

He describes the graph in detail, and the meaning he drew from the exercise.

'Premiership in '80, miss the finals in '81, sack the coach. Grand final in '82, lose the grand final, '83, sack the coach – a favourite son, Francis Bourke. Between there and Northey's [appointment] in '93, five coaches, no progress. The reason is – and it's my thesis after speaking with several respected Richmond people – that we never really addressed the underlying issues. The underlying issues were: we needed to modernise the club, meet the demands of an elite team in a national competition, focus and align the organisation, build the culture, grow the business, get the recruiting right.

'And then the line goes up again with Northey, then red dot. [In] '96, what happens?'

I don't need to say we finished ninth.

'Now it wasn't the club's fault, they didn't sack him – they created an environment where he felt he had to [walk]. It comes to 2010 and we get to Damien, and up we go [on the graph]. So end of '15, you put a question mark. Where are we?'

Gale thought a one-year extension was a cop-out. He wanted to make a 'strong decision'. A two-year extension to 2018 would give Hardwick the confidence and strength to 'work through any tough situation when it inevitably comes'.

A woman was in charge around the boardroom table now. Peggy O'Neal had been elected president after the first finals series, in 2013. She did not have an inflated view of her position, unlike her headline-seeking male peers at other clubs. She told her board that as directors, they were all equally responsible for the decisions they made.

While Northey was on Gale's mind, the case study that informed O'Neal's thinking was the appointment of the coach before Hardwick, Terry Wallace. It happened before she joined the board, but her understanding was the decision was a 'captain's call' by the management and it was presented to the board for rubber stamping. Wallace was considered one of the game's elite match day coaches, but he chased short-term success at a time when Richmond needed to rebuild. After four and a half seasons without a finals appearance he was shown the door.

O'Neal did not want an ad hoc hiring process or to impose her or Gale's choice on the board. She wanted every director to have their say, and for the decision to be made by consensus. O'Neal saw herself as the chair of the board, not the boss; a distinction understood in the corporate world but that many football clubs still have trouble grasping.

A two-year contract extension to 2018 meant that Hardwick could have a season that did not meet the expectations of the members.

'We asked, "What is going to happen if it goes backwards?"' O'Neal says. The answer was they would stick with Hardwick. 'By taking our time and having several discussions over a number of months, no individual could say, "You misled me, I didn't have all the information, you just pushed this through one day," or, "You just came in and told us what you'd done." This important decision was made by the entire board and we all stood behind it.'

10

THE COACH

Damien Hardwick came to the Tigers via the lucky road of rejection. Richmond was the third job he applied for, following knockbacks from Essendon and Melbourne. If he had been chosen by the Demons or his old club, the Bombers, he might have been fated for scandal instead of a premiership.

Hardwick's résumé was stronger than the applicants who beat him to those other jobs. He had played in premierships under Kevin Sheedy at Essendon in 2000 and Mark Williams at Port Adelaide in 2004, and he was an assistant coach at Hawthorn under Alastair Clarkson.

Essendon had him on their shortlist to replace Sheedy at the end of the 2007 season. Hardwick impressed in his first interview but lost his composure when his computer failed him at his final presentation.

'My understanding is that while he was applying for the job, he wasn't allowed in at Hawthorn,' Essendon's then chief executive, Peter Jackson, revealed. 'They took his computer off him, so he had to borrow one to redo his presentation, because his original one was all on his work computer. I got the impression he was burning the candle at both ends trying to get it going, then on the day, he wasn't familiar with the computer, and it didn't start up properly, and Damien can get a bit annoyed with himself.'

Instead, Essendon hired former Richmond captain Matthew Knights. With his appointment, the sash of boardroom impatience changed from yellow to red; Knights took the Bombers to the finals in his second season as coach, in 2009, but was sacked a year later. Whether Hardwick would have been the better choice is hard to say – Essendon did not have a strong team.

Melbourne was another bullet dodged for Hardwick. He made their coaching shortlist in 2007, but was overlooked for Dean Bailey, who coincidentally had been an assistant at the two premiership teams Hardwick played for, Essendon and Port Adelaide. The Demons had the mad idea that they could best rebuild their playing list by winning no more than four games in 2009, which was the threshold for a bonus number-one pick in the national draft.

The practice was called tanking, and while the AFL concluded that Melbourne 'did not set out to deliberately lose in any matches during the 2009 premiership season', it did find that the club's general manager of football operations, Chris Connolly, and its coach, Dean Bailey, 'had acted in a manner which was prejudicial to the interests of the [game]'. By the time of the finding Bailey was an assistant at Adelaide. He was suspended from coaching for sixteen games.

Hardwick returned to the treadmill of job interviews in 2009. Having added a premiership as an assistant at Hawthorn to his résumé, he was now in a buyer's market. A number of clubs were looking for a coach who had been part of Hawthorn's transformation from basket case to premiership in four seasons. North Melbourne and Port Adelaide were both interested in Hardwick, but Richmond was his plan A, and he won the job a week after his thirty-seventh birthday.

As a player, Hardwick had been a ruthless defender at Essendon and then a calculating midfield pest at Port Adelaide. In the 2002 semi-final, playing for his new team against his old, he provoked a melee before the opening bounce by roughing up his former teammate at the Bombers, Blake Caracella. Hardwick confessed to the AFL tribunal that he had rung his friend ahead of the game to tell him he was 'out to get him'.

He repeated the tactic in the 2004 grand final against Brisbane, goading the Lions into overreaction. Brisbane's Brownlow medallist, Simon Black, one of the fairest players in the game, was subsequently suspended for striking Hardwick.

Sheedy described Hardwick as a baby-faced killer. Before he became a full-time senior footballer, he had worked as a humble teller at the Commonwealth Bank. 'The little old ladies in the bank were happy handing over their money to him, but if they had known what he was doing out on the ground, they would have been shocked.'

His coaching persona was a combination of bank teller and teacher. Brendon Gale tells me that Hardwick loves his statistics – he thinks that Hardwick and I would have an interesting chat. But when I bump into the coach after interviewing Neil Balme at the club, he says he is still considering my interview request. It's not yet six months, but the premiership 'felt like six years ago', Hardwick says, and he is reluctant to talk about it again. Balme encourages him, but Hardwick does have a point. There's little benefit in looking back when his mind has already turned to the coming season.

Later, Hardwick tells a mutual friend who had volunteered a good word for me that he is tired of hearing himself speak about the premiership. After more than three decades in the media, that was a first for me: a public figure who did not want to be interviewed on their greatest professional achievement. It tells me that his ego is in check.

The big question I wanted to ask, from one data nerd to another, was whether he had noticed the moody pattern in his coaching record. Each season contained a long losing streak. I have a theory that he took the losses too personally, that his disposition affected the players, and that it was only after he learned to control that side of his character that he was able to help them win a premiership.

Midway through his first season as coach Hardwick told journalist Rohan Connolly that he found he was too emotionally involved in a game. He was 'the loneliest bloke on the face of the earth' after his first game as coach, against Carlton, ended in a thrashing. 'I remember going to bed that night and I actually felt crook, thinking: "What have I got myself in for?"'

He endured eight more losses before achieving his first win, against Port Adelaide. That victory felt better than any of his three premierships as player and coach. 'That was the best song I've sung. I nearly teared up. It was just so emotional for the players, they'd put in so much hard work, I was so happy for them and to actually get to sing that song. Jeez it's a great song.'

The media consensus was that Richmond would win the wooden spoon in 2010. But once the team got a taste of victory, the rookie coach and his young players drove each other on. As Hardwick's confidence rose, starting in round twelve, Richmond won four games in a row. Among the scalps were two finalists that season, Sydney and Fremantle.

A slow start followed by a revival became the new normal for Richmond. The apotheosis of the Hardwick way came in 2014. That season was divided into equal parts of darkness and light. Ten losses from the first thirteen games before a jaw-dropping run of nine wins in a row. No other side in the game's history has overcome a deficit that large to reach the finals. The 2015 season had a shorter slump and a longer recovery – two wins from the first six games; nine wins from the next ten.

But there were warning signs of the implosion to come. By 2015, Hardwick had become publicly cranky in defeat. 'It was as poor an effort as I've seen from our footy club for a long time,' he said after a loss to the Demons. In previous seasons, he would not give the media the pleasure of knowing when he was upset with his players.

Those conversations remained private. In 2015, he either stopped pretending, or was too angry to bite his tongue.

At three-quarter time in a close game against Greater Western Sydney, he gave his team an old-fashioned spray. At one point he drove an open hand into a player's chest, as if slamming a lectern. It wasn't a punch, but nor was it a blokey slap of encouragement. The tirade inspired a comeback, and perhaps Hardwick rationalised that the tough love was a necessary evil, but the pressure of expectation and Hardwick's response to it was eating away at the bond between the coach and his team.

When the 2015 season ended in that third successive loss in an elimination final, Hardwick exploded at his players in the changing room. 'Never, never, never again,' he yelled.

The first finals defeat, against Carlton in 2013, could be explained by inexperience. The second, against Port Adelaide in 2014, was just one of those things – the players were drained after their nine-match winning streak and Port, playing on their home ground, were simply too good. But the loss to North Melbourne in 2015 could not be excused.

Playing before a crowd of 90 000, Richmond established an early lead, then folded. The shock was in the timidity of the performance. The Kangaroos harassed their younger, more talented opponents, and the Tigers went into their shells.

Among those missing in action was Richmond captain Trent Cotchin. He played the worst game of his career, touching the ball just nine times. His opponent Ben Jacobs had no interest in getting the ball himself; his job was to stop Cotchin. Tagging is an occupational hazard for all elite players, but it is best negotiated collectively, with teammates helping to break the tag by putting themselves between the stalker and their target. But Cotchin had little support on the day. He took responsibility for his performance, but they all shared the blame.

Trent Cotchin joined Richmond as the second pick in the 2007 draft, and by the time Hardwick arrived he had established himself as the team's best player. Cotchin was the youngest to win three best and fairest awards at Richmond and in 2013, at age twenty-two, became the club's youngest captain in more than 100 years.

That record would earn most people a lifetime of hyperbole from the media. But Cotchin polarised football opinion. Many commentators thought he was too nice to lead Richmond. Even within the club, there were some who wondered if he was given the job too soon. Mark Williams, who joined Hardwick at Richmond to be one of his assistant coaches, suggested that Cotchin might play better and have a greater influence on games 'without the responsibility of captaincy'.

Cotchin approached the game with the same intensity as Hardwick had as a player, but without the rule bending. If they had been contemporaries, Hardwick would surely have made a beeline for Cotchin on the field and niggled Mr Clean until he snapped.

But off the field they both led an atypical footballing life. Each man had married young and when training finished they would laugh off the peer pressure to kick on, preferring an evening at home with their families over a night on the town with their teammates. Their bond as coach and captain was like that of father and son and it recalled Tom Hafey's relationship with his three most devoted players, Kevin Bartlett, Francis Bourke and Kevin Sheedy. But they won a premiership at their first attempt, and then three more in the next six years. Hardwick and Cotchin carried the baggage of three finals losses together as coach and captain.

Ahead of the 2016 season, Cotchin's wife Brooke posted a public message of encouragement on her Instagram account. 'Those closest to you know that there are not many people that have values & morals like you have,' she told Trent. 'Let the haters hate because there isn't many people like you out there!'

The hating resumed in round two, after Richmond lost to Collingwood with the last kick of the game. The Tigers had led by 17 points late in the final quarter but made a number of 'cataclysmic mistakes', according to Hardwick. What angered him more, though, was the media's treatment of Cotchin afterwards. He had been Richmond's best player on the night, and would receive a vote in the Brownlow medal for his effort. But he was being judged by the impossible standard of the captain as superhero. The 38 kicks and handballs he garnered were meaningless because he didn't collect the 39th possession that would have saved the game for his team.

'I sit there and am flabbergasted by the criticism he cops,' the coach said of his captain. 'We win a lot of football games because of this bloke, so people need to actually take a deep breath and start to look at some other targets.'

Brooke Cotchin posted a follow-up message after Richmond's third consecutive loss. 'To have to listen to the constant criticism you have had to put up with especially of late has been incredibly hard.'

Former Brisbane Lions captain Jonathan Brown weighed in. 'Our partners and our loved ones, they are there to support you at home, through the tough times, which is great, they do a fantastic job the girls,' Brown said. 'But they need to stay out of it publicly.' Football was a 'man's game' and to see a player defended by his wife added to the perception that Richmond has 'a soft underbelly, sometimes from the leaders'.

This is the charmless side of football; its tedious cult of manhood and relentless search for players to publicly shame for the unpardonable sin of losing. At the time I didn't read the articles about Cotchin because I'd stopped reading newspapers altogether. Going through that commentary now for this book has been disorienting. The majority of the copy was shrill, pedantic and juvenile, and would have shamed even the most callous schoolyard bully.

I don't think the journalists concerned paused to consider the absurdity of their scrutiny. Cotchin hadn't taken drugs, or king hit an opponent, or ignored a young fan seeking an autograph. He wasn't a politician who had broken an election promise or rorted his electoral allowance. He was just the polite captain of a football team that was struggling.

The media pile-on reminded me of something Jeff Kennett had told Michael Gordon for his book on Hawthorn's eleventh premiership, *Playing to Win*. Kennett was explaining the difference between being president of a football club and premier of Victoria.

'[As premier] you spend more money, you've got more levers to pull, the responsibility is greater, but the emotion among the community is almost non-existent. The only time they get upset or have an emotion is when you do something wrong, or sometimes in an election they get excited, but rarely.

'But in a football club, where the size of the finances is miniscule compared to being in office, the emotion is through the roof.'

Neil Balme and Damien Hardwick shared a knowing look during our brief encounter. You wouldn't believe the pressure that envelops a football club after a loss, they told me.

I wouldn't, but I have seen what public and internal pressure does to politicians. It forces the weak and the cynical to adopt positions they don't believe in. But this does not necessarily threaten their career prospects; politicians who compromise their beliefs can still win elections. A footballer or cricketer cannot afford to cut ethical corners in the same way – just ask the Australian test cricketers who were caught ball tampering in South Africa – nor can they pretend to be someone they're not.

Trent Cotchin thought he could deal with the pressure honourably, by ignoring it. But it ate away at him until it threatened his love of the game. 'I think I plummeted without knowing that I'd plummeted after the 2016 season finished,' he told the *Herald Sun*.

'Articles were still being written about me and the club. We'd had a horrible year, we were all in a bit of a freefall.'

A defining moment for Cotchin was the funeral of former president Neville Crowe, who had passed away just six days after the pitiful end to Richmond's 2016 season.

'I think the emotion of Neville's funeral, combined with the emotion surrounding what he did to save the club in the 1990s, plus the difficulty of the season and all the cloudiness about who I was and who I wanted to be, it all just got to me.'

He wondered whether he should give up the captaincy. 'Was I the right fit for the club? I felt as unclear and as uncertain as I had ever been in footy.'

At the funeral, he sought out Damien Hardwick. The two had a long talk and a good cry. 'He threw his arms around me, told me he loved me and would support me.'

In 2016, Damien Hardwick became more distant from his players with each defeat. He delivered laboured old-school rev-ups before games and ranted and raved after them.

The author Konrad Marshall detailed one example in his captivating account of life inside the Richmond Football Club, *Yellow & Black*. The Anzac Eve game against Melbourne in 2016 was to reignite their season. After three losses in a row, Hardwick was adamant that they would not be beaten again.

'You take off the jumper at the end of the game, what do you want it to say? "Whoever wore me today gave everything. No short steps."'

When the players returned to the dressing room having now suffered their fourth consecutive defeat, he wouldn't let his tortured analogy go. The jumper, he said, had delivered its verdict: 'We are weak as piss as a football club.'

Hardwick told Brandon Ellis and Bachar Houli that he loved them but they needed to go harder at the ball. He told

Alex Rance he had played like 'an idiot'; Dustin Martin like a 'school boy'.

'I sit here and I rant and rave and show bravado, but I can't walk down the street tomorrow. I'm embarrassed to don my colours. I never thought I'd say that. Ever! Hat down, sunglasses on – you should never feel that.'

Four defeats in a row became six in a row before Richmond finally snapped its losing streak with a stirring after-the-siren win against Sydney. That inspired a brief run of five wins in six games. But the Tigers were too far behind to make a serious charge at the top eight and their final position of thirteenth on the ladder was the lowest since Hardwick's first year as coach.

If the team had remained competitive throughout the season, the media might have accepted the spin that this was just a hiccup. But as the season reached its insipid denouement, the players appeared to give up. Two games in particular drew the ire of the members – an 88-point surrender against Greater Western Sydney in Canberra and a 113-point annihilation by the Sydney Swans at the SCG in the final round.

After the game against the Giants, Kevin Bartlett used his soapbox at Melbourne radio station SEN to warn that Richmond faced an existential crisis. 'Such a pathetic performance has now put everyone at the club on notice. For it was an effort that could kill off the coach, it could kill off the board, kill off recruiting managers, kill off assistant coaches and kill off members.'

After the end of the regular season, a challenge to overthrow Peggy O'Neal's board was indeed launched. The timing ensured that the media would continue to feast on the Tigers even though they were not playing in the finals.

The rebel group featured two former premiership players, Bruce Monteath, who had captained the 1980 premiership team, and Bryan Wood, who had been one of the big three to leave the club after the 1982 grand final.

'We are thirty-five years into a five-year plan. People laugh at it but unfortunately it's true,' Monteath said.

The leaders of the coup wanted to know what Hardwick's game plan was. They didn't want to sack him immediately, because it would have been too expensive to pay out the final two years of his contract, but they couldn't guarantee his job beyond the 2017 season. In fact, Hardwick was referred to as a 'dead man walking'. They criticised the club's recruiting record, but they wanted to keep Brendan Gale.

It was a confused pitch. *The Australian*'s Patrick Smith described it as the 'most inept bid for power in AFL history'. But the rebels did reflect the reaction of many members who were prepared to cut their losses with Hardwick and start again with a new coach. O'Neal received a number of tetchy messages to that end, urging her to leave the country 'and take Damien with you'.

At Richmond's best-and-fairest award function, Hardwick told the members that good clubs don't fracture after one bad season. 'You need to trust our leaders in Brendon and Peggy and make sure we back them up at every opportunity,' he said. They were 'two of the best administrators' he had seen in his time in football.

O'Neal addressed the challenge indirectly by vowing to avoid the mistakes of the past. 'Should we start making reactionary decisions based purely on emotion? Clearly not,' she said. 'We surely have matured as a club and we can't let anger and finger-pointing define our future. We must be in this together – it's the only way.'

O'Neal and Gale stared down the challenge and the rebels eventually withdrew. The AFL breathed a little easier. As one senior AFL figure had been telling O'Neal, 'it would not be a good look if the first female president was rolled like Julia [Gillard]'.

Any previous Richmond administration would have imploded in these circumstances. Any contemporary political party would have knifed their leader and reshuffled their frontbench. But O'Neal and Gale conducted themselves like politicians from another age.

They were more Bob Hawke than Graeme Richmond. They gathered evidence, sought advice, waited for it to be delivered, took time to consider their response and had a united board behind them. They were not panicked by the media coverage, or the Richmond members.

Gale says he learned to detach himself from the emotion of the game. It wasn't easy to let go. As a young player 'I thought everything mattered, that every week mattered'. But a decade on the field, and another decade and a half off it, had taught him the power of patience. 'What really helps is having a board that is exceptional, and committed to the machinery and process of good governance. The commitment to a process is liberating.'

Gale had commissioned a review of the club's football department midway through the 2016 season. Had he waited until the end of the season, when the media was baying for blood, he would have been forced to make policy on the run. Instead, he was able to consider a restructure at his own preferred pace. This proved critical for the next season. The coach and the players could prepare for 2017 without the disruptions of seasons past when Richmond was breaking in new presidents, board members, and coaches.

The key structural announcements from the review were the appointment of Neil Balme to run the football department alongside Dan Richardson and a turnover of the assistant coaches working under Hardwick. Mark Williams was the highest profile departure. Among the new arrivals were Hardwick's former teammate and sparring partner Blake Caracella, who had been an assistant coach at Geelong, and Justin Leppitsch, who returned to Richmond as an assistant after three unsuccessful seasons as senior coach at Brisbane. They brought a fresh perspective to the club, informed by success. Caracella's résumé was as impressive as Hardwick's – a premiership alongside Hardwick at Essendon, another at Brisbane under Leigh Matthews, and a premiership at

Geelong as assistant coach. Leppitsch had played in Brisbane's three consecutive premierships in the early 2000s.

But the most important part of the review was the frank private conversation it allowed O'Neal and Gale to have with Hardwick. 'We were able to provide considered but direct feedback to Damien, and he was able to take that from a position of trust and support. However, to be fair, Damien had already arrived at some of the same conclusions himself,' Gale tells me. The discussion was constructive because the coach knew his job was safe. Helping him become a better coach was in everyone's interest.

O'Neal says Hardwick understood that he had to get better at teaching and listening. 'He had that in some aspects of his life, but he wasn't bringing it here.'

She says nothing prepares a coach for the big job. 'When you become more responsible, in any field, the people part is always the hardest part. What you're trained to do, what you love to do and what attracted you to that vocation is only a small part of what you do in the end. The rest of it is getting everyone happy to work, and making sure you have standards.'

Gale says Hardwick increasingly shut himself off from his players in 2016. He sought certainty in the data, and in more elaborate game plans. It was his default response to pressure: work harder. During the losing streak he consumed the statistics, watched and re-watched the clips from the last week's defeat and studied the form of the coming opponent. When he began coaching he had promised his players he would keep the door open, and while it technically still was, his body language said 'I'm too busy'. He realised he had lost himself in the detail and alienated the players with his anxiety.

'He learned the most important thing about coaching and leadership is getting people to follow you,' says Gale. 'And that's engagement, that's emphasis on authentic relationships, all those things that are often uncertain.'

It was a message he had already heard at home in 2016. His wife Danielle told him: 'You've changed, you're not the guy that I married.' She wanted her happy-go-lucky husband back.

Gale explains that players no longer accept the aggressive style of coaching that he and Hardwick grew up with. That coach had been an authority figure, and he governed by yelling because that's how it was always done. Today's players are less deferential. They still want to be led, but they expect the coach to relate to them, to explain himself and to respect their opinions. They crave connection with the coach.

One of the first AFL coaches to empower his players was Neil Balme at Melbourne in the 1990s. At the time the knock on Balme was that he was too soft and his failure to secure a premiership with the Demons was seen as a repudiation of his approach. The successful coaches in that decade were the most demanding – Mick Malthouse at the West Coast Eagles, Denis Pagan at North Melbourne, Malcolm Blight at Adelaide and Kevin Sheedy at Essendon.

Balme sees empathy as a simple matter of football logic. 'I don't think I was too soft, but it's very easy to be over-demanding,' he says. 'I understand the guy who is going for the ball is in charge of your destiny [as a coach], so you've got to empower him somehow, because he's got all the responsibility. You need him to want to do it for the right reasons, you need him to want to do it for you.'

He says it is even more important now to treat players with respect because they have been raised to question authority.

'They don't demand it, but they kind of expect it. They would never quite know how to express that to you. [But] if you treat them without respect, all it does is smash them. If you smash them, they won't feel good about themselves, and if you don't feel good about yourself you won't play good footy. It's a very challenging game. Physically it's demanding. Mentally it's demanding.'

The other reason the players need to be treated with respect is the game requires their full-time attention. When he played in the

1970s, football was important, but it was still just a game. Players still worked full-time jobs elsewhere and the clubs were essentially volunteer organisations, with only a handful of paid staff.

When Balme coached Melbourne in the 1990s, he had three full-time employees in the football department. At Richmond today, he runs a football department with thirty people working under him.

'Footy hasn't changed, the other stuff has. But the challenge for the players, [when] they have to commit full-time to footy, [is] how do you manage the rest of their lives?'

But no one ever won a premiership through empathy – until 2016.

While the Tigers were working out how to help Hardwick become a better coach, the Western Bulldogs were rewriting the rules for footballing success. That was the other big question I wanted to ask Hardwick: what did he learn from Luke Beveridge, the coach who had inspired his young players to an improbable, romantic premiership the year before Richmond's?

The Bulldogs were not the most talented team that year, but they were the most unified. They chased, tackled and ran with the ball with a sustained intensity not seen before. Their game plan wasn't violent, but it was physical. More skilled, more experienced sides were exhausted by the frenzied pressure applied by the Bulldog pack.

Every coach watches the trophy presentation at the end of a grand final and wishes it was them. They could not have helped noticing that Beveridge had broken the mould. He gave his medal to his injured captain, Bob Murphy, and took a step back to allow Murphy to raise the premiership cup with the playing captain, Easton Wood. On Beveridge's face was the satisfied grin of a parent watching two children graduate.

Beveridge had told author Martin Flanagan that none of the coaches he played under had really influenced him. 'I don't think any of them had the full package.' But he did have a soft spot for

John Northey, who had coached him at Melbourne. 'He recognised the importance of the emotional side of the game. We played for Swooper because we loved him. Some part of every player plays for the coach.'

For his part, Bob Murphy explicitly drew a link between the Bulldogs and Tigers when reflecting on the game's recent history in a newspaper column previewing the 2018 season. He wrote that in 2016 Beveridge started a cultural shift in the game and Hardwick 'rammed it home' in 2017.

'These teams have displayed a new kind of masculinity, a tenderness and affection that we haven't seen before in our game. Words like vulnerability and mindfulness are all of a sudden not just hip, but seemingly important cogs in the quest for victory. This is a radical change.'

Beveridge did it this way from the outset. Hardwick had to change himself before he could become a premiership coach, while Trent Cotchin had to learn to be himself to become a premiership captain.

One of the keys to Richmond's resurgence had been there all along, but it was missed in the meltdown of 2016. In 2014, when the team had tumbled to sixteenth on the ladder, Damien Hardwick decided to release the handbrake. 'Just go and play,' was his message to his team. They won the next nine games. He still had a game plan for them to follow, but he wanted them to enjoy themselves.

In their summer of self-analysis in 2016–17, Hardwick and Cotchin, their friendship further strengthened by their heart-to-heart at Neville Crowe's funeral, accepted that they had been the problem. They promised the team they'd make amends. The coach would strip back the game plan to make football fun again. The captain would stop being a killjoy.

In previous seasons, Cotchin would frown if the players

celebrated too hard after a win. He did not want them to get ahead of themselves. Now, he would join in. 'I've realised it's okay to be happy about winning,' he wrote. '[It's] a game after all. We should enjoy it, we should have fun with our mates.'

Cotchin had an unexpected boost to his self-esteem in December 2016. He was retroactively awarded the 2012 Brownlow medal as Essendon captain Jobe Watson was stripped of the honour following his involvement in the supplements scandal. Although the circumstances were awkward, Cotchin decided to embrace his retrospective success.

In the 2017 season, Cotchin changed his game. He tackled, crashed into opposition midfielders and hunted the ball. He had never been a selfish player, but that year he became totally selfless. Indicative of his new approach was his vow to help his friend Dustin Martin win a Brownlow medal as well.

Hardwick and Cotchin shared a mentor, former Nike executive Ben Crowe, and through their discussions the coach and the captain learned not only to accept their imperfections as human beings but to share those insights with the group. Honesty, they would discover, increases a leader's authority by securing the trust and respect of the team.

Hardwick had been encouraged by the club to take a short leadership course at Harvard University. He returned for pre-season training with an idea to create a unique connection across the team; one that would mirror the connection O'Neal and Gale had already established across the club's administration. The players were asked to get up before the group, one at a time, and offer examples from their lives of a hero, a period of hardship and a highlight. Hardwick went first and reflected on his love for his wife and his parents. Cotchin was next and he shared his vulnerabilities.

The players responded to the honesty of their leaders by opening up about their own experiences. It had a transformative effect on the group.

Brandon Ellis spoke of his father's fight with cancer, the shame of growing up poor and being bullied at school, and the day he was drafted by Richmond. Bachar Houli revealed how the birth of his daughter made him appreciate his own parents, and urged his teammates to ring their mothers and tell them they loved them. Jack Riewoldt, inspired by the coach's honesty, discussed the grief in his life, including the recent death of his cousin Maddie. Nick Vlaustin talked about his Dutch grandfather who had been a prisoner of war at Changi and had worked on the Burma railway.

'To see the head coach, who always seems so tough and so strong, talk about his family and show that he's vulnerable really opened my eyes,' Vlaustin said later.

In a single pre-season the Tigers had changed from the old Australian sporting value of stoic mateship to genuine brotherly love. Brendon Gale says the younger players drove that cultural change at the club. 'You and I had silent fathers. Put your head down, do your job. These kids are very now. They have all this information at their fingertips. They are less anchored. They crave connection, they crave intimacy. They are more tactile.'

Every club has its nice guys. Richmond was uniquely positioned to harness their talent with a female president, a chief executive who did not court attention or play backroom games, and a coach and captain who were solid family men. No other club had had this combination before.

If I were to summarise why this Richmond premiership team was special in a young footballer–friendly tweet, I'd write: 'A woman in charge, a coach who hugs and a playing list that is drawn from every corner of Australia.'

Hardwick also learned to share power. He allowed his new assistants to devise a more aggressive, less complicated game plan for the team. The old method had involved slow, considered ball movement – when the team's confidence was low, the mistakes were excruciating to watch. The new method was based around defence first, but with a licence to run once Richmond got the ball. The revolutionary aspect of the game plan was the reliance on small, speedy forwards to trap the ball in Richmond's attacking half.

Hardwick scrapped the macho pre-match speeches in favour of storytelling. Before the Anzac Round rematch against Melbourne in 2017, he didn't implore them to play for the jumper; he told a dad joke. He confessed that he couldn't beat his seventeen-year-old daughter when they played Connect Four because her strategy was to block every move he made.

'It drives me insane,' he said. 'Deny, deny, deny. That's all she does. So, Dad gets frustrated. Dad makes a shit move. Dad loses. She goes in with a defensive mindset and she either wins – or has a draw. With my offensive mindset, I either win – or lose.'

He teased out the analogy to explain the plan for the night. They would pressure the slick Demons until they made a mistake, then punish them on the counterattack. And that is how it played out.

The game was emblematic of the early part of the 2017 season, when Richmond won without necessarily playing well. The Demons had established a 23-point lead late in the third quarter. In previous seasons that might have been enough to break the Tigers, but Richmond came back with 5 unanswered goals in the final quarter. In the end they won comfortably by 13 points. It was their fifth victory in a row, their best start to a season since 1995.

On the only previous occasion that Hardwick's Richmond opened a season with consecutive wins, in 2013, the three victories were promptly offset by three defeats. This time, the pendulum had further to swing back, and the public was transfixed by the repetition of misery. Richmond lost four in a row between rounds six and nine. It was a masterclass in suffering as the players explored every angle of defeat. Comedian Wil Anderson coined a new term to describe what was now a familiar pattern of false hope followed by a letdown: 'Richmondy'.

The first loss of the season was a routine 76-point thrashing, to Adelaide, the top team. The second – an unlucky 5-point defeat to the reigning premier, the Western Bulldogs – could almost be called honourable. Then it went pear-shaped. The ghost of fadeouts past was calling to Richmond. Having clawed back a big deficit, they lost to lowly Fremantle following a goal after the siren, then blew a big lead against Greater Western Sydney when a last-minute Tigers goal was ruled out by the video umpire. The combined margin of the last three defeats had only been 10 points. The epitome of Richmondy.

But Hardwick had no intention of repeating the mistake of 2016 by 'laying the boots' into his players. Privately he told his players that he was proud of them and that he trusted them to learn from their losses.

Neil Balme observed the coach's fatherly optimism. 'That could have derailed the whole year but at no stage during those [losses] did he waver from his belief in front of the players. Easy to lose [that belief], but he didn't. Also some coaches bullshit the players, but they would have seen through it.'

They responded with wins against Essendon and North Melbourne.

When the Tigers then dropped another game after leading big, against Sydney, Hardwick was again philosophical. 'We're very competitive. We'll keep the games close,' he said. 'We're not going to win games by 10 goals, we're not going to lose games – hopefully – by 10 goals.'

Former Tigers coach Danny Frawley accused his old team of choking. 'Every coach in the competition would love to play Richmond in a final at the moment because [of] their mental disintegration.' But what commentators could not see was that steps had already been taken to retrain the muscle that had previously failed the players under pressure – the brain.

11

DARING TO DREAM

The other key that was waiting to be turned in 2017 was mindfulness. A small but influential number of players had been training individually with mindfulness expert Emma Murray. They could measure the resulting improvement on the field with more possessions and more kilometres covered on game day. Defender Dylan Grimes was the first to work with her, in 2015, and he encouraged others to follow his lead. By 2016, Murray was helping the team's best player, Dustin Martin, but not the captain or his deputies.

Past premiership teams had used hypnosis or meditation to gain a competitive edge over their rivals. The most notable examples were Ron Barassi's North Melbourne in 1975 and Tony Jewell's Richmond in 1980. For decades, individual players practised mindfulness without realising it. Kevin Bartlett would visualise a game before he played it. On the eve of the 1980 grand final, he stepped into his backyard with a football in his hand and for an hour he imagined all the passages of play he would be involved in. 'I snapped goals, I threw the ball on the ground and picked it up as though I was roving off the packs. I took set shots,' he recalled.

'It may sound strange, but some of the things I visualised the night before happened in the grand final.'

But the idea of training the mind in an organised way was too exotic for most clubs. In this respect, football lagged behind other sports. From golf and tennis to basketball and even rugby league, individuals and teams had been including some form of mind coaching in their training schedule since the 1980s.

What prompted Richmond to make mindfulness a compulsory part of its regime were those three losses to the Bulldogs, Dockers and Giants in 2017.

'You don't lose three games by less than a kick if it's a physical problem,' Murray tells me. She had conducted sessions with the entire playing group ahead of the 2017 season, but once the season itself began players were given the choice to continue working with her or do their own thing. 'But those who really needed it were not knocking on the door.'

Following the loss to the Giants, she had a frank meeting with Neil Balme. He thought the club was already committed to her program, but she explained that it had slipped out of the schedule. Balme decided to put it back in. From now on, Murray would meet two times a week with all the players, first to review the game they had just played and, later in the week, to prepare for the next opponent.

When she first spoke to Grimes in 2015 Murray assumed he was ready for the many layers and concepts of mindfulness. Although the defender was an eager student, Murray realised that teaching young athletes to become masters of mindfulness was too ambitious. Their goal was to become better footballers, so she adapted her program to their needs. 'I had to evolve to design mental strategies and tools to help them play better football.'

Murray didn't create the connection between the coach, the captain and the playing group – that was Damien Hardwick's initiative. But she helped to reinforce it. Her twice-weekly sessions taught players how to recognise when they lost focus in a game and how to reclaim it.

'The two big things that will take you out of flow is fear of failure and focus on outcomes.'

The post-game reviews became sophisticated exercises in taming their demons.

'They were sharing, talking to each other about "When I went to fear of failure, when I went to focus on outcomes." "What took me there, what did I feel like there, how did I get back out?"'

'They were getting better as individuals by shining a light on this stuff as a group. They were learning each other's stuff so they could help each other on-field and become stronger as a unit.'

She cites the example of Grimes and his two backline colleagues, David Astbury and Alex Rance. 'Those three guys have higher emotional intelligence than most guys in the AFL, and that is just random that those three guys ended up together. Bringing three of them together can be very heated. But it can also mean they are three people who want to work it out and make it work. If every marriage worked like those three . . .' She laughs before summarising their approach: 'They put their shit on the table and they clear it; they put their shit on the table and they clear it.'

The Tigers might have won the premiership without Murray, but they would not have won it in the same compelling manner, as a band of twenty-two loving brothers.

'What we learned from Richmond,' she says, 'and it's so applicable to politics and business – you think what wins is the concrete thing that you are doing. In AFL they think what wins is being fitter, being stronger, being better with the ball.' But she argues that there is little room for substantial improvement on the physical side of the game. Where Richmond gained a significant advantage was in the area that had been viewed as a weakness, the mental side of their game.

'Mindfulness isn't about being soft, it's about being present,' Murray says. 'By no means does Richmond avoid tough conversations, or accountability or anything like that. It's just not [done] in a fashion that sends us as a human into that shutdown, survival mode.'

The fadeout against Sydney didn't trigger a second losing streak, nor did the team snap into premiership-winning form. The highs and lows of the past, the tantalising wins and the season-ending losses, had been replaced by a stability that was very out of character for Richmond. All year Hardwick had told the players he wanted them to come to work each day at Punt Road 'with a smile and walk away with a smile'. Not dwelling on the defeats, but not getting too comfortable after the wins either.

They won their next two matches against Carlton and Port Adelaide, then suffered their second thrashing of the season against St Kilda. After fifteen games, the Tigers sat sixth on the ladder with nine wins and six losses. Previous Richmond teams coached by Gieschen, Frawley and Wallace had fallen to ninth from similar positions. Previous Hardwick teams had missed the top four.

But this team was writing its own history. Apparent setbacks were being seen as opportunities for experimentation. All year, Hardwick and his assistants searched for a tall forward to replace the injured Ben Griffiths. As the game plan gelled, they realised they didn't need a second big man alongside Jack Riewoldt. In fact, an extra small forward would increase the anxiety levels of opposition defenders and make Richmond even quicker across the ground. Without a second tall forward, the ruckman Toby Nankervis would be relieved by midfielder Shaun Grigg, who was too short to seriously contest a ball up.

No other team, not even the 2016-model Bulldogs, had broken with tradition to this extent. And none of the teams Richmond met in the finals could cope with this game plan. They were still playing an older, more lumbering version of football.

Genuine innovation in team sports is rare. The old VFL had just two transformative moments that forever changed the way the game was played. In 1902, Collingwood developed the first organised system of play. It began with the accidental discovery of the stab pass: a low, skimming kick that players could use to deliver the ball to a teammate who had run into an empty space on the field, thus avoiding a contest with an opponent. The Magpies stormed to the premiership that year, losing just one of the ten games they played under their new method. Teams have been using short passes ever since.

The next revolutionary change came in the 1970 grand final, when Ron Barassi told his Carlton players to handball at all costs. The Blues were trailing Collingwood by 44 points at half time and the effect of the new game plan was seismic. Carlton staged the greatest premiership comeback the game had ever seen to win the grand final by 10 points. With this shift, the handball became as important as the kick.

Richmond's breakthrough in 2017 was to reverse the positions on the field. The forward line attacked by defending. When Jack Riewoldt flew in marking contests he would often deliberately knock the ball to the ground to create opportunities for his smaller, speedier teammates. Through fierce tackling the forwards trapped the ball in their half of the ground, until one of their party broke free to shoot for goal.

It remains to be seen whether the Tigers have fundamentally altered the game in the manner of that early Collingwood side and Barassi's Carlton. But other clubs will have noticed that the creativity in the game plan was part of a larger story of transformation at every level of the club. Richmond had taught itself to think with the non-male side of its brain and validated one of my pet theories of public life: the next big improvement in the operation of government and business will come by unleashing true diversity. With women in positions of authority and with leaders prepared to share power, Richmond put itself in a position to win its first premiership in thirty-seven years.

The media finally noticed that the Tigers might be building to a premiership when they hosted the Giants at the MCG in round eighteen. Coincidentally, I had been invited onto the ABC's *Grandstand* radio program before the game. Nathan Burke, the St Kilda champion, thought I was crazy to suggest the Tigers might go all the way. My argument was that the season had been unusually even. No team stood out, and of the likely finalists, Richmond had been the most consistent team all season.

I wasn't there for my opinion. Every week, they asked a non-football person in the public eye to talk about their life as a supporter. I was serving in a dual capacity as fan and interviewer, because the special guest was Julia Gillard.

It was a nasty, wet Sunday afternoon. I watched the first quarter from the members' area and felt a shudder of embarrassment as the Giants kicked 3 goals while the Tigers never looked like scoring. I walked around to the Ponsford Stand at quarter time to meet up with Mum and my brother-in-law. After a brief consultation, we agreed we'd leave early if the Giants smashed us. I had long lost my innocent insistence of staying until the end. We spoke too soon, because Richmond was just about to start its roll. We kicked 8 of the next 9 goals and were 27 points in front at three-quarter time.

Earlier in the year, the Giants had pinched the game from a similar position. On this sodden afternoon, there was a small wobble but no collapse. *The Age* declared that 'this was the type of win in torrid conditions from which real belief is built'. The significance for the season was that Richmond was back in the top four, where it would be assured of a double chance.

Revenge against the Giants was part of a four-match winning streak going into round twenty. The Tigers had still not figured out how to kick big scores, but they were only one more loss away from cracking that code too. All year they improvised, all year they promised to learn more from their defeats – a 14-point loss against Geelong in round twenty-one proved to be the final blessing. Richmond midfielder and forward Josh Caddy suffered a minor injury and would miss the last two matches of the home and away season. He was replaced by Jacob Townsend, who proved to be a revelation.

In its previous thirteen victories, Richmond's average winning margin had only been 26 points; in only four of those had they scored more than 100 points. In his first senior game of the season, Townsend kicked 6 goals against Fremantle, contributing to a 104-point winning margin. The next round, against St Kilda, he kicked 5 goals, and Richmond won by 41 points.

A latecomer to football, Townsend was the unlikeliest piece in the premiership puzzle. He grew up playing rugby league in the southern New South Wales town of Leeton before switching to football when he was thirteen. Drafted by the Giants ahead of their inaugural season in 2012, he was delisted after four underwhelming years at the club. Richmond picked him up in the 2015 draft to add strength to the midfield that had failed to handle the pressure of North Melbourne in that elimination final. But Townsend could not secure a regular spot in the senior team in 2016 and, with a year left on his contract in 2017, remade himself in the VFL as a defensive forward who could kick straight. All year he waited for a chance to prove himself. When it came, he exceeded everyone's expectations, including his own. The 11 goals he scored in the final two games of the regular season came from just 19 kicks. Not very Richmondy at all.

Every premiership team needs an element of luck to complement its good management. Richmond's good fortune was to play its opening final against Geelong at the MCG, even though the Cats had finished higher on the ladder. But Geelong's home ground was ruled out by the AFL because it was too small for the crowd of 95 000. The advantage of playing at the MCG was multiplied by

Richmond's supporter base. The Tigers had 18 000 more members than the Cats and on the night it felt as if Richmond's collective voice was twice as loud as Geelong's.

Pushing against these propitious breaks was the baggage. Richmond had not beaten Geelong since 2006, and the last time the two sides had met at the MCG, in the 2016 season, the Tigers surrendered a 35-point lead at three-quarter time to lose by 4 points. Add the layers of doubt from those three consecutive elimination final defeats and Richmond went into the game as the underdog. The *Herald Sun* published the tips from thirty experts and celebrities, and the count was nineteen to eleven in Geelong's favour. The Richmond tally was inflated by the tips of Trent Cotchin and Kevin Bartlett, who predicted a 67-point winning margin for the Tigers.

The game opened with a goal to Townsend after just two minutes of play. Damien Hardwick identified a moment in that first quarter that assured him his players were united. '[Richmond's] Brandon Ellis and [Geelong's] Patrick Dangerfield came together in a huge collision,' he said after the game. 'Patty gets a pat on the bum from one of his teammates. Seven guys come to Brandon Ellis [to congratulate and encourage him]. That's the love and the unity that our team had for each other.'

The game was low scoring, but it remained Richmond's to lose. Two late goals to Geelong just before half time reduced the margin to 9 points. The Cats sensed a momentum shift and in the third quarter they launched a fierce counterattack. The old Richmond would have panicked, but this team revelled in the challenge. Geelong launched raid after raid, but the bombardment yielded just 1 goal.

The core of this epic contest was between four men – the respective captains and superstars of each team. Trent Cotchin and Dustin Martin versus Geelong's skipper Joel Selwood and the reigning Brownlow medallist Patrick Dangerfield. Often they travelled in pairs. Either the captain extracted the ball from the thicket of bodies and passed it off to the superstar, or the superstar got it himself and lit up the stadium with a locomotive run towards the goal.

One of the notable differences between the two teams was how the Richmond players repeatedly mobbed Dangerfield, while Geelong could not contain Martin. Late in the third quarter, both teams exchanged quick goals. With only seconds remaining, Martin followed the play into the Geelong forward line. When the ball came to him he missed the mark but instinctively pulled the ball back to him like a yo-yo. With the ball tucked under his right arm, Martin used his free left hand to push off his Geelong opponent like a skateboarder launching off a ramp. The crowd exploded as he took one bounce, then a second. He whipped a kick to Jack Riewoldt who swung the ball into the goal square. Waiting to receive the pass was Dion Prestia, who had run half the length of the ground. Prestia marked the ball, turned, and dribbled the easiest, most emphatic goal of the final.

As the siren sounded to end the third quarter, Richmond was 13 points ahead. When the players walked back to their huddles, all eyes were on Martin. He straightened his back and puffed his chest. I learned later that this was one of the routines he had developed with Emma Murray to maintain focus in a game.

The trust between the Richmond players is what made these passages of play so engrossing. They blocked and they pushed until Geelong surrendered the ball. When one of the Tigers emerged with ball in hand, his teammates switched to attack mode, running ahead of the play to where they expected the ball to go.

Richmond's final winning margin was 51 points, with Cotchin and Martin leading the way. Neil Balme was surprised at how good Richmond had become. I ask him for a highlight of the finals series and he recalls the teamwork. 'There would be three minutes [of play] of us not getting it, but crashing in, crashing in, causing this, causing that, and then someone [finally] gets a kick.'

He knew Geelong well, with three premierships at the club as an administrator. But he couldn't believe how impotent Richmond made them look. 'They had ten chances to go forward, and we just wouldn't let them go forward. It was really quite amazing.'

Brendon Gale had been a jumble of nerves before the game. 'This was the team that had tormented us,' he tells me. His three children were seated in a separate section of the ground, while he was being hosted by the AFL and their A-list guests. As the lead blew out in the final quarter, his wife Jane checked whether it was safe to bring their son and two daughters to watch the last minutes with him. 'Yes, we're home,' he told her. When the family were reunited, the eldest daughter, who was normally ambivalent about football, was 'bawling her eyes out'. 'We won!' she screamed to her father.

With the monkey of the first final off his back, Damien Hardwick reset his expectations for the season, from making the finals to winning the premiership; from thirteenth in 2016 to first in 2017. The club's new mantra became 'Why not us?'

The preliminary final against Greater Western Sydney was more free-wheeling, but it followed a similar outline to the Geelong game: early goals to Richmond, a counterattack from the Giants, followed by a tug of war until the Tigers broke their opponent and started scoring at will. Against the Cats, the Tigers had to wait until the last quarter before the game opened up for them. Against the Giants, the avalanche began at the midpoint of the third quarter. Four goals in fifteen minutes secured a 31-point lead by the end of the quarter. A stadium-rocking goal to Martin in the opening minute of the final quarter settled the issue. The teams swapped goals for the remainder of the match and the Tigers won by 36 points.

Once victory was beyond doubt, Hardwick brought four key players to the bench as a safeguard against a late injury. He had done the same thing against Geelong. The irreplaceable quartet were

Cotchin, Martin, the ruckman Toby Nankervis and the defender Alex Rance.

The difference between the Richmond of 2017 and all the Richmonds of the previous thirty-six seasons – teams that had lost finals, or finished ninth, or won the wooden spoon – was the sense of fun in the playing group.

'In grand final week we had blokes saying "Shit, I hope this doesn't finish,"' Neil Balme says.

Damien Hardwick told the players to embrace every aspect of the week, from Dustin Martin's Brownlow medal victory on the Monday night to the grand final parade on the Friday. There was no point pretending that this was just another ordinary week in their lives as footballers. Better to enjoy each moment in its own right and move on to the next event, the next team meeting, the next training session.

Emma Murray says this approach helped the players maintain their focus. 'All year the Richmond guys were working on being present and in the game. In grand final week there are lot of things pulling our attention in other directions. "That's okay," we said. "Normalise it."'

The last time Richmond failed in a final, against North Melbourne in 2015, a number of players had woken up on the morning of the game with 'heavy legs'. Back then, the group had no common language to address their nerves.

'They were locked away in their own prison freaking out about it, thinking it's not going to be a good day today, it's going to be hard work,' Murray says. 'Come 2017, that was put on the table, everyone knew why it happened, and how to get out of it. No player went missing in the grand final.'

For his pre-game address, Hardwick took his players to the summit of Mount Everest. He told them they were on the

Hillary Step, the place where more people lose their lives than any other part of the climb, because they take their eyes off their feet.

'You're on the Hillary Step with 40 feet to go. The summit is there, but we know to do it we've got to walk each individual foot to get us up to the summit. We don't ever take our eyes off our feet.' He would use this analogy to maintain their focus throughout the game. Thirty steps to go at quarter time, twenty at half, ten at three-quarter time.

He reminded them of their journey to the grand final. 'We know what's made us a great football club this year, and it's the ability to work for each other, it's embracing the imperfection of who we are. I love what you've done, I'm so proud of you.'

He told them they deserved to be there. 'Everyone from pillar to post has said you can't do it. You're not tall enough. You've got no forward line. You're too young. We've proven most of them wrong thus far. Our goal is silverware but our expectation is we embrace who we are. We are quick, we are powerful, we celebrate what we do and enjoy it.'

The result was already written on the faces of the two teams as they took their positions for the national anthem. Both sets of players were suitably earnest. The Tigers formed one chain, with each player linked to their teammate with an arm over a shoulder or around the waist. The Crows stood side by side like Dr Who Cybermen. The Adelaide players maintained their rigid formation for an extra ten seconds after the song had finished. A united team facing a team of perfectionists.

The only discernible difference between the grand final and Richmond's two previous finals was the timing of the Tigers' first surge. After a fumbled first quarter, which Adelaide won by 9 points, Richmond wrested control of the game in what had previously been its weakest quarter, the second. The Tigers kicked 4 unanswered goals to take a 9-point lead into half time.

The first ten minutes of the third quarter decided the game. Goals to Jack Graham, Shaun Grigg and Kane Lambert came in exhilarating succession. Adelaide captain Taylor Walker interrupted the party with a goal midway through the quarter, but Richmond replied with another run of goals – 2 at the end of the third quarter and another 2 to open the fourth. In just under an hour of play, Richmond had scored a thumping 11 goals and 5 behinds to Adelaide's solitary goal and 7 behinds.

Few teams in the game's history have dominated a grand final in this way, with destructive continuity of play across quarters. The half-time and three-quarter time breaks did not disrupt Richmond's concentration or allow Adelaide to regroup. During the regular season, Adelaide had been the team that scored goals quickly, while Richmond scratched out narrow victories. The Crows didn't suddenly lose their form in the grand final; their first quarter was promising. But their slick game plan, which relied on clean movement of the ball, crumbled under Richmond's wall of united pressure.

The final ten minutes of the game were a blur of tears. After Dan Butler's cheeky banana kick extended Richmond's lead to 46 points, the camera caught Brendon Gale crying, and then sharing a triumphal embrace with his children. Gale's old teammate Matthew Richardson, now a boundary rider for the Seven Network's commentary team, was also sobbing.

The final winning margin of 48 points was not quite a thrashing. But it concluded the most dominant display in a final series by any team since Kevin Sheedy's Essendon in 2000, which, coincidentally, Hardwick and his assistant coach Blake Caracella had played for together. In twelve quarters of finals football against Geelong, GWS and Adelaide – three teams that had beaten Richmond in the home and away rounds – the Tigers kicked 44 goals and 38 behinds. Their opponents scored exactly half as many goals in total, 22, and 35 behinds.

After the players had received their medals, and sung the club song, the twenty-two who had won the grand final linking arms with the rest of the playing group, Hardwick spoke to them like a gushing fan. 'The manic nature of the way you played the game, it's just so exciting,' he said. '[You] guys can have your thing tonight, all your celebrations – I'm going home to watch the tape.'

It would be a mistake to think that Richmond discovered how to win a premiership suddenly. At one level, the horror of 2016 provided the perspective and motivation for 2017. By backing Hardwick, Brendon Gale and Peggy O'Neal created a golden thread of confidence throughout the club.

'The courage that Brendon and Peggy instilled in Damien meant Damien could instil belief in the players after those [narrow] losses [earlier in the season],' Emma Murray says.

But premiership clubs aren't built by a single year's epiphany. 'This has been five or six years of shared struggle, of trial and error, but all the time strengthening unity and trust,' Gale says.

The turnover in the playing list supports that idea, with a rebuild followed by a major renovation between 2010 and 2017. Of the forty-four players that Hardwick began with in 2010, only eighteen were still on the list when Richmond made its first finals series under him in 2013. And only nineteen of the players from that 2013 list remained at the start of the 2017 season.

Of twenty-two who played in the grand final, only four had been at the club before Hardwick became coach – the defender Alex Rance, the midfielders Trent Cotchin and Shane Edwards, and the full forward Jack Riewoldt.

The premiership team that Hardwick assembled contained two distinct groups – eight players who were brought into the club in the first phase of the rebuild between the 2010 and 2013 drafts, and a further ten who were added to the playing list after the losing final against Port Adelaide in 2014.

Half the side – eleven of the twenty-two – had played at least 100 games before the grand final. Only seven of the twenty-two had played fewer than fifty games. By contrast, the 1967 premiership team had just four veterans who had played more than 100 games, while twelve of the twenty had played fewer than fifty games.

Yet the 2017 champions were young by contemporary standards. The oldest players in the team, Shaun Grigg and Bachar Houli, were only twenty-nine years old on grand final day. Only one other club in the national competition had won a premiership with a side where every player was under thirty – Collingwood in 2010.

If Richmond's history is any guide, these mighty Tigers will have a few more premierships to celebrate before the next long drought.

12

THE NEW RICHMOND

I swear it wasn't me. Every time we replay this argument at home, I plead for mercy. Seriously, I didn't sing the Richmond song to our poor defenceless baby daughter. I'm not that mad.

'Well, where did she pick up that tune?' the footy sceptic demands.

'Your mother-in-law?' I shrug.

Our girl was a fan of the Beatles, the Beach Boys and the Wiggles before she latched onto football. Her first word was 'Dorothy'. I thought she'd said 'doddy', as in Daddy. But she meant Dorothy the Dinosaur. There was a phase early on when she insisted on hearing the *Pet Sounds* album every night before she went to sleep. The sounds of the steam train, the bells of the level crossing and the barking dogs at the end of 'Caroline No' would be her signal to close her eyes. Her first fully formed sentence was the 'Nah, na, na, na-na-na-nah' chorus to 'Hey Jude'.

I've forgotten the game that was being televised, but one night as Richmond took the field she was humming along to the club song. She didn't know the words yet, but the melody had clearly caught her attention. Later, when I quizzed Mum, she said she only sang it to her once or twice while babysitting when a game happened to be on the TV.

I wasn't sure that I wanted our little girl to love the Tigers. Why subject her to the torture of following a club that was a magnet for ridicule? But there was the social side of football to weigh up.

After returning to Melbourne from Canberra in 2000, I resumed the habit of regular attendance. I formed a little band of family and friends to watch Richmond play, adding and losing members from show to show. We'd see anywhere between two and ten games, depending on the season. But it wasn't really about the footy, not in the way it had been for me as a child. It was an extended family catch-up, with food, because Mum always brought a snack for an afternoon game or a generous helping of Greek pita for a night game.

Conversations change when you are reading the play rather than the other person's face. They're more open, less hurried.

The core of our group was Mum, myself and my brother-in-law. My nephew and niece joined once they were old enough to understand the choice they were faced with on any given round. A day locked up at home versus an adventure to the footy; a day doing whatever they wanted at home versus a miserable afternoon watching Richmond lose to Essendon by 101 points.

I could not deny our daughter at least one day at the footy with her favourite people in the world. Her first game, in 2012, picked itself. It came with the most tantalising diary clash. Richmond was playing Melbourne at the MCG while the original Wiggles – Greg was back in the yellow skivvy – were at the Princess Theatre in the city. The Wiggles were due on stage at 1 p.m. while the game started at 1.45 p.m. I couldn't resist the opportunity to spoil her.

The plan was we'd watch the entire Wiggles show, then take the train from Parliament station to Richmond for the second half of the game. Her grandmother, uncle and the cousins would be waiting for us on the city side of the ground, in the Ponsford Stand.

While the Wiggles performed, I checked the score on my phone. Doomsday scenario: Melbourne had taken the lead. When I was her age, in the black and white 1970s, if you weren't at the ground the only way to follow a game was on the radio. Now I was hitting refresh on my phone every minute or so to see if the score changed. A goal to us. Time to turn off the phone.

We arrived just on half time, with Richmond 8 points in front. We located the family and they received the new recruit with a smother of hugs. As we took our seats, my brother-in-law advised us that Richmond was useless in the first half. 'Useless,' he repeated. If they keep this up, they will lose again. 'Let's see if your niece changes our luck,' I joked.

'Okay darling, here come the players for the start of the third quarter.' Within a minute, the Tigers had scored a goal and all was good in the world.

As research for this chapter the two of us watched the highlights and played a little memory game: who kicked the first goal she saw in person? I had got it into my head that it was Dustin Martin, launching one of his missile kicks from outside the 50-metre arc. But she insisted that it was her favourite player, Trent Cotchin. As we neared the moment of truth I prepared to say 'I told you so.' But dammit, she was right. She had a better recall of the game than her journalist father.

Richmond scored 9 goals in her first quarter of football and another 5 in her second, winning by 59 points. I should have given myself five parenting stars for a perfect introduction to the game. But I knew Richmond would torment her, just like every other supporter who's had the misfortune of being born into the club's longest premiership drought.

Brendon Gale often wondered if his job as Richmond CEO was in his family's best interests. They could never be regular fans, with the inalienable human right to disengage during a losing streak, because he brought every defeat home with him. Even when he told them not to worry, they'd win next week, his children could feel his disappointment.

And those defeats followed them to school. Their class mates would tell them 'the Tigers suck' or 'your dad's a loser'. Gale says there was no malice. Kids tease each other all the time. But his children couldn't help but be affected.

He tried to maintain a sense of perspective, reminding his children that football is only a game, while never really believing his own rhetoric. 'We're not curing cancer here. There are far more important things, but it just consumes you.'

I've had this conversation with a number of parents who have raised footy fans, whether by their own initiative or, as in my daughter's case, because of the influence of her grandmother's home cooking. There is a time in every one of those children's lives when the result of a particular game feels like a death in the family. Gale tells me the loss that crushed his son was the 2015 elimination final against North Melbourne. He was so upset after that game that they decided to give him the day off school on Monday.

I have a couple of my own memories that game: two photos of my daughter. The first shows an energetic young girl pulling faces before the game as Mum and the gang take their seats. She is wearing her Richmond junior-member T-shirt, a Tiger headband with little ears, and war paint – a block of black, yellow and black on each cheek. The second photo was taken at a street corner as we were nearing the end of our silent walk home from the train station. The Tiger paint looks like the charcoal smudge of a child labourer who has just emerged from a nineteenth-century coal mine.

'You don't want Mum to see that sad, empty face,' I'd told her. 'Let's pretend we had a great day despite the loss.'

This particular game was personal – her best friend at school that year was a North Melbourne supporter.

The possibility of defeat didn't enter her mind until midway through the last quarter when the Kangaroos established a

2-goal buffer. Her first instinct was to overcompensate with optimism. But I had seen enough of Damien Hardwick's Tigers to know when they were choking, and I believed this would be an era-defining choke.

'I don't think we can win now,' I said. 'Let me know if you want to leave before the end.'

She shook her head and flashed me that 'don't embarrass me' look of hers. 'No, we can still win,' she said.

A moment later, another North Melbourne goal settled the issue. She dissolved into tears. It was a sudden, unexpected, unstoppable geyser of grief. I gave a discreet nod to the aisle and offered to carry her out. Walking towards the exit, with the face of my little Tiger cub disappearing into my shoulder, I thought back to my seven-year-old self and that devastating preliminary final loss to St Kilda in 1971.

I revealed that shameful secret on the way home, to assure her that she had been magnificent by comparison. 'You know I kicked my dad's uncle?' I said, and proceeded to tell her the story of my footy tantrum. That confession restored her humour for a second. 'You are an idiot,' she giggled.

The best footy story she tells against me is about the drive home from the Swans game in 2016, which Sam Lloyd won for us after the siren. The tribe had already given up on the season and I didn't bother asking them if they were going to the MCG that evening. Our losing streak was at six, while Sydney had won its past three games.

We only went because my daughter asked. She had a new Richmond flag she kept forgetting to bring and wanted to see if she could wave us to victory. So we hopped in the car and took the rat run to the station, where we parked and waited for a train.

We had an agreement to pull out early if the game was going badly, and it did. The Swans kicked the last 5 goals of the third quarter. I asked if she wanted to go home, but I wasn't really asking. 'We need to get you to bed.'

The comeback unfolded as we walked to the station. One goal, then another, then a third. Scores were level.

'Do we go back or make a run for the train to catch the end of the game on TV?' I asked.

'Let's go home,' she said.

We were 2 goals in front when we boarded the train, but 2 goals behind when we reached our station. We had been following the game on my phone. Once in the car, we switched on the radio. A minute from home Ben Griffiths kicked a goal and suddenly victory was possible again. We roared.

'Dad, two hands on the steering wheel!' she screamed. In her retelling, the car swerves towards the footpath before I remember my responsibilities and pull it back on course. But I swear I was only doing 30 km/h, and my hands were in the air for only a millisecond.

We tiptoed inside the house, hoping not to wake the footy sceptic, and turned on the TV. Phew, there were five minutes left in the game. 'If we win, let's not get carried away. Mum will kill us.' But when Lloydy kicked that goal after the siren, of course we jumped and screamed, and hugged, and jumped and screamed.

We were too pumped up to go to sleep. My phone pinged for the rest of the evening as I exchanged messages with friends who'd stayed at the game, who left early like we did or who had watched it at home the whole way. Friends who follow other clubs sent their unsolicited congratulations. We know it's only a game. But we don't need to qualify our love of footy after a game like that.

Every club has a media-friendly minority of supporters who take defeat so personally that they have to share it on talkback radio. The Richmond fans who called in during the wilderness years became notorious for their self-loathing. They would count off the decades they had been watching the Tigers without reward before declaring the end of their relationship with football. As one caller said after a loss in 2016, 'I am just so damned angry it's not funny. I've taken my membership cards for my three sons and myself, and I've just put them in the microwave.'

The voices of the agitated were almost exclusively male, and were most likely born between Tom Hafey's departure in 1976 and the Save Our Skins campaign in 1990. Too young to remember the 1980 premiership, but old enough to have followed Richmond throughout Matthew Richardson's brilliant, erratic career. By 2016 this cohort had become the highest-risk group for a Tiger mid-life crisis: aged between twenty-five and forty. As another said that season, 'They've finally done it, they've finally broken my heart. I've followed this side for thirty years and had some pretty tough times in those thirty years. But this is it.'

These blokes provided great copy although I'm sure they would be among the first to renew their memberships when a new season approaches. But even if some did abandon the cause for good, the movement they were supposed to represent was a figment of the football media's imagination. In the real world, something more remarkable was happening: Richmond supporters of all ages kept coming to games.

You'll recall that between the 1980 premiership and the first wooden spoon in 1987, Richmond home attendances collapsed by almost two-thirds (64 per cent). If that trend had repeated in the twenty-first century, surely the media would have jumped all over it. Certainly the club and its supporters would have noticed. But even in hard times, Richmond never returned to the black hole of the late 1980s.

Consider the period between the preliminary-final season of 2001 and the wooden spoon of 2007. Attendances only fell by 17 per cent. And the Tigers sold 30 000 memberships in 2007, a new record for the club at the time.

During the microwave season of 2016, home crowds fell by 15 per cent compared with the previous season. Yet Richmond still had the third-largest home crowd after Adelaide and Collingwood. And the supporters were reaffirming their loyalty in a more substantial way, as the Tigers now had 72 000 members.

These days the attendance gap between the most successful and most miserable seasons has narrowed. The gap hasn't disappeared entirely, but it is small enough to suggest a change in behaviour in the twenty-first century. If it were only true of Richmond fans, I would be tempted to diagnose our loyalty as a collective madness. But in recent years Collingwood and Essendon supporters have also maintained the faith when their clubs were rooted around the bottom of the ladder.

The change is driven by a broader demographic trend – the fall in Australia's birth rate – and it is best understood by comparing the corporatised present to the joyful swarm of young faces that went to football in the 1970s. If you go back and watch replays of big games at the MCG, from the mid-1990s onwards you can hear the noise from the grandstands become more primal as the crowds aged along with the wider community. Football today is a Midnight Oil reunion concert: it's watched by an older audience reclaiming its youth. In the 1970s it was closer to a Wiggles show.

It is in fact the combination of the two, the parents and their children coming to the football together, that propped up Richmond crowds in the twenty-first century, even before Gale, O'Neal and Hardwick made the club great again.

My non-football friends think I am a fanatic, but my family's spectating life is the norm in Victoria. The cycle of attendance from my childhood to my daughter's, with Mum as our pita-making pied piper, repeats across generations of households. Other codes have their own versions of this ritual, but not on the same scale, because no other game and state are as entwined as football and Victoria.

The peak of the baby boom in Australia was 1971, the same year I went to my first game. Children like me helped to underwrite the attendance boom between 1971 and 1981. But we stopped going, or at least reduced the number of games we saw, once we entered the workforce, which in my case was the cleaning job at the cinema and then journalism. This would not have mattered if the birth rate had remained stable – crowds would have stayed at record levels. But the birth rate fell, sharply, leaving fewer children to replace those who had grown out of the game.

Of course this is not the only reason why Richmond's support fell off a cliff in the 1980s. The club's wretched form was the primary driver. But even if Richmond had remained a superpower, attendances would have declined somewhat because of demography.

Yet those losses were bound to be reversed once the birth rate stabilised and the spoiled generation returned to the football with their own children. The initial trigger for the recovery may have been the form spike under John Northey in the mid-1990s. But the family connection meant the stands would remain occupied even when the club zig-zagged between ninth and last.

But there is a second social force that has lured people back to the game. Football is filling the void in our public life that was created by the loss of faith in our political and religious institutions.

Faith in democracy has crashed to its lowest level on record. The main political parties are being punished with their lowest primary votes in the post-war era. And in the 2016 census the most common response regarding religious beliefs was 'no religion'. In this cynical and secular age, football has assumed greater responsibility as supporters, and players, ask their clubs to become agents of social change. Richmond under Peggy O'Neal and Brendon Gale was among the first to recognise the shift in attitudes, and to translate that into a new model of engagement beyond football.

Like all clubs, Richmond surveys its members as rigorously as the political parties conduct focus group research of swinging voters. Gale tells me that people buy Richmond memberships because they think they offer 'value for money' and because they want to make a financial contribution to their club. That's the pragmatic side of the calculation. The other side is emotional. Gale goes on to explain that the surveys show people want to see the club's values align with their own. The club represents them, he says. Members want to be informed and they don't want to be embarrassed by off-field behaviour. They also want to see their club contribute to the community.

'It's not just about winning [or] losing anymore,' Gale says. 'Performance does matter, but members want their club to stand for something.'

For the first century of its existence, Richmond's membership sales were only a fraction of attendances at Punt Road and then the MCG. The club made little effort to market season tickets because fans would reliably show up on game day. As the spoiled generation returned to football in the 1990s, the number of members jumped from 8000 in 1994 to 29 000 five years later. The next surge was in 2009, the year Ben Cousins came to Richmond, when almost 37 000 became members.

With Brendon Gale's data-informed approach, memberships have grown every year since 2011. In 2012 the membership total exceeded the average home crowd for the first time. Support for the Tigers is strongest in the southeast of the city, along the train lines and freeways from high-income Richmond out to middle-class Mount Waverley, Scoresby and Knox, and on to the new growth suburbs in the Casey Cardinia shire.

Richmond, once proudly Catholic and Labor, now reflects a wider cross-section of the community. There are significant clusters of members living in electorates held by the Greens, Labor and the Liberals. Other clubs have been on a similar journey to diversity, although from different directions. Carlton is no longer associated with the Liberal establishment, while Collingwood crossed the Yarra in a figurative sense when club president Eddie McGuire moved to Toorak.

Peggy O'Neal describes Richmond as 'a place for everybody'. She notes, with understandable pride, that the entire spectrum of the population is part of the Tiger family, from Indigenous and Muslim Australians to the gay and lesbian community. Richmond was the first AFL club to sponsor the Midsumma Festival. It has the most prominent Muslim in football, Bachar Houli. And it uses its position to bring attention to social issues; the club has partnered with the Alannah and Madeline Foundation, a national charity that protects children from violence and bullying.

Richmond now runs an Indigenous leadership school, the Korin Gamadji Institute. A delegation from the club was invited to address the United Nations Permanent Forum on Indigenous Issues in April 2018. Gale sees a virtuous circle in the KGI. It's not designed as a talent scouting exercise for the club, but it does help Richmond players and staff 'gain perspective from these kids'. 'We are in a privileged position to do things, to make us a better country,' says Gale.

That's a credit to the Tigers. But if I take off my membership lanyard and put on my old press pass, I also see a warning that our social safety net is in need of repair. No government or electorate should be satisfied with a world in which Indigenous Australian parents would rather send their children to a football club than a state school.

The evolution from a singular focus on sport to a wider social engagement is not unique to Richmond, or to football. In the NRL, the North Queensland Cowboys are one of the most trusted institutions in their region. Cowboys CEO Greg Tonner has never met Brendon Gale, and before I spoke to him he had no idea what Richmond's community programs involved. But the Cowboys had independently reached a similar conclusion about where to devote their time off the field. The club now runs a boarding house for secondary students from remote communities in northwest and Far North Queensland.

Tonner grew up in Townsville and was a senior executive at Optus, based in Sydney, before he was headhunted for the Cowboys job. His work in the private sector told him that consumer attitudes have shifted in recent years, from self-interest to a desire for meaning. 'What people are moving towards are purposes greater than themselves that are authentic and provide leadership and respect for community,' Tonner says.

This, he explains, has profound implications for sporting clubs. The successful ones will be those 'that can align their leadership teams and can stay true to their values and be accountable for behaviour, and not fall into the trap of winning at any cost'.

Writing about sport more broadly in the 1960s, Donald Horne said it was 'the one national institution that has no 'knockers''.

'Sport to many Australians is life and the rest is shadow. [To] many it is considered a sign of degeneracy not to be interested in it.'

I imagine Horne saw our obsession with sport as a sign of character weakness. But he was writing at a time of complacency. As fans project a higher purpose onto their clubs, I detect an urgency in the preoccupation with football today. Personally, I would prefer politics lifted its game, but the longing for football to provide leadership is genuine. And it helps explain why Richmond's 2017 premiership felt like a mass movement.

Our football family had broken up for the end of the 2016 season. Mum came over to watch the telecast of the grand final between the Western Bulldogs and the Sydney Swans. While we cheered the underdog, she was annoyed. 'Why couldn't Richmond do this?' It was a fair question, framed by exasperation, not jealousy.

My daughter picked up the gist of the conversation and announced: 'I want to barrack for the Bulldogs next year.'

'They can be your second team', I replied. 'But we won't be going to the football again if you drop the Tigers.'

I explained that neither her grandmother nor I had any interest in watching another team. Yes, that was a little mind game.

Cut to round three of the 2017 season. I was flying to Newcastle for the writers' festival while the tribe was reconvening without me for the game against West Coast at the MCG. My talk on Australian politics would run from 4.15 p.m. to 5.15 p.m., so there was no practical way to follow the final quarter.

Backstage at Newcastle's Civic Theatre, waiting for the MC to introduce me to the audience, I allowed myself a quick update before turning off the phone. Richmond was 1 goal in front at three-quarter time. Okay, now I was distracted. It's a rugby league town, but they laughed when I suggested that if there were any Richmond people in the house, they should feel free to interrupt with the final score. But only if we won. No one did, and so I assumed the game was lost.

At the end of the session there was no time to check the result as I joined my fellow authors at the book-signing table. A tall chap waited patiently until I had finished talking to the last of the generous readers.

'Do you know the score?' he asked me.

'No, I haven't had a chance to turn on my phone, but you better tell me.'

He clenched his fist and smiled. 'Go Tigers.'

Later that evening, I called home for a match report. My daughter was definitely still a Tiger. She gave me a breathless account of the most amazing goal she had seen in her life. 'We all jumped out of our seats. I thought I was about to fly.'

I caught the clip on the TV in my hotel room. Daniel Rioli, pressed against the boundary line, was pursued by two Eagles defenders. He flicked out a hand pass to Dion Prestia, who looped it back to Rioli, now running towards the Punt Road End goals. Another defender was closing, but Rioli had already taken aim and fired. It was the most audacious banana kick, the ball spinning left to right, because there was no other way to weave it through the goal posts from that tight an angle. And my daughter was right, the Richmond crowd celebrated with the most incredible noise.

My moment of quiet parental pride came in round eight, when we lost to Fremantle after the siren. 'Now we know how the Sydney supporters felt last year,' she volunteered. The game was teaching her perspective, and empathy.

Throughout that winter, conversations with friends would veer between the assumedly high probability of a Richmond implosion and the absurd possibility of a premiership. After a win, we'd have to remind one another of those three elimination finals losses. Let's not get ahead of ourselves, we agreed.

But by July we were thinking of September. My non-Richmond friends would get straight to the point as the finals approached: would I cry if we won it, and how would the city cope with a hundred thousand feral Tiger fans?

The only previous final I had seen Richmond win was in 2001, against Carlton. More notable than the result was the context; the game was played just three days after the terror attacks on New York, Washington and Philadelphia. The minute's silence before the opening bounce was broken by a solitary idiot near our section yelling, 'Carn'a Tigers!' I thought of blokes like him – consumed by footy – when the Geelong team entered the field for our 2017 qualifying final.

Ordinarily, Richmond supporters give an opposing team a moment's peace to run through their banner and for their fans to sing the club song. But that night against Geelong, they booed. It wasn't just a few stray voices, but thousands. An insistent, startling boo that I had not heard before in all my years watching football. After the game, Geelong chief executive Brian Cook wrote to Brendon Gale to pass on complaints he had fielded from Geelong supporters who felt intimidated by the Tiger Army.

The Grateful Dead had a theory that the audience was an extension of the band. 'The magic only happens when we're on stage performing, and it only happens between the band and the audience,' guitarist Bob Weir explained. Against Geelong, the Richmond supporters didn't just cheer the goals and marks, they applauded every tackle and smother as if to reinforce the game plan in the minds of the players. When Richmond goaled, the wall of noise took shape as one of two words: a long ecstatic 'Yes!' or, if the play involved our number four, 'Dusty!'

In that qualifying final, the energy of the crowd was directed towards the field. In the preliminary final against Greater Western Sydney, it was shared with the person sitting next to you. Supporters didn't rise like a singular wave to celebrate a goal, they formed a boiling ocean of yellow and black, turning to a loved one or friend to exchange hugs and high fives. In every row there were photographers: pointing a phone camera at the players on the ground, at their own group, or squeezing two or more faces together into a selfie.

This is the final that brings a tear to my eye when I watch the replay because I am drawn to the passion in the stands. Everyone is wearing their colours. There are Richmond jumpers, hoodies, T-shirts, scarves, beanies and caps. There are more flags being waved than a political rally in a one-party state.

The AFL probably thought it was doing the game a favour by fast-tracking the development of the Giants. It granted the new franchise draft concessions between 2011 and 2013, at the expense of clubs that were rebuilding their lists at the time, including Richmond. The calculation was that early success would bring new fans to the game in the difficult Sydney market. But it carried the obvious risk that the first final the Giants played at the MCG would be against a team that had the entire crowd on its side. Karma insisted that it would be Richmond, one of the teams the AFL had sacrificed in order to pamper the Giants.

The crowd of 94 000 comprised about 90 000 Tigers, 2000 Giants and 2000 neutrals. All 2000 Giants were seated behind the city-end goals, to create a false impression of mass. But who were they kidding? Without opposing fans to speak of, the MCG became one massive, uninhibited Richmond cheer squad. Damien Hardwick said the glass window that's meant to insulate the coach's box from the noise outside actually shook when Kane Lambert kicked the opening goal of the game. The roar that greeted Dan Butler's goal late in the final quarter was measured at 126 decibels. Louder than a jet engine, though not quite as loud as an AC/DC concert. The club song at the end was as exhilarating as any Springsteen show I've been to (and I've been watching him for almost as long as Richmond.)

As we walked towards Richmond station, police sirens wailed along Punt Road. Road blocks were being improvised to cope with the fans who were swarming onto Swan Street with no intention of going home.

Neil Balme swore by the theory that crowds don't influence games. 'The crowd doesn't get a kick,' is how he puts it. 'But if they were going to [influence games], it was certainly in those three finals.'

As he watched the grand final parade, from the top of the city to the MCG, he wondered if Adelaide players would be intimidated by the endless sea of yellow and black. More than 100 000 people attended the parade on the Friday. On grand final day, the MCG was filled with 100 000 spectator while another 16 000 were across the way at Punt Road Oval, watching on three big screens. Every pub and virtually every house, terrace and apartment in Richmond had the television on.

Our tribe, like the team itself, was unchanged for all three finals. Mum, my daughter, my niece, my brother-in-law and myself. On grand final day we met at Mum's station and took the train in together for old time's sake. Just outside the gate I asked Mum to pose for a quick selfie with me, which I posted on Twitter. Later that night, one of her Greek friends called to say she'd 'seen her on the internet'. She had no idea what she was talking about.

That evening I took the girls back to Richmond for a glimpse of the street party. It was a marvellous, chaotic scene best experienced without lingering. Swan Street was a mess. We turned right into Lennox Street and I showed them the house where their grandfather had once lived as a young migrant. Every few metres we high-fived a group going the other way, into the cauldron of Swan Street. Boisterous teenagers, fabulously inebriated old Tiger couples, girls on a night out, a group of young Asian Australians. Everyone was singing the song. One group was at the line 'In any weather you will see us with a grin,' another was at the chorus 'Yellow and black!'

We turned right again at Bridge Road, past restaurants filled with celebrating Richmond fans. More high fives. We reached the town hall to check out the spot-lit Tiger mural and then doubled back down Church Street, where we confronted the funniest sight of the evening: a barber offering free Dustin Martin haircuts, and the queue stretched halfway up the block.

The last time football inspired street parties on this scale was the 1920s and 1930s, when people had virtually nothing else to look forward to. Obviously Richmond is a different place today. It is younger, better educated, better paid and now not as Catholic as the nation. The cafes on Swan Street are more representative of the people than St Ignatius' on Church Street.

The median household income is $1973 per week – 37 per cent higher than the national figure of $1438. More than half the workers living in the suburb (57 per cent) are either professionals or managers, compared to a national total of 35 per cent. Yet the affluent celebrated as hard as their predecessors during the depression judging by the beautiful noise coming from the courtyards and balconies of Richmond on grand final night.

One explanation for the explosion of emotion is the 37-year wait. The other is the way the Tigers played.

But there were two much larger forces at work that made this premiership spectacular, and gave it meaning beyond football. The first was Richmond's population boom, which restored the suburb to a grandeur it last enjoyed in the 1880s. Since 2001, the population has almost doubled, recovering the losses of the previous fifty years. That gave the street party scale.

The second factor was the political climate.

I can't help but think that the people needed the distraction of this particular premiership in this particular year – the first year of the Trump presidency and umpteenth year of malaise in Australian public life.

Richmond's premiership contained the very elements of leadership and community that are missing in our politics today – power exercised without ego, a united team, a dash of charisma and a committed supporter base.

The identification with football echoed the 1920s and 1930s not because there was nothing else in peoples' lives, but because nothing else in public life today so easily demonstrated what should be the universal Australian values of fair play and openness.

Football was all people wanted to talk about in days leading up the grand final. Afterwards, friends would ask if I had recovered. 'I'm taking it one replay at a time,' I told them.

This premiership continued to resonate throughout the summer of 2017–18 as the cup went on tour around the nation. Thousands of Richmond fans lined up to be photographed with the trophy in Tasmania, country Victoria, Sydney, the Gold Coast, Darwin and Perth. More than half the adult population of Australia watched the 2017 grand final on TV, websites or phone applications.

I was impressed by my team's star power – until I checked the fine print of the survey. The audience was concentrated in the footy states; 68 per cent of Victorians and Tasmanians saw the game,

65 per cent of South Australians and 54 per cent of Western Australians. In the rugby league states, fewer than one in three people tuned in – 28 per cent in New South Wales and 27 per cent in Queensland. The nation remained as divided as ever, even on this glorious day.

CONCLUSION

I've taken the liberty of adapting Malcolm Fraser's advice to journalists in the 1970s to put sport on the front page – I'm placing politics squarely at the back of this book. I wanted to tell Richmond's story first before offering my opinion about what is broken in politics; a separation of church and state, so to speak.

The comment on politics begins with what should be a joke, but isn't. Richmond is better run than the country now, while the Labor and Liberal parties have been behaving like the Tigers of old, executing prime ministers even after they've won an election.

In an inversion of the instincts that govern both enterprises, Richmond finally gave up the self-destructive urge for quick fixes in the same year politics confirmed it no longer had the wit to think beyond the next Newspoll. Trust in government went into freefall at the 2010 election after Labor sacked Kevin Rudd. Damien Hardwick began coaching Richmond that year, although by his own self-deprecating admission he had no idea what he was doing.

But while Hardwick and the club learned on the job – sifting the playing list, tweaking the game plan, building the business and creating a model for collective leadership that could inspire a premiership – politics repeated its mistakes. Australia had five prime ministers between 2010 and 2015, including three who were dumped by their own party rather than voters. Richmond had five coaches between 1981 and 1986.

But politics didn't suddenly throw itself into this abyss. It has been sleepwalking towards a crisis of relevance since the early 1990s (the same time, coincidentally, that Victorian clubs started processing the shock of the national competition). I count seven steps. Each one violated a convention of democracy, removing one of the checks on the system and thereby reducing the effectiveness of government.

The first step, I have to confess, was taken by my old newspaper *The Australian* in 1992 when we doubled the frequency of the Newspoll survey of federal voting intentions. By moving from a monthly to a fortnightly survey, we disrupted the rhythm of national affairs. The problem wasn't the opinion poll itself – newspapers had been publishing them for half a century – but the attention we paid to it. The fortnightly poll became a news event, and its findings warped public debate.

Once media organisations decided that polls were news, they excused themselves from the responsibility of covering public policy at the level of detail needed to inform the community. When a government or opposition released a new initiative the first question was no longer what it would mean for individuals and society but whether it would influence the voting behaviour of this or that target group. Political reporting eventually became one extended footy tipping competition.

And once the media started covering politics like sport, it was inevitable that politics would begin to assume the worst aspects of sport, from the short-termism of scapegoating the coach to the unthinking loyalty of the fanatic who is blind to the sins of their own team while calling for a royal commission to investigate their opponents.

Leadership challenges became more common with the fortnightly Newspoll. The Liberals were the first opposition party to have three leaders in a single parliamentary term, between 1993 and 1996. Labor did the same in opposition between 2004 and 2007.

Before long the leadership instability of opposition was transferred into government. Each side gave the Richmond treatment to its prime minister. Kevin Rudd brought Labor to power in 2007 after eleven years in opposition, but like John Northey, who returned Richmond to the finals for the first time after thirteen years, he was gone before the next election.

Rudd's successor Julia Gillard won minority government in 2010, but Rudd took his old job back before the 2013 election. He, in turn, lost office to Tony Abbott – who was dumped by his own party in 2015. Malcolm Turnbull even publicly cited Abbott's poor Newspoll numbers as one of the reasons for calling the challenge against the prime minister.

The second step into the abyss is long forgotten, but it marked a change in the relationship between politics and the public service. Liberal senator Bronwyn Bishop used a parliamentary inquiry to humiliate the Commissioner of Taxation, Trevor Boucher, a public servant who had served both major parties with distinction. Bishop was an opposition backbencher at the time and would not have been thinking beyond that night's television news, which would broadcast her attack and make her a household name. But the slow death of public service independence began on that day. Others followed Bishop's example, assuming this was how politics was always conducted, with the elected bullying the expert. When the Coalition returned to office four years later in 1996, John Howard sacked the heads of six government departments.

The third step into the abyss was the 1993 election. Paul Keating won it with a scare campaign against something he once believed in, the consumption tax. The lesson Tony Abbott drew from this exercise was that he could one day become prime minister with an entirely negative platform.

He was right, but he forgot the other side of the Keating example. As part of his program to defeat the John Hewson–led opposition, Keating had promised to deliver personal tax cuts. He realised only after the election that he could not honour that commitment without breaking the budget. So he broke the promise instead. As Keating subsequently admitted to me, the 1993 post-election budget, which cancelled one half of those tax cuts, helped to kill his government at the next election. Abbott found himself in a similar hole after winning the 2013 election. He had promised no spending cuts, but slashed spending anyway in the 2014 budget. He never recovered his authority after that.

The fourth step was taken by John Howard in 2001, when he decided that voters could be bought off without savings in the budget to offset the expenditure. The age of entitlement began here, with its self-defeating assumption that every single voter should be a winner. The first in the handout queue were young home buyers, then retirees. After the 2004 election, the mining boom gave the budget a temporary boost, but Howard spent that windfall as well, first by increasing family payments, then on a series of tax cuts that ultimately left budget in deficit. Like the Richmond administrations that tried to buy a premiership in the 1980s, Howard passed on the bill to the next government.

Howard was the first prime minister to use the budget as an explicit tool of short-term bribery outside an election year. On his government's re-election in 2004, he told the Liberal members of parliament that they should treat every day of the next term as a day on the hustings. 'The moment you start campaigning for the next election is today,' he said. 'I'm a great believer in perpetual campaigning.'

The fifth step was Labor's election of Mark Latham as opposition leader in 2003. This was the first leadership ballot decided by factional revenge rather than policy differences or electoral concerns, and it established the precedent for the removal of Rudd in 2010.

The sixth step into the abyss was John Howard's WorkChoices legislation. He had no mandate for it. Before the 2004 election he had explicitly ruled out major changes to the industrial relations system. But he had control of the Senate and couldn't resist the temptation to destroy the trade unions. It cost Howard the next election, but the cost to the system was far greater. From here on, every incoming government would allow its predecessor's agenda to dictate its own policy making. The first term of a new government would be devoted to undoing as many of the previous government's policies as possible.

The seventh and final step was the national brain snap over climate change policy at the end of 2009. Both sides had agreed to act on climate change. During the 2007 election the only argument between Howard and Rudd was over the start date for a market-based system to reduce greenhouse gas emissions. But following the election, prime minister Rudd and new opposition leader Turnbull proved incapable of negotiating in good faith. Their egos were simply too big for the task.

Once Turnbull lost his job to Abbott, Rudd had the option of calling an early election in the summer of 2010, which the Coalition concedes he would have won. But he blinked and, by April, he walked away from what he had previously termed the great moral challenge of climate change. His personal poll numbers collapsed as a result and his colleagues took the opportunity to remove him, even though Newspoll said Labor was still ahead.

The public has made its displeasure with politics clear by dismissing governments after just one or two terms in office, and by lodging an increasing number of protest votes for the minor parties. The way to see this is to draw a line at 2010. Before Rudd's sacking, the government of the day, whether Labor or conservative, lost just two of the seventeen federal, state and territory elections held in the preceding seven years. In the seventeen elections after Rudd's sacking, through to 2017, the government of the day was ousted ten times.

The minor parties recorded just 14.4 per cent of the primary vote at the 2007 federal election, which Rudd won. In 2016, the minor parties achieved a vote of 23.2 per cent, a post-war record, and Turnbull came within a seat of losing the fifteen-seat majority he had inherited from Abbott. In 2007, 43 per cent of voters thought that government could be trusted. By 2016, that figure had crashed to just 26 per cent.

My frustration with politics today is its belligerent immaturity. Our leaders have fallen for the old football trap of mistaking tribal identity for strength. The parties assume the electorate is too diverse to unite, so they divided it to prop up their respective base votes. Like the football coaches of old, leaders are reduced to the equivalent of yelling at voters to respect their authority.

Politics is a game of persuasion. The best politicians I've observed are willing to field hostile questions from people who may never vote for them. I think of Keating going on talkback radio in 1993 to debate callers who opposed his native title legislation, or Howard wearing a bullet-proof vest during the gun law reform debate of 1996 when he faced a hostile crowd of farmers who wanted to keep their firearms. Football had little to teach politics in the 1990s because political leaders did not fear scrutiny, and had the confidence of their beliefs to promote unpopular policies in the national interest.

Today, governments release policies without consultation then dump them at the first sign of pushback from vested interests. The system lost its bearings when Rudd folded on climate change. A decade on, Australia has had no substantial reform introduced that's survived a change of government, with the notable exception of Julia Gillard's National Disability Insurance Scheme.

The main parties expect journalists and public servants to back their team no matter what. They assume that anyone who questions them, or offers an alternate view, does so out of bias against them. I grew up in a press gallery in which politicians relished interrogation; as treasurer, Keating would conduct hour-long press conferences and not leave until he had exhausted his inquisitors. Those encounters kept him match fit. They shaped his public language more decisively than the abuse he delivered to the opposition in parliamentary question time because he was forced to clarify his policies.

The internet gave politicians the option to avoid the press gallery. They could use social media to talk directly to the public without the interruption of nitpicking journalists such as myself. But that hasn't improved the conversation. The direct feedback from the public unsettled them and they followed the path of least resistance. Now they speak only to those who agree with them. This has further alienated the swinging voter, who prefers their politics without the harangue of partisanship. I know this is easy to write, but our leaders would be better off if they submitted themselves to more scrutiny, learned to listen and had the patience to keep explaining.

In the past, a defeated government would undertake years of soul searching to find out why they lost, and what they needed to fix in their platform to recover the support of the community. The understanding that it would take at least two terms to reclaim office meant that policy renewal would be a long-term project, much like building a premiership-worthy playing list.

But since 2010 the expectation has been for an early return to power, and this has shifted the incentives for both sides of the chamber. New governments start on the defensive, fearful of the first opinion poll that turns against them. Oppositions have no time for reflection – they go on the attack from day one, because they calculate that chaos will accelerate the demise of the new government.

Parties don't learn from their mistakes; they repeat them. I know from direct contact with the present generation of politicians that they are sick of being told that Australia was once governed by grown-ups. So rather than repeat my old advice that they should study the records of the last great reforming prime ministers of Australia – Bob Hawke, Paul Keating and the early John Howard – I now offer the example of my football club. The Richmond model of collaborative leadership isn't a new one, it's a reminder of that better way of governing in an unexpected setting.

It begins with the recognition that the problem starts with the parties themselves. Richmond could not fix its playing list until it accepted the need to reform the club's administration. Good people did not work at Punt Road because of its vindictive, blokey culture; the main parties cannot attract good people to stand for parliament while they continue to treat politics as sport.

Richmond set long-term goals for financial stability and increased membership as a precondition for premiership success. The main parties cannot expect to run successful governments without first getting their policies to add up and using those platforms to restore their primary votes.

Once Richmond became competitive on the field, it had to learn how to manage expectations and respond to setbacks. If Brendon Gale and Peggy O'Neal had thought like politicians in 2016, they would have sacked Damien Hardwick and never discovered that a premiership was just a season away.

I am not suggesting that parties never remove their leaders. But what Richmond showed is that leaders are most effective when they are given time to learn on the job, and they, in turn, are prepared to share power.

Ultimately, the parties have only themselves to blame for concentrating power in the prime minister's suite. They took the presidential style of campaigning, which centres on the leader's personality ahead of the party's platform, to the illogical conclusion of making government solely about the prime minister.

Leaders today insist that every word that comes out of their government reflect the daily talking points issued by their office; Damien Hardwick's worst season as coach, 2016, was the one when he tried to do everything himself. In the Hawke–Keating era, ministers were allowed to run their portfolios without micro-managing from the prime minister's office. 'One of the things I admired [about Bob Hawke] – he let me do things,' Paul Keating told me.

The present generation of politicians look at the 1980s through the wrong end of the telescope, seeing the Hawke–Keating reforms to open up the economy and reduce the size of government as the perfect game plan for all conditions. No tweaking required to adapt to shocks in the global economy, or to moderate the greed of players in the free market.

This is one of the reasons why football clubs have found themselves to the left of the parliament: politics has moved too far to the right of the people, leaving no meaningful role for government in the twenty-first century. Another is that the parliament looks nothing like the people it serves. It is remarkable that Australia, a nation much more ethnically diverse than the United States or Britain, has a parliament that is whiter than the US Congress or the British House of Commons.

Like the Tigers of old, too many politicians today view the community beyond their boundaries of identity as enemy territory, to be punished.

The new Richmond did not need to set itself against the world to succeed. It did the reverse, it embraced diversity. With a playing list and membership drawn from all parts of Australia, it proved that an active policy of inclusion is more unifying than any hackneyed appeal to tribal loyalty. As Brendon Gale reflects on the club's remarkable journey back from the wilderness, he points to a framed poster above his desk. It contains the pictures of the ten previous Richmond premiership teams, from 1920 to 1980.

'That is old Richmond,' he tells me. 'We are incredibly proud of our past. Our predecessors built a great club and we are so grateful for it. But this is a different Richmond.'

Gesturing to Punt Road Oval, he says for the club to move forward it had to prove something important to its supporters: there's another way to win.

NOTES

This book has involved a deep dive into the archives of Richmond, the club and the suburb.

Unless stated, the scores and attendance records for VFL, AFL, and rugby league are sourced from afltables.com.

Where comparisons are made across eras, and between the codes, I've used my own calculations based on the raw data. Some of my tables are shared below.

The Richmond population data is based on my calculations from each census release, which is available under 'Historical Census Data' at abs.gov.au.

For the sake of brevity, I haven't repeated here all the newspaper sources for match reports, as those sources are already stated in the book. The full articles can be found by searching a line or two from the quoted passage in the National Library of Australia's Trove archive, trove.nla.gov.au.

For an overview of Richmond's club history, see the informative *Tigerland Archive* by Rhett Bartlett and Trevor Ruddell: tigerlandarchive.org.

The club's chronology is available on their website at richmondfc.com.au/club/history/chronology while the AFL's official chronology is at afl.com.au/afl-hq/the-afl-explained/chronology.

The interviews with Brendon Gale, Peggy O'Neal, Neil Balme and Emma Murray were conducted over the summer of 2017–18. Greg Tonner was interviewed in February 2018 and Megan Davis was interviewed in May. They are quoted in the present tense.

If I have left out anything important, or if you have further questions, please contact me on Twitter: @gmegalogenis.

INTRODUCTION

x **'As my confidence grew . . .'** My Twitter prediction was posted in two grabs on 30 July 2017.

'Getting a bit of feedback on the footy. Consensus is I should keep the lid on. Bugger that. I'm tipping a @Richmond_FC premiership. #gotiges

'It's the reverse moz. A bit like my call in 2008 that Australia would miss the GFC. Most people laughed, but everyone wanted me to be right.'

xi **'Collectively, the eighteen clubs . . .'** The trade union data is contained in 'datacube 16' in the the Australian Bureau of Statistics' '6333.0 – Characteristics of Employment, Australia, August 2016'. Union coverage in the private sector fell by 6 per cent between 2014 and 2016 to an all-time low of 941 500.

AFL club memberships increased by 4 per cent between 2016 and 2017 to a new record high of 907 500. (afl.com.au/news/2017-08-16/afl-club-membership-tally-hits-new-high)

Based on these trends, the lines will cross by August 2018, with AFL clubs having more members than the trade unions in the private sector.

The membership figures of the political parties are notoriously difficult to verify, because the parties themselves are reluctant to release this information.

The estimates of 54 000 for Labor and 50 000 for the Liberals are sourced to Troy Bramston, 'Membership reforms see recruits rally to Labor cause', *The Australian*, 13 May 2015.

At the time of writing, in late May 2018, it's not clear if Richmond will reach 100 000 members, but even if they fall short of that milestone, it's a remarkable achievement.

CHAPTER ONE

6 **'Tom Wills . . .'** Biographical details here: adb.anu.edu.au/biography/wills-thomas-wentworth-4863

'He shared his concerns . . .' The Wills letter to the sporting weekly *Bell's Life in Victoria* is quoted and analysed by Geoffrey Blainey in *A Game of Our Own*, Black Inc., 2010, pages 19–20.

7 **'The following April . . .'** 'Telegraphic Despatches', *The Argus*, 18 Apr 1859, page 5. In the same column of despatches, there was a report of an escaped tiger terrorising residents of Little Bourke Street in Chinatown. 'It appears that a person who keeps a species of menagerie in Bourke-street recently imported the animal in question from Singapore.' The tiger wounded 'an unfortunate Chinaman' before being recaptured by its owner.

8 **'The first rules . . .'** *A Game of Our Own*, pages 221–239.

'*The Argus* mocked . . .' 'Melbourne v. Richmond', 14 May 1860, page 5.

10 **'The official position . . .'** The research by Jenny Hocking and Nell Reidy is detailed here: meanjin.com.au/essays/marngrook-tom-wills-and-the-continuing-denial-of-indigenous-history/.

See also: abc.net.au/news/2017-04-13/historian-reveals-marngrook-influence-on-afl/8439748.

11 **'Consider this description . . .'** Ken Edwards, *A Bibliography of the Traditional Games of Australian Aboriginal and Torres Strait Islander Peoples*, University of Southern Queensland, Faculty of Education, 2012. Available here: eprints.usq.edu.au/24914/13/Edwards_2012_PV.pdf.

'This is the theory . . .' Roy Hay, 'Indigenous players didn't invent Australian rules but did make it their own,' *The Conversation*, 25 May 2017.

15 **'In July 1877 . . .'** *South Australian Chronicle and Weekly Mail*, 28 July 1877, page 16.

18 **'In its review . . .'** *The Argus*, 6 September 1886, pages 4–5.

19 **'Melbourne held two . . .'** Geoffrey Searle, *From Deserts the Prophets Come*, Monash University Press, 2014, page 42.

'Up to this point . . .' GDP per capita calculated from raw tables on the Maddison Project Database: rug.nl/ggdc/historicaldevelopment/maddison/releases/maddison-project-database-2013.

CHAPTER TWO

21 **'The depression was a global event . . .'** The Americans took seven years to recover the losses of their depression. See: eh.net/encyclopedia/the-depression-of-1893/.

Australia's depression lasted twice as long on this measure, which makes it our worst economic crisis in history.

23 **'Richmond had what turns out to be . . .'**

Janet McCalman, 'Richmond,' *eMelbourne*. emelbourne.net.au/biogs/EM01245b.htm

'Richmond,' *Victorian Places*. victorianplaces.com.au/richmond

29 **'The tipping point for open rebellion . . .'** My account of the formation of the VFL is drawn from the helpful list of articles 'VFL formation' on Trove: https://trove.nla.gov.au/list?id=79321.

31 **'In 1901, the players took a vow of sobriety . . .'** I picked up this titbit from the *Tigerland Archive*: 'Richmond's new head trainer, Joseph McCormack objects "to the use of whiskey" by players at half time. It is resolved that whiskey may only be used after the match.' Interestingly, that year there was a push from some residents to change the name of the suburb to East Melbourne. The push failed.

34 **'He captained Eastern Suburbs . . .'** Rugby league's opening round was held on Easter Monday, 20 April 1908, with two games each at Birchgrove and Wentworth Ovals. Messenger did not play that day.

Richmond made its VFL debut two weeks later, on Saturday 2 May, with a win against Melbourne. While 3000 people went to each rugby league ground, Richmond attracted a crowd of 8000 to its game at Punt Road.

'Indeed, Deakin commemorated . . .' Alfred Deakin's speech was quoted in 'Football Jubilee,' *The Argus*, 29 August 1908, page 17.

CHAPTER THREE

38 **'Week after week . . .'** Vic Thorp's memoirs were serialised over seven editions of the *Sporting Globe* between 30 July and 10 September 1938, on page 5. These articles are available on Trove.

39 **'The catalyst for the split . . .'** Dan Minogue's account of his move to Richmond and the 1920 premiership season was published in a column titled 'Left sick bed to win a premiership,' *The Sporting Globe*, 28 August 1937, page 8.

41 **'The story got taller . . .'** Janet McCalman, *Struggletown: public and private life in Richmond 1900–1965*, Hyland House Publishing, 1998, page 140.

42 **'In the dressing room . . .'** Jack Archer's address as published in Rhett Bartlett, *Richmond F.C.: "The Tigers": a century of league football*, Geoff Slattery Publishing, 2007, Page 43.

43 **'Sir Arthur Conan Doyle . . .'** The author's praise of Australian football was front-page news in the *Melbourne Herald*, 2 October 1920, under the headline 'Best Game of All'.

44 **'Herbert had a crayfish in each hand . . .'** As told by Vic Thorp in the second article of his series in the *Sporting Globe*, 6 August 1938, page 5.

'The 1925 grand final . . .' *The Argus*, 12 October 1925, page 6–7.

49 **'The most popular clubs of the era . . .'** Here are the average home crowds for the first 15 seasons of the VFL's 12-team competition, between 1925 and 1939:

1. Carlton 21 730
2. Richmond 20 234
3. South Melbourne 17 883
4. Melbourne 17 264
5. Collingwood 17 147
6. St. Kilda 16 898
7. Fitzroy 15 160
8. Essendon 15 152
9. Footscray 13 890
10. Geelong 11 838
11. North Melbourne 10 258
12. Hawthorn 9843

51 **'We were locked in . . .'** Tony Hardy, *Finding Jack Dyer*, Slattery Media, 2013, pages 23–24.

53 **'The economics of football . . .'** For a summary of player payments from the Depression onwards, and the various recruiting laws, see:

Lionel Frost and Peter Schuwalow, 'Labour market regulation and professional sport: The case of the Victorian Football League's Coulter Law, 1930–1970,' Monash University, Department of Economics discussion paper 42/10.

Ross Booth, 'History of Player Recruitment, Transfer and Payment Rules in the Victorian and Australian Football League,' Monash University, Department of Economics.

54 **'the grand final of 1934 . . .'** *The Sporting Globe*, 13 October 1934, page 3 and page 6.

56 **'. . . the world's first super team'** Sam Walker, *The Captain Class,* Penguin Random House, 2017. The appendix lists the sixteen tier-one teams in chronological order:

Collingwood, New York Yankees (baseball), Hungary (international men's soccer), Montreal Canadiens (National Hockey League), Boston Celtics (National Basketball Association), Brazil (men's soccer), Pittsburgh Steelers (National Football League), Soviet Union (international men's ice hockey), New Zealand All Blacks (rugby union), Cuba (international women's volleyball), Australia (international women's field hockey), United States (international women's soccer), San Antonino Spurs (NBA), Barcelona (professional soccer), France (international men's handball) and the New Zealand All Blacks, the only team to appear twice on the list.

CHAPTER FOUR

61 **'Both suburbs were transformed . . .'** A tale of two tribes from the 1971 census. Here are my calculations of the ethnic faces of nine football suburbs (Carlton and North Melbourne were not counted separately from the City of Melbourne in the census). The first figure is the Australian-born as a share of the total population, the second figure is the largest overseas-born group as share of total population. Listed in order of most to least diverse:
Fitzroy, Australia 49.4 per cent, Italy 14.2 per cent
Collingwood, Australia 54.9 per cent, Greece 21 per cent
St. Kilda, Australia 56.8 per cent, UK and Ireland 13 per cent
Richmond, Australia 57.6 per cent, Greece 19.5 per cent
Footscray, Australia 62.7 per cent, Yugoslavia 10 per cent
Melbourne, Australia 65.2 per cent, Italy 8.3 per cent
South Melbourne, Australia 67.4 per cent, Greece 11.6 per cent
Essendon, Australia 71.5 per cent, Italy 10.7 per cent
Hawthorn, Australia 74.1 per cent, UK and Ireland 8.2 per cent
National average: Australia 80 per cent, Britain 8 per cent, Italy 2.3 per cent, Greece 1.2 per cent, Yugoslavia 1 per cent

62 **'There is a telling portrait . . .'** *Struggletown*, page 268.

64 **'. . . I don't think he was a coach'** *Richmond F.C.*, page 71.

64 **'Get up you weak so-and-so . . .'** *Fighting Fury: The history of the Richmond Football Club from Dyer until today,* AFL DVD, 2003, updated edition.

65 **'They kept coming to watch . . .'** Here are the average home crowds between 1946 and 1964, before the Tigers moved to the MCG. The growth in attendances compared to the club's pre-war record, between 1925 and 1939, is recorded in brackets. Note how Richmond's crowds flatlined.

1. Melbourne 33 140 (+92 per cent)
2. Collingwood 25 896 (+51 per cent)
3. Carlton 24 276 (+12 per cent)
4. Essendon 22 751 (+50 per cent)
5. Footscray 21 687 (+56 per cent)
6. Richmond 20 545 (+2 per cent)
7. Geelong 20 428 (+73 per cent)
8. St. Kilda 19 215 (+14 per cent)
9. South Melbourne 18 869 (+6 per cent)
10. Fitzroy 17 173 (+13 per cent)
11. Hawthorn 15 420 (+57 per cent)
12. North Melbourne 14 778 (+44 per cent)

CHAPTER FIVE

94 **'. . . we weren't some hick club'** Elliot Cartledge, *The Hafey Years,* Weston Media Communications, 2011, page 280.
'But the club secretary Alan Schwab . . .' *Fighting Fury.*

CHAPTER SIX

101 **'Carlton and Hawthorn were the main beneficiaries . . .'** Blogger Billy P. Hickey used the old country zones to create playing lists for twelve teams in 2016 and found that Hawthorn would still be the big winner, although Carlton would not do as well. thehickeystand.com/2016/05/14/thc-12-vfl-country-zones-and-how-they-would-have-screwed-your-club-today/

106 **'I don't think I played as well . . .'** Michael Roach's comment reported in Patrick Carlyon, '10 tales of Tiger heartache: Richmond's pain from 1980 to today,' *Herald Sun,* 29 September 2017.

108 **'. . . on the verge of bankruptcy'** Peter Costigan, 'Magpies set business example,' *Canberra Times,* 30 September 1990, page 6.

Michael Roberts and Glenn McFarlane, *In Black & White: 125 moments that made Collingwood,* Nero, 2016, pages 190–191.

CHAPTER SEVEN

118 **'In Geelong, I told Gary Ablett about Margaret Thatcher . . .'** John Button, *As it Happened,* Text Publishing, 2000, page 400.

120 **'Robert Menzies, too . . .'** 'Sir Robert Gives "Rules" a Boost,' *Canberra Times,* 9 January 1967, page 6. Menzies donated a football and a Carlton jersey to the University of Virginia. The jumper had the number 43 on its back, which was then not in use.

122 **'Keating did not pretend . . .'** George Megalogenis, 'Paul sums up Pies' plight,' *Melbourne Sun,* 24 March 1990, page 1.

CHAPTER EIGHT

128 **'We just looked at each other . . .'** Michael Gordon, 'The day Nicky Winmar drew the line,' *The Age,* 16 April 2013. See also: theage.com.au/national/victoria/when-nicky-winmar-did-this-25-years-ago-i-m-proud-to-be-black-20180414-p4z9mx.html

129 **'Keating was into his fourth season . . .'** The Redfern address, 10 December 1992. keating.org.au/shop/item/redfern-speech-year-for-the-worlds-indigenous-people---10-december-1992

The speech to launch the Aboriginal All-Stars vs Collingwood game, 11 February 1994: pmtranscripts.pmc.gov.au/release/transcript-9116.

131 **'The players' association . . .'** Statement cited in 'Pies boss – there is no proof,' *The Age,* 30 April 1995, page 1.

132 **'Tony Shaw . . .'** Ashley Browne, 'Tony Shaw – Still telling it in Black & White,' *The Age,* 5 May 1995, page 26. Shaw subsequently retracted his criticism of Long.

'Former Richmond player . . .' Mal Brown's comments cited in Patrick Smith, 'Racism claim calls for action,' *The Age,* 29 April 1995, page 36.

'On the fringe . . .' B.A. Santamaria, 'A slur on good sense,' *The Weekend Australian,* 20 May 1995, page 25.

134 **'Hibbins took particular exception . . .'** For a defence of Gillian Hibbins's chapter, see John Hirst's column 'An Indigenous Game,' *The Monthly,* September 2008. themonthly.com.au/issue/2008/september/1331684674/john-hirst/comment-indigenous-game

And Martin Flanagan's reply to her chapter, 'The History Wars and AFL Footy,' *The Age* blogs, 15 May 2008. theage.com.au/flanagan/archives/2008/05/the_history_wars_and_afl_footy.html

135 **'Football crowds did not boo . . .'** Adam Goodes' Australian of the Year 2014 acceptance speech: youtube.com/watch?v=3EV-cLb_Ttg.

See also 'Australian of Year 2014: Adam Goodes, Sydney Swans footballer, recognised for anti-racism advocacy and youth work', *ABC News*, 26 January 2014. abc.net.au/news/2014-01-25/adam-goodes-named-australian-of-the-year-for-2014/5219118

136 **'In a short video profile . . .'** youtube.com/watch?v=6b-ByVi6uAg

'The attorney-general . . .' Senate Question without notice, from Labor Senator Nova Peris to Senator George Brandis, 24 March 2014. Coincidentally, the opening round of the 2014 AFL season, which stretched over two weekends from 15 March to 23 March, was completed the day before this debate.

137 **'He coined the phrase . . .'** Rachel Olding, 'Counter-terrorism adviser: Abbott's IS "death cult" label is counter-productive,' *Sydney Morning Herald*, 11 May 2015.

138 **'. . . commissioners were split'** Chip Le Grand, 'Adam Goodes: division drives AFL Commission's insipid response,' *The Australian*, 3 August 2015.

139 **'. . . belated apology'** The AFL made its first public statement in support of Adam Goodes on 28 July 2015, after he was booed by West Coast supporters at a game in Perth. afl.com.au/news/2015-07-28/afl-statement-on-adam-goodes

The AFL's formal apology to Goodes was reported on its website on 17 March 2016. afl.com.au/news/2016-03-17/gillon-mclachlan-says-sorry-to-adam-goodes-for-not-acting-sooner-against-booing

141 **'Almost half the Australian population . . .'** The exclusive data on our changing ethnic face was supplied to me by the Australian Bureau of Statistics for my essay in the first edition of *Australian Foreign Affairs*, October 2017. The full table is in that publication. australianforeignaffairs.com/essay/2017/10/the-big-picture

144 **'On the weekend that Adam Goodes did not play . . .'** 'Richmond, Western Bulldogs to wear Dreamtime AFL guernsey in support of Adam Goodes,' *ABC News*, 30 July 2015. abc.net.au/news/2015-07-30/richmond-to-wear-dreamtime-afl-guernsey-for-adam-goodes/6658794

CHAPTER NINE

157 **'The TV news in Melbourne . . .'** John Northey's departure is covered at the end of *A Tiger Tale,* AFL DVD, [1995]. I knew I was fan again when I bought the original VHS video when it was first released.

159 **'We finished ninth again . . .'** youtube.com/watch?v=KBD49n36F9k

168 **'The worst 47 seconds . . .'** 'Former Sydney Swans coach Paul Roos analyses Richmond implosion against Gold Coast Suns,' *Fox Sports*, 17 July 2012.

171 **'A two-year extension . . .'** richmondfc.com.au/news/2016-03-16/richmond-extends-hardwicks-contract

CHAPTER TEN

173 **'. . . lost his composure'** Rohan Connolly, 'Essendon top job hopes crashed with Hawks' PC,' *The Age*, 17 April 2009.

174 **'tanking'** afl.com.au/news/2013-02-19/afl-full-statement-melbourne-tanking-penalties

175 **'. . . out to get him'** Len Johnson, 'Hardwick's joke cost him $8000,' *The Age*, 18 September 2002. Port Adelaide won the semi-final against Essendon by 4 goals. Blake Caracella had 21 disposals and a goal. Damien Hardwick touched the ball just nine times.

'. . . a baby-faced killer' Glen McFarlane, 'Damien Hardwick seen as the man who can end Richmond's premiership drought,' *Herald Sun,* 20 April 2013.

176 **'What have I got myself in for?'** Rohan Connolly, '"What have I got myself in for?",' *The Age*, 19 June 2010.

179 **'. . . Jonathan Brown weighed in'** 'Jonathan Brown responds to Trent Cotchin's wife Brooke's public support of Richmond captain,' *Herald Sun*, 18 April 2016.

180 **'The media pile-on . . .'** Michael Gordon, *Playing to Win,* Slattery Media, 2014, page 72.

'I think I plummeted . . .' Hamish McLachlan, 'Considered and wise Trent Cotchin fighting footy stereotypes,' *Sunday Herald Sun,* 1 April 2018.

181 **'. . . the emotion of Neville's funeral'** 'Trent Cotchin on the pressure of the Richmond captaincy and learning to enjoy the good times,' *Sunday Herald Sun,* 1 May 2017.

Coincidentally, Cotchin was born in the year of the Save Our Skins campaign, 1990.

181 **'You take off the jumper . . .'** Konrad Marshall, *Yellow & Black: a season with Richmond,* Slattery Media, 2017, pages 170–171.

183 **'. . . Hardwick told the members'** Lauren Wood, 'Damien Hardwick delivers passionate speech at Richmond best-and-fairest,' *Herald Sun,* 9 September 2016.

187 **'But he did have a soft spot . . .'** Martin Flanagan, *A Wink from the Universe*, Penguin Random House, 2018, page 44.

188 **'. . . a new kind of masculinity'** Bob Murphy, 'How To Win A Flag: the game has changed,' *The Age*, 20 March 2018.

190 **'Nick Vlaustin talked . . .'** Caroline Wilson, 'The Making of Damien Hardwick,' *The Age*, 29 September 2017.

191 **'Before the Anzac Round rematch . . .'** *Yellow & Black,* pages 169–170.

192 **'Former Tigers coach . . .'** Kate Salemme, 'Richmond criticised for crumbling under pressure in wake of fourth narrow loss this season,' *Herald Sun,* 18 June 2017.

The first two reader responses to that article suggested that the supporter mood had not improved since 2016. Steven: 'Peggy should go with Dimma about the same time Eddie goes down the road with Bucks' David: 'As [a] Tiger supporter, we still havent got an 'Eat em Alive' mentality . . . Danny is right in many ways.'

CHAPTER ELEVEN

193 **'Kevin Bartlett would visualise . . .'** *Richmond F.C.*, page 186.

200 **'Patty gets a pat on the bum . . .'** richmondfc.com.au/video/2018-03-12/dont-believe-in-never-richmond

203 **'For his pre-game address . . .'** richmondfc.com.au/video/2018-03-15/tigers-break-the-fall-

CHAPTER TWELVE

214 **'The voices of the agitated . . .'** See the 'Don't Believe in Never' video above.

215 **'The peak of the baby boom . . .'** In '4102.0 – Australian Social Trends, 2004' the ABS reports: 'In 1971, Australia's largest ever cohort was born – 276 400 births.'

216 **'Faith in democracy . . .'** *Trends in Australian Political Opinion Results from the Australian Election Study 1987–2016*, see table marked 'trust in government' australianelectionstudy.org/trends.html

216 **'no religion'** ABS, '2071.0 – Census of Population and Housing: Reflecting Australia – Stories from the Census, 2016'.

218 **'A delegation from the club . . .'** richmondfc.com.au/news/2018-04-04/richmond-invited-to-present-at-the-united-nations

219 **'Writing about sport . . .'** Donald Horne, *The Lucky Country*, Penguin Books, 1964, page 32.

222 **'The Grateful Dead . . .'** David Gans and Peter Simon, *Playing in the Band,* St. Martin's Press, 1996, page 171.

224 **'Richmond is a different place today . . .'** The latest snapshot of the suburb, from the 2016 census: censusdata.abs.gov.au/census_services/getproduct/census/2016/quickstat/SSC22158.

226 **'. . . divided as ever'** From Roy Morgan's research: roymorgan.com/findings/7356-afl-grand-final-viewers-september-2017-201710020358.

CONCLUSION

229 **'Each side gave the Richmond treatment . . .'** The period of greatest instability at Richmond was between 1981 and 1985, with the following coaches sacked at the end of the season: Tony Jewell 1981, Francis Bourke 1983, Mike Paterson 1984 and Paul Sproule in 1985. The political equivalent between 2010 and 2015 saw Rudd sacked in 2010, Gillard sacked in 2013, Rudd defeated at a general election in 2013, and Abbott sacked in 2015.

230 **'So he broke the promise . . .'** The saga of the 'L.A.W.' tax cuts, first announced in 1992, stretched over three elections. Paul Keating paid one half of the tax cuts early after the 1993 election but deferred the second half to later in the decade. Later he repurposed those delayed tax cuts as a government contribution to workers' superannuation accounts. But he lost office in 1996 before that promise was due to be honoured. John Howard's government adopted the Keating policy, but then changed its mind and broke the promise in the run up to the 1998 election.

'The moment you start campaigning . . .' John Howard, address to the party room, 18 October 2004. http://pandora.nla.gov.au/pan/10052/20050221-0000/www.pm.gov.au/news/speeches/speech1128.html